European Framework Agreements and Telework: Law and Practice, A European and Comparative Study

ENCH

BULLETIN OF COMPARATIVE LABOUR RELATIONS 62

European Framework Agreements and Telework: Law and Practice, A European and Comparative Study

Editor: Roger Blanpain

Contributors:

Michele Colucci
Christian Dirkx
Chris Engels
Alvin Goldman
Frank Hendrickx
Antoine Jacobs
Morin Jackie
Emma Keating
Alan Neal
Birgitta Nyström
Jean-Emmanuel Ray
Jacques Rojot
Andrzej Swiatkowski
Di van den Broek
Manfred Weiss

KLUWER LAW INTERNATIONAL

A C.I.P. Catalogue record for this book is available from the Library of Congress.

ISBN 9789041125606

Published by:
Kluwer Law International,
P.O. Box 316, 2400 AH Alphen aan den Rijn,
The Netherlands
sales@kluwerlaw.com
http://www.kluwerlaw.com

sold and distributed in North, Central and South America
by Aspen Publishers, Inc.,
7201 McKinney Circle,
Frederick, MD 21704, USA

Sold and distributed in all countries by
Turpin Distribution Services Ltd.,
Stratton Business Park,
Pegasus Drive, Biggleswade,
Bedfordshire SG18 8TQ,
United Kingdom

Table of Contents

Chapter 3
Implementation of the European Framework Agreement
on Telework

Part II
National Reports 75

Chapter 4
Australia 77
Emma Keating and Di van den Broek

Chapter 5
Belgium 93
Roger Blanpain

Chapter 6
Belgium

A discussion on the Collective Bargaining Agreement
No. 85 on Telework, Implementing the European
Framework Agreement on Telework
Chris Engels

Chapter 12
Poland 205
Andrzej Swiatkowski

Chapter 13
Sweden 217
Birgitta Nyström

List of Contributors

Roger Blanpain, Professor at the Universities of Hasselt, Belgium and Tilburg, the Netherlands

Michele Colucci, Agent at the Legal Service of the European Commission, Professor of Labour Law at the University of Salerno, Italy

Christian Dirkx, Human Resources Manager, IBM Belgium/Luxembourg

Chris Engels, Lawyer and Partner, Claeys & Engels law firm, Professor at the University of Leuven, Belgium

Alvin Goldman, Professor at the University of Kentucky, USA

Frank Hendrickx, Professor at the University of Leuven, Belgium and Associate professor at the University of Tilburg, the Netherlands

Antoine Jacobs, Professor in Labour Law, Social Security and Social Policy at the University of Tilburg, the Netherlands

Emma Keating, Student, School of Business, University of Sydney, Australia

Jackie Morin, European Commission, Social Dialogue

Alan Neal, Professor of Law at the University of Warwick, United Kingdom

Birgitta Nyström, Professor of Private Law at the University of Lund, Sweden

Jean-Emmanuel Ray, Professor at the University of Paris I, France

Jacques Rojot, Professor at the University of Paris II, France

Andrzej Swiatkowski, Jean Monnet Professor of Labour and Social Security Law at the Jagiellonian University, Cracow, Poland

Diane van den Broek, Lecturer, School of Business, University of Sydney, Australia

Manfred Weiss, Professor at the University of Frankfurt am Main, Germany

Introductory Remarks

I. EUROPEAN VOLUNTARY AGREEMENTS: FROM SOFT TO LIQUID LABOUR LAW?

The European Forum on Telework took place on 1 and 2 September 2006 in the Palace of the Royal Flemish Academy in Brussels, with the support of the Academy. The forum focused on various aspects of European labour law.

A. THE SIGNIFICANCE AND IMPORTANCE OF FRAMEWORK AGREEMENTS

First, on a fundamental one: the significance and importance of framework agreements between the European social inter-industry partners, namely the Union of Industrial and Employers' Confederations of Europe (BUSINESSEUROPE), the European Centre of Enterprises with Public Participation and of Enterprises of General Economic Interest (CEEP) and the European Association of Craft, Small and Medium-Sized Enterprises (UEAPME); employer organizations; and the European Trade Union Confederation (ETUC) — trade unions — as a source of European labour law.

A first agreement was concluded on telework (2002), a second on stress at work (2004). Future framework agreement topics may include lifelong learning and gender equality.

Blanpain et al., European Framework, Agreements and Telework, pp. 1–8.
©2007, Kluwer Law International BV, The Netherlands.

B. AUTONOMY

These agreements testify the 'autonomy' of the European social partners. Indeed, the social partners act on their own without institutional help from the Commission, the Council of Ministers or the European Parliament integrating their agreements into legally binding European directives. These 'voluntary' agreements stand on their own.

C. VOLUNTARY

These framework agreements are labelled 'voluntary' in the sense that they intend not to create legally binding obligations between the concluding parties, or impose them on their national constituents. They merely put, it seems, a 'moral' obligation on the European social partners to recommend the content of the agreement to their national members — employer associations and trade unions — namely to implement the European agreement in their own countries in accordance with local law and practice.

The main question is then whether these agreements constitute a new way of developing European employment law, or the main way? Legally binding directives seem difficult to agree upon between 25 Member States, even with a system of majority voting. So could framework agreements do the job, underlining, at the same time, the important legislative role social partners may play at European level, and giving an additional dimension to the European social dialogue?

The first question, then, concerns the role of framework agreements in the shaping of European labour law: an additional way or a main way?

Secondly, the agreements are voluntary. But this is nothing new. Indeed, all framework agreements are voluntary. Here voluntary does, however, have another meaning, namely that the agreements, as mentioned above, do not intend to create legal obligations between contracting parties. This seems to be an English approach, as under English law collective agreements do not create legal obligations, as parties do not intend to do so.

Is this also the case in relation to the constituent members of BUSINESSEUROPE, UEAPME, CEEP and the ETUC? The telework agreement states that it *shall* be implemented by the members of the contracting parties. This seems to imply an obligation. The question is whether it is a legal obligation. This could be the case, depending on the by laws of the contracting European organizations, and whether or not membership implies that the national constituents are bound by the decisions of their mother organizations. If this is the case, could then the European mother oblige the national daughter to comply? Could a teleworker or a member of a daughter do so and engage in legal action in order to obtain appropriate social protection as provided for by the European framework agreement?

The answer to these questions will co-determine the effectiveness of the *framework agreement approach.*

D. DOES THE VOLUNTARY APPROACH WORK?

A third question is equally important but of a more practical nature: does he scheme work? How do the national social partners implement the European framework agreement? How effective are the local ways?

It is, self evidently, a fact that these ways differ enormously from Member State to Member State.

Indeed, in some countries the legislator plays a role; in other countries inter-industry wide collective agreements have been concluded, some of which have been extended by governmental decree and are enforced by way of penal sanctions. In still others there are sectoral agreements or even mere recommendations.

A number of questions arise: Are all workers covered by the benefits of the framework agreement? And are we heading for a social Europe with two speeds, one where the social protection is guaranteed and eventually sanctioned penally, and another where mere recommendations are the rule?

E. TELEWORK

Another set of questions relate to telework itself. One of the main questions concerns the definition of telework. According to the framework agreement, regular telework is meant to be performed away from the premises of the employer. This is a very wide definition covering telework at home or at premises chosen by the workers, as well as mobile workers performing e.g. at the premises of a client, and teleworkers employed at satellite offices. In certain countries, like Belgium, however, telework is limited to work at the home of the teleworker or at premises chosen by the employees. Is it a problem that, in these instances, a more restrictive definition has been retained at national level?

Moreover, non-structural, non-regular, occasional telework is not covered. It seems that in practice most telework is done in an informal way. How can we move forward with this information? And where should we draw the line between regular and non-regular telework?

Other points dealt with in the framework agreement concern the voluntary character of telework, employment conditions, data protection, privacy, equipment, health and safety, organization of work and training, and collective rights issues, which also raise a number of questions.

Still others arise when an international relationship is involved: the teleworkers work in one country and the employer is situated in another Member State.

So a lot of ground had to be covered in this European Forum on Telework!

II. PROGRAMME OF EVENTS AND EXCHANGE OF VIEWS

The programme of the European Forum on Telework[1] was as follows:

1 September 2006

Welcome and Introductory Remarks
Professor Roger Blanpain, Universities of Hasselt and Tilburg

Telework in Motion

- The IBM case, *Mr Christian Dirkx, Human Resources Manager*
- The General Motors case, *Mr Bob Schelfhaut, Human Resources Manager*

Soft Law and Voluntary Agreements
Mr Jackie Morin, European Commission, Social Dialogue

Soft Law and Voluntary Agreements
Mrs Thérèse de Liedekerke, Director of BUSINESSEUROPE, Social Affairs Department
Mrs Maria Helena André, ETUC

The European Framework Agreement on Telework
Prof. Manfred Weiss, University of Frankfurt

Telework in the USA
Prof. Alvin Goldman, University of Kentucky

IMPLEMENTATION OF THE FRAMEWORK AGREEMENT INTO NATIONAL LAW

- The Way of Implementation of the Agreement (Legislation, Collective Agreement, Guidelines . . .)
  The Netherlands, Prof. Frank Hendrickx, University of Tilburg
  United Kingdom, Prof. Alan Neal, University of Warwick
  Poland, Prof. Sebastian Koczur, Jan Dlugosz Academy[2]
- Definition of Telework and Scope of Application of the Agreement, including the Public Sector
  Belgium, Prof. Frank Hendrickx, Universities of Leuven and Tilburg
  Germany, Prof. Manfred Weiss, University of Frankfurt
  France, Prof. Jacques Rojot, University of Paris
  Italy, Prof. Michele Colucci, University of Salerno
- The Voluntary Character of Telework. Organisation of Work. Equal Treatment
  Belgium, Prof. Chris Engels, University of Leuven

---

1. Professor Birgitta Nyström (Sweden) sent in a paper, which is published in this book.
2. Replacing Professor Andrzej Swiatkowski (Poland), who sent in a paper which is also published in this book.

Italy, *Prof. Michele Colucci, University of Salerno*
United Kingdom, Prof. Alan Neal, University of Warwick
- Data Protection and Privacy
  Belgium & the Netherlands, Prof. Frank Hendrickx, Universities of Leuven and Tilburg
  Germany, Prof. Manfred Weiss, University of Frankfurt

2 September 2006
IMPLEMENTATION OF THE FRAMEWORK AGREEMENT INTO NATIONAL LAW

- Equipment and health and safety
  France, Prof. Jacques Rojot, University of Paris
  Poland, Prof. Sebastian Koczur, Jan Dlugosz Academy
- Follow up
  Belgium, Prof. Chris Engels, University of Leuven
  France, Prof. Jacques Rojot, University of Paris
  Italy, Prof. Michele Colucci, University of Salerno
- Collective rights
  United Kingdom, Prof. Alan Neal, University of Warwick
  Italy, Prof. Michele Colucci, University of Salern,
  The Netherlands, Prof. Antoine Jacobs, University of Tilburg
  Poland, Prof. Sebastian Koczur, Jan Dlugosz Academy

III. CLOSING REMARKS

Roger Blanpain

The discussion was too dense and rich to be summarized in detail, so we have limited ourselves to some of the main points.

A. VOLUNTARY AGREEMENTS

The road of the voluntary agreements, engaged in by the European social partners, seems to be 'the' new way of developing European labour law. These agreements are voluntary in the sense, the ETUC explained, that they, the social partners, choose freely to deal with the topic of telework — full stop! The ETUC added that it had a mandate from its national constituents to negotiate an agreement and that these national members were bound to an effective follow up, leading to an implementation of the agreement in the national framework of law and/or practice.

The European Commission said that the European social partners rightly underlined that they were acting on the basis of Article 138 of the EC Treaty, which gives the partners a full European mandate to negotiate agreements, according to European law.

As a consequence, we may have to deal with a (new) category of a source of European labour law, a new kind of European Act, open to interpretation by the (European) Court of Justice.

Both the social partners stressed that they left it to the national 'actors' to implement the European agreement as these actors (legislator, government, social partners at all levels, etc.), saw fit. This self-evidently leads, as mentioned earlier, to a great variety in the way of implementation, from legally binding rules to mere recommendations. This did not seem problematic to the European partners, as this outcome corresponds to the local ways and the expectations of the local actors.

Both social partners seemed to fully agree on the approach, content and outcome. Moreover, they worked hard to convince and encourage local partners to come to results.

This development, however, leaves the future of European labour law in a rather weak situation.

B.   The Future of European Labour Law

The implementation of the European agreements, according to national — very weak — ways, means that since binding European directives are not any longer possible, European labour law depends for its development on:

    (1) The social partners agreeing on non-controversial issues;[3] and
    (2) Local ways, which do not guarantee all workers the same rights to social protection. The national ways may rely on soft law, if not on totally *liquid* approaches.

Some participants to the forum wondered whether the 'voluntary European agreements' are merely serving the needs of the European social partners looking for a 'credible' role and usefulness at European level, instead of aiming at setting (firm) social standards on which workers can rely.

The question was also raised as to whether the Telework Agreement has really added value, since the various points dealt with in the agreement, such as the voluntary character of telework, the health and safety aspects, privacy, training and so on, are already guaranteed in most national legal systems.

CONCLUSION

So European labour law can be seen as almost at a standstill, due also to the (overtowering) role of managerial power aiming at more flexibility and refusing new (rigid) labour market rules, thus affecting social protection.

In a sense, these developments also express the overall need to consider the revision of existing labour law, given the changing framework where social

---

3. They could not agree on information and consultation and on temporary work agencies.

protection is geared away from static 'job security' to a more dynamic 'employ-ability', aiming at employment security, and providing workers with increased competencies to find new jobs in an ever faster, changing labour market.

It seems also that the only real source of (classic) European labour law in the future is the European Court of Justice, which is continuing to interpret the existing European employment provisions, including general principles of law, in a tradi-tional and pro-European way.

Indeed, politicians seem powerless to generate traditional social protection at national level, as they want to attract foreign investment at all costs. Social partners seem less and less representative, leaving room for management to take appropri-ate (socially-economic balanced) action, while defending their own interests. Management has more social responsibilities than ever.

Labour law faces difficult times, entering a period — as soft law evolves — of even more subtle forms of 'liquid' law.

We are heading for a 'new world of work' with less (traditional-rigid) social protection, towards a more open labour market, where skills and personal efforts will be rewarded.

Roger Blanpain
President of the Human Sciences Section
of the Royal Flemish Academy of Belgium

Part I

European Reports

Chapter 1

The European Social Dialogue: A General Introduction

Jackie Morin

When the Social Dialogue (SD) was launched, more than 20 years ago, the aim was to develop a framework for transnational collective bargaining.

The then President of the European Commission, Jacques Delors saw this prospect as a dream.

For more than 20 years, Social Dialogue developed continuously, with a strong personal involvement and commitment from EU social partner organizations and with the overall support of the European Commission

This is because Social Dialogue is the way the EU deals with a number of issues in the economic and social fields, based on a commonly shared governance approach:

- At the Barcelona European Council, Heads of State mentioned Social Dialogue as a substantive component of the European social model;
- During the Hampton Court discussions (2005) on the modernization of our social model, the contribution of the SD at all levels was strongly highlighted.

Blanpain et al., European Framework, Agreements and Telework, pp. 11–30.
©2007, Kluwer Law International BV, The Netherlands.

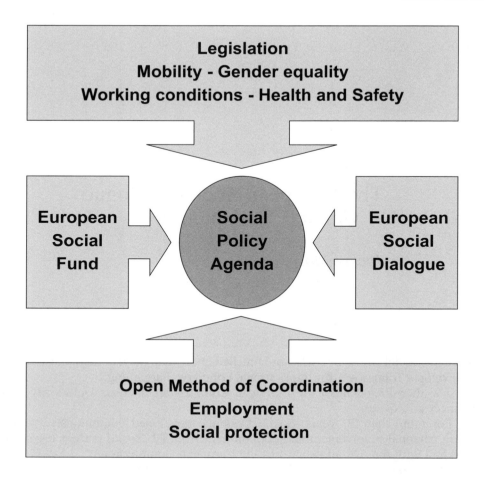

The fact that we meet today to discuss the implementation of the European Social Dialogue autonomous agreement on telework demonstrates clearly that the European Social Dialogue is a success story.

Of course, there are difficulties and divergences on analysis and approaches between the Social Partners, but the European Social Dialogue is developing and we are much further compared with the first joint opinions adopted in 1986.

This development is recognized in the Social Policy Agenda, which builds the European approach on the basis of the relationship between the 4 main social policy tools.

In addition, the European Commission's attitude is to give preference to a negotiated approach in each situation where the Social Partners are ready to take the lead.

What place for social dialogue at European level?

ART 138 of the Treaty

The Commission has a responsibility
to promote consultation of the social partners
at community level and to take every
useful measure to facilitate their dialogue,
taking care to ensure a balanced
support of both sides.

The Commission consults social partners first.

Social partners can engage in a dialogue.

ART 139 of the Treaty

The Community level dialogue between
the social partners can lead,
if they wish, to contractual relations,
including agreements.

They can be implemented either
by an EU instrument or through
national channels.

The Treaty on the European Community recognized the role of the Social Partners at EU level. It introduced the principle of horizontal subsidiarity, i.e., the possibility for the Social Partners to bring solutions as an alternative or as an addition to action by the public authorities.

Articles 138-139 of the Treaty have 4 dimensions:

- They give an active role to the Commission in promoting the Social Dialogue. This means providing logistical support, promoting and enabling a favourable environment for the Social Dialogue.
- They give a right to the European Social Partners (ESP) to be consulted. ESP speak first on social partnership issues. There have been more than 20 consultations since 1993.
- They recognize the contractual dimension at EU level and foresee the possibilities of concluding agreements between the ESP.
- They introduce a strong extension mechanism.

Main communications from the EU Commission

- Communication of 1993 : *Representativity and list of organisations*
- Communication of 1998 :*Institutionalisation of the sectoral dialogue*

In line with these treaty provisions and prerogatives, the Commission adopted a series of Communications in order to clarify:

- Who are the SOCIAL PARTNERS at EU level;
- To propose and establish appropriate structures;
- To propose a typology of Social Dialogue outcomes.

European social partners

General cross-industry organizations
&
Cross-industry organizations representing certain categories of workers or undertakings

ETUC, UNICE, CEEP, UEAPME, CEC, Eurocadres

Specific organizations Eurochambres

Sectoral organisations representing employers
EUROCOMMERCE, AEA, POSTEUROP, COPA, HOTREC, FBE ...
&
European trade union organizations
UNI-Europa, EPSU, EFFAT, EMF...

European Capacity to act in a voluntary way

Being composed of national organizations recognized as **social partners**

Adequate structures

The first Communication in 1993 addressed the question of the representativeness of the Social Partners.

To be considered as representative, the European organisations should be represented in all or most of the Member states and be composed of national organisations themselves considered as representative social partners under their national systems.

The mapping of European actors is not yet finalised but a lot of ground has been covered over the last ten years.

Today, there are two large families of European Social Dialogue: cross-industry and sectoral, comprising around 70 European organisations.

There is a regular update of the list of organisations which are consulted and new representativeness studies are to be carried out in the future by the Dublin Foundation.

1. The European Social Dialogue: A General Introduction

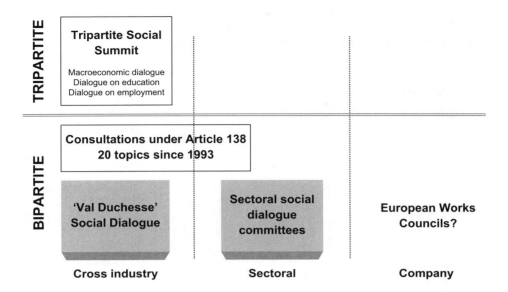

STRUCTURES

Two Communications in 1998 and 2002 proposed the creation of:

- The Tripartite Social Summit (TSS);
- Sectoral Social Dialogue Committees (SSDC): on the basis of the Val Duchesse Social Dialogue for sectors.

Today, we have a functional and balanced structure:

- Tripartite / bipartite;
- Cross industry / sectoral.

The weakest dimension is the company one. This is why the Commission is currently analysing the possibilities for promoting transnational collective bargaining.

1 Cross industry social dialogue committee

32 Sectoral social dialogue committees

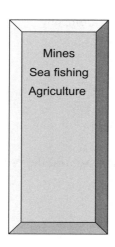

Mines
Sea fishing
Agriculture

Gas (*)
Steel
Chemical
Woodworking
Textile/clothing
Tanning/leather
Sugar
Shipbuilding
Furniture
Footwear
Electricity
Construction

Hospitals (*)
Live performance
Insurance
Inland Navigation
Industrial cleaning
Horeca
Commerce
Civil aviation
Banking
Audiovisual
Temporary work
Telecoms
Sea transport
Road transport
Railways
Private security
Postal services
Personal services
Local government

The more spectacular recent developments have occurred in the framework of the sectoral social dialogue, where new committees are created each year.

Today, we have 32 sectoral social dialogue Committees. The last one was launched in the steel sector in June 2006 and we are analysing requests for the creation of new committees in the Hospital and Gas Sectors.

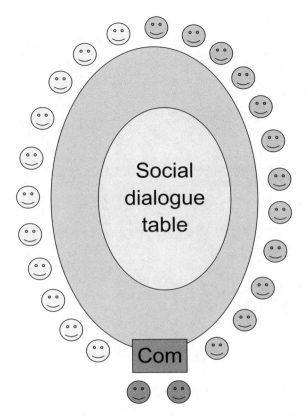

Social
dialogue
table

Com

The Commission : 'support'

SDC are autonomous, bipartite bodies.
Social Partners decide on the content and the outcomes.

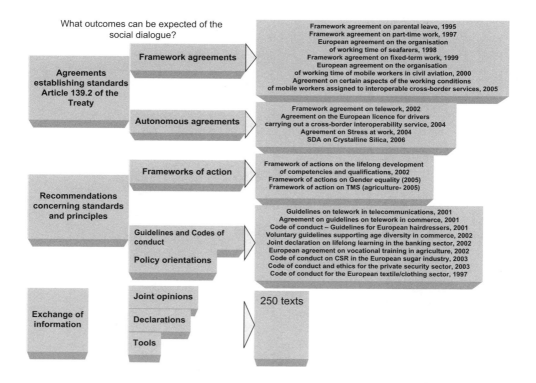

The Commission provides logistic support (rooms, interpretation and administration). It helps in organising the preparation of the meetings and on follow-up. In a number of Sectoral Committees, it chairs the meetings.

RESULTS

The 2004 Commission Communication on 'Partnership for change in an enlarged Europe' related to Social Dialogue outcomes.

The main message is that the outcomes of Social Dialogue should be analysed in relation to their objectives and the implementation clauses they contain.

In this context, it is possible to distinguish between three types of texts.

- Declarative texts: in the past 90 per cent of the texts belonged to this category. The aim is to make the joint position of the Social Partners known to EU Institutions, Member States or the national members of the Social Partners.

- Recommendations addressed to the Social Partners' national members. These texts are EU level frameworks for action and contain guidelines to that end. They provide for reporting on actions at national level – each year – and an evaluation report after a certain period (three, four, or five years).
- Agreements on the basis of article 139.2 of the Treaty.

Social dialogue outcomes

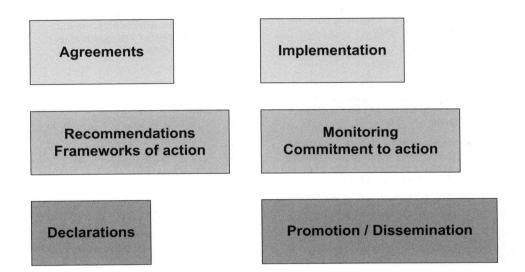

The Commission encourages the social partners to refer to the appropriate (legal) wording when finalising a joint negotiated text and to plan the appropriate follow-up procedure.

Implementation by way of a European Council Directive, for example, is limited to agreements between the Social partners.

6 Agreements establishing minimum standards implemented by Council decision	4 Agreements establishing minimum standards implemented by the procedures and practices specific to management and labour and the Member States 'autonomous' agreements

6 Agreements establishing minimum standards implemented by Council decision

- Framework agreement on parental leave, 1995

- Framework agreement on part-time work, 1997

- European agreement on the organisation of working time of seafarers, 1998

- Framework agreement on fixed-term work, 1999

- European agreement on the organisation of working time of mobile workers in civil aviation, 2000

- Agreement on certain aspects of the working conditions of mobile workers assigned to interoperable cross-border services, 2005

4 Agreements establishing minimum standards implemented by the procedures and practices specific to management and labour and the Member States 'autonomous' agreements

- Framework agreement on telework, 2002

- Agreement on the European licence for drivers carrying out a cross-border interoperability service, 2004

- Agreement on Stress at work, 2004

- Agreement Crystalline Silica, 2006

Implementation reports by the social partners

Today, we have ten EU negotiated agreements:[1]

- 5 cross-industry;
- 5 sectoral;
- 6 are implemented through a Council decision (the last one was in mid 2005);
- 4 are autonomous : the first one : telework;

---

1. Agreement Crystalline Silica, 2006. More than 2 million workers in many different sectors across Europe will be covered by the first European multi-sector agreement to be signed today. It will protect workers exposed to crystalline silica dust, which can lead to silicosis, a potentially fatal lung condition. Silicosis is also linked to other dangerous lung conditions, such as emphysema and lung cancer. The agreement aims to reduce workers' exposure to crystalline silica dust through good practice in the workplace.

1. The European Social Dialogue: A General Introduction

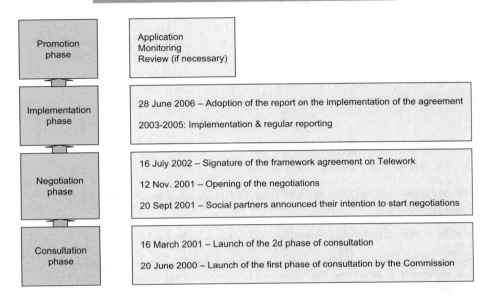

The telework agreement is the result of the launch by the Commission of a consultation on the basis of article 138 of the Treaty.

It is important because, without denying the autonomous character of the agreement, there is a Commission initiative at the beginning of the process and also a responsibility in the follow-up.

The negotiation phase was rapid and we are at the end of the implementation phase.

We are now entering into the real existence of the agreement, namely the period of concrete application, of promotion and monitoring, of possible challenges and possibly review.

The agreement on telework

IN THE CONTEXT of article 139 of the Treaty, this European framework agreement shall be implemented by the members of UNICE/UEAPME, CEEP and ETUC (and the liaison committee EUROCADRES/CEC) in accordance with the procedures and practices specific to management and labour in the Member States.

This implementation will be carried out within three years after the date of signature of this agreement.

> **Report** based on national reports from 20 EU Member States and 2 EEA countries (IS, NO).
>
> Final joint report not yet received from CY, EE, LT, SK and SI.
>
> The report looks at actions carried out to translate the agreement and to disseminate it. It analyses the choice of instruments taken in each country to implement the agreement. It examines the way in which individual provisions have been implemented, looking at each article of the agreement.

The text of the agreement includes a deadline for its implementation.

The Social Partners finalised the implementation report (June 2006), based on joint national reports from 20 Member States.

1. The European Social Dialogue: A General Introduction

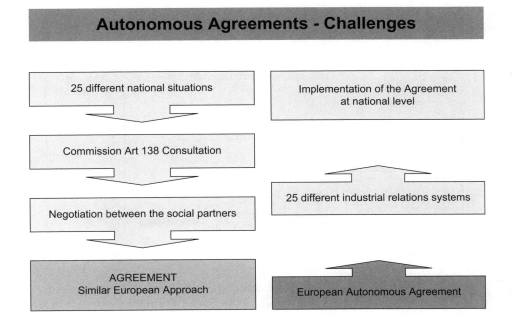

The first challenge for the implementation of the agreement is a validity test for this type of agreement.

The left column shows that there is a need to deal with 25 different national situations. The right column shows that implementation of an autonomous agreement depends on 25 different industrial relations systems. This is the first time that this has been attempted at European level.

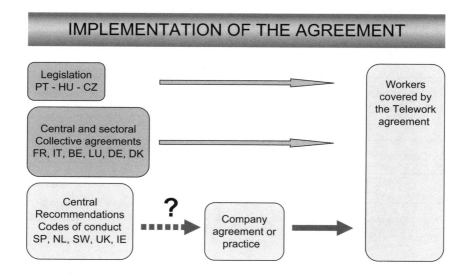

Second Challenge: centralised/decentralised industrial relations systems.

Some examples given in the report of the Social Partners show that in some countries, centralised systems of implementation where chosen. In that case, they influence directly the employment relation of the workers.

In some other countries, with decentralised systems of industrial relations, the active follow-up by companies is required. There is no information available on the real impact of eventual codes of conduct or recommendations on the real conditions of workers.

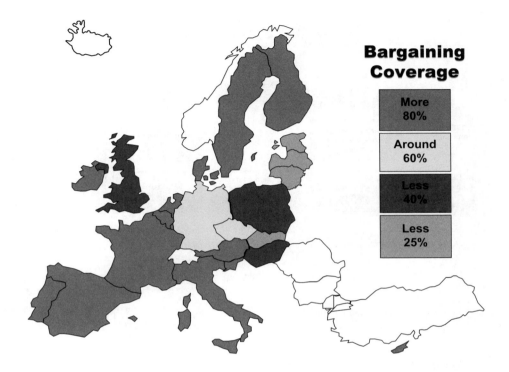

NB the legends should read: Over 80 per cent, around 60 per cent, less than 40 per cent, below 25 per cent

Third Challenge: Capacity of the Social Partners to reach the workers.

Depending of their representativeness, the capacity of the national social partners to influence practices through national industrial relations systems vary a lot: from more than 80 per cent of the workforce to less than 20 per cent.

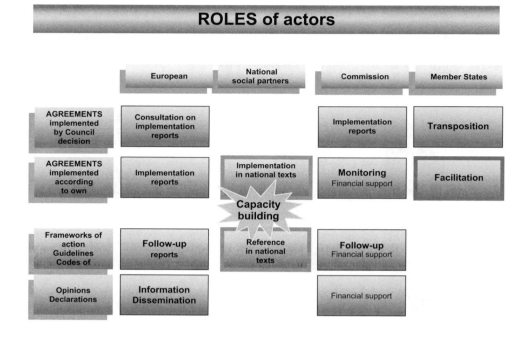

Fourth Challenge: Capacity to mobilise all actors.

With more and more complex texts adopted by the social partners at EU level, with follow-up implications and implementations procedures, the question of the inter-relationship between European and national dialogue becomes central.

To be implemented autonomous agreements need the full involvement of the national organisations. This raises the question of the quality of the industrial relations systems at national level as well as of the administrative capacity of the national actors.

This is why the European Commission has proposed to introduce the possibility to support social partners' initiatives in the new ESF[2] regulation 2007-13.

The role of the Member States is also important in supporting the implementation process.

---

2. European Social Fund.

1. The European Social Dialogue: A General Introduction

The Commission's role

COM (2004)557 final – 12/08/2004
With regard to autonomous agreements negotiated as a result of an Article 138 consultation

'Upon the expiry of the implementation and monitoring period, while giving precedence to the monitoring undertaken by the social partners themselves, the Commission will undertake its own monitoring of the agreement, to assess the extent to which the agreement has contributed to the achievment of the Community's objectives. Should the Commission decide that the agreement does not succeed in meeting the Community's objectives, it will consider the possibility of putting forward, if necessary, a proposal for a legislative act'.

The Commission should be in position **to assess** whether the Community objectives have been reached	**Way to promote** Social dialogue results and paying tribute to Social partners' work

There is **no obligation** on Member States or Social partners to notify implementation instruments to the Commission

The Commission has announced (COM (2004) 557) its intention to undertake its own monitoring of the agreement.

3 aspects were underlined:

- The Commission is not in a process similar to the implementation of an EU Directive.
- The Commission needs to be able to assess whether the Community' objectives have been reached, taking into account the fact that the telework agreement originated in a Commission consultation process.
- The Commission will promote this agreement through support given to the social partners who wish to organise national meetings and through the encouragement within sectors for the social partners to integrate the agreement in their discussions.

Autonomous Agreements - Expectations

What cannot be expected	What can be expected
100 per cent coverage	Coverage by all signatories
The same tool in each Member State	Respect of national industrial relations traditions
	Action in each Member State

CONCLUSIONS

An autonomous agreement is not a Directive, nor is it a text without a legal effect for the workers covered.

It has its own identity, but some aspects still need to be confirmed.

There are already some very positive signals. The first is the serious report established by the Social Partners.

The Commission will now undertake its own analysis, on the basis of the information already collected by the social partners and complemented by existing sources. At the end of this exercise we should be able to draw conclusions on the ability of autonomous agreements to reach Community objectives.

The objective of the Commission is to increase confidence and understanding regarding autonomous agreements, which are an innovative way to develop the European social dialogue and its influence.

More information ...

- **EUROPA website for social dialogue**
  http://ec.europa.eu/employment_social/social_dialogue/

- **Report 'Industrial Relations in Europe 2004'**
  http://ec.europa.eu/employment_social/
  social_dialogue/reports_en.htm

- **Report Industrial Relations in Europe 2006**

Chapter 2

The European Social Dialogue And Voluntary Framework Agreements

Roger Blanpain

I. A NEW STRATEGY

A new strategy between the social partners in the area of social dialogue was embarked on at the initiative of BUSINESSEUROPE, by way of the conclusion of *voluntary* agreements between the social partners. The first one concerns tele-work (16 July 2002), the second work-related stress[1] (8 October 2004).

A. AIM

The agreement on telework reads in its preamble as follows:

> In the context of the European employment strategy, the European Council invited the social partners to negotiate agreements modernising the organisation of work, including flexible working arrangements, with the aim

---

1. This agreement is, like the one on telework, a voluntary agreement. It will be implemented in accordance with the procedures and practices specific to individual countries rather than by an EU directive and aims to establish a framework within which employers and employee representatives can work together to prevent, identify and combat stress at work. See Andrea Broughton, IRS, 'Social partners sign work-related stress agreement' (October, 2004) at <www.eiro.eurofound.ie>, accessed 8 December 2006.

Blanpain et al., European Framework, Agreements and Telework, pp. 31–40.
©2007, Kluwer Law International BV, The Netherlands.

of making undertakings productive and competitive and achieving the necessary balance between flexibility and security.

The European Commission, in its second stage consultation of social partners on modernising and improving employment relations, invited the social partners to start negotiations on telework. On 20 September 2001, the ETUC (and the liaison committee EUROCADRES/CEC), BUSINESSEUROPE/ UEAPME and CEEP announced their intention to start negotiations aimed at an agreement to be implemented by the members of the signatory parties in the Member States and in the countries of the European Economic Area. Through them, they wished to contribute to preparing the transition to a knowledge-based economy and society as agreed by the European Council in Lisbon.

This voluntary agreement aims at establishing a general framework at the European level to be implemented by the members of the signatory parties in accordance with the national procedures and practices specific to management and labour. The signatory parties also invite their member organisations in candidate countries to implement this agreement.

Implementation of this agreement does not constitute valid grounds to reduce the general level of protection afforded to workers in the field of this agreement. When implementing this agreement, the members of the signatory parties avoid unnecessary burdens on SMEs.

This agreement does not prejudice the right of social partners to conclude, at the appropriate level, including European level, agreements adapting and/or complementing this agreement in a manner, which will take note of the specific needs of the social partners concerned.

B.   Implementation and Follow Up

Here the preamble reads as follows:

In the context of article 139 of the Treaty, this European framework agreement shall be implemented by the members of BUSINESSEUROPE/UEAPME, CEEP and ETUC (and the liaison committee EUROCADRES/CEC) in accordance with the procedures and practices specific to management and labour in the Member States.

This implementation will be carried out within three years after the date of signature of this agreement.

Member organisations will report on the implementation of this agreement to an ad hoc group set up by the signatory parties, under the responsibility of the social dialogue committee. This ad hoc group will prepare a joint report on the actions of implementation taken. This report will be prepared within four years after the date of signature of this agreement.

In case of questions on the content of this agreement, member organisations involved can separately or jointly refer to the signatory parties.

The signatory parties shall review the agreement five years after the date of signature if requested by one of the signatory parties.

C. Comments

This agreement raises many questions of a legal and political nature. Legal questions first – what is a voluntary agreement? Indeed, all agreements are voluntary. It probably means in this context that the agreement is not legally binding, so that it has only 'moral consequences' for the parties involved and is not enforceable before the courts. In this case the agreement would constitute a sort of voluntary code of conduct. No legal action would be possible against a signatory party or a member if a member did not implement the agreement.

The second question is whether the signatory parties can oblige their constituent members to implement the agreement. (This will depend on the mandate the signatory parties have from their members.) This does not seem to be the case here, so no legal obligations can be ascertained.

Regarding the interpretation of the agreement, member organizations can refer to the signatory parties.

The conclusion is self evident. The agreement imposes no legal obligation whatsoever and depends completely on the goodwill of the member organizations, who may implement the agreement at their will.

Moreover, many difficulties arise. Implementation will take place according to national practice. For countries where nationwide collective bargaining is prevalent and extension procedures are available this might not be a problem. In those countries, workers may enjoy the rights which are contained in the European agreement on telework. For other countries, like the UK, where those mechanisms do not exist, national collective bargaining may provide only a very partial answer, and codes of conduct may be another way of implementing the agreement.

This presents very soft law for which the European Court will not have to intervene, as there is no legally binding European rule subject to interpretation. Nor is there a role for European Parliament in this scenario.

So a European regulation on European collective bargaining is necessary, unless this new road of 'voluntarism' is one of the ways to modernize European labour law, namely by way of non-enforceable agreements. This is, however, to my mind, too soft and undermines further the already weak European social model. The ETUC was right to question this development, but the European Commission hailed the agreement as a landmark deal: 'Not only will this initiative benefit both workers and businesses, but is the first European agreement to be implemented by the social partners themselves'.

II. THE VOLUNTARY AGREEMENT ON TELEWORK OF 16 JULY 2002[2]

On 16 July 2002, in Brussels, the central EU-level social partner organizations formally signed a new EU-level framework agreement on telework. The agreement concluded consultation and debate on this topic since 2000.

---

2. A. Broughton, IRS, 'Social partners sign teleworking accord' (July, 2002) at <www.eiro. eurofound.ie>, accessed 8 December 2006.

The European Commission estimates that there are currently 4.5 million employed teleworkers (and 10 million teleworkers in total) in the EU.[3]

At the initiative of the Union of Industrial and Employers' Confederations of Europe (BUSINESSEUROPE), a so-called 'voluntary', meaning non-legally binding, agreement was concluded.

The signatories were the European Trade Union Confederation (ETUC); the Council of European Professional and Managerial Staff (EUROCADRES)/ European Confederation of Executives and Managerial Staff (CEC) liaison committee; BUSINESSEUROPE/the European Association of Craft, Small and Medium-Sized Enterprises (UEAPME); and the European Centre of Enterprises with Public Participation and of Enterprises of General Economic Interest (CEEP).

Emilio Gabaglio,
General Secretary of the ETUC
(on behalf of the trade union delegation)

Georges Jacobs,
President of BUSINESSEUROPE

Andrea Bonetti,
President of UEAPME

Rainer Plassmann,
General Secretary of CEEP

A.   General Considerations

In the context of the European employment strategy, the European Council invited the social partners to negotiate agreements modernizing the organization of work, including flexible working arrangements, with the aim of making undertakings productive and competitive and achieving the necessary balance between flexibility and security.

As indicated above, the European Commission, in its second stage consultation of social partners on modernizing and improving employment relations, invited the social partners to start negotiations on telework. On 20 September 2001, ETUC (and the EUROCADRES/CEC liaison committee), BUSINESSEUROPE/ UEAPME and CEEP announced their intention to start negotiations aimed at an agreement to be implemented by the members of the signatory parties in the Member States and in the countries of the European Economic Area (EEA). Through them, they wished to contribute to preparing the transition to a knowledge-based economy and society as agreed by the European Council in Lisbon.

---

3. Agreements were concluded earlier in the telecommunications sector (2001) and in the commerce sector (2001).

2. The European Social Dialogue and Voluntary Framework Agreements

Telework covers a wide and fast evolving spectrum of circumstances and practices. For that reason, social partners have chosen a definition of telework that covers various forms of regular telework.

The social partners see telework both as a way for companies and public service organizations to modernize work organization, and as a way for workers to reconcile work and social life and give them greater autonomy in the accomplishment of their tasks. If Europe wants to make the most out of the information society, it must encourage this new form of work organization in such a way that flexibility and security go together and the quality of jobs is enhanced, and that the chances of disabled people on the labour market are increased.

This voluntary agreement aims at establishing a general framework at European level to be implemented by the members of the signatory parties in accordance with the national procedures and practices specific to management and labour. The signatory parties also invite their member organizations in candidate countries to implement this agreement.

Implementation of this agreement does not constitute valid grounds to reduce the general level of protection afforded to workers in the field of this agreement. When implementing this agreement, the members of the signatory parties avoid unnecessary burdens on SMEs.

This agreement does not prejudice the right of social partners to conclude, at the appropriate level, including European level, agreements adapting and/or complementing this agreement in a manner which will take note of the specific needs of the social partners concerned.

B. DEFINITION AND SCOPE

Telework is a form of organizing and/or performing work, using information technology, in the context of an employment contract/relationship, where work, which could also be performed at the employer's premises, is carried out away from those premises on a regular basis.

This agreement covers teleworkers. A teleworker is any person carrying out telework as defined above.

C. VOLUNTARY CHARACTER

Telework is voluntary for the worker and the employer concerned. Teleworking may be required as part of a worker's initial job description or it may subsequently be engaged in as a voluntary arrangement.

In both cases, the employer provides the teleworker with relevant written information in accordance with Directive 91/533/EEC, including information on applicable collective agreements, description of the work to be performed, etc. The specificities of telework normally require additional written information on matters such as the department of the undertaking to which the teleworker is attached, his/her immediate superior or other persons to whom he or she can address questions of professional or personal nature, reporting arrangements, etc.

If telework is not part of the initial job description, and the employer makes an offer of telework, the worker may accept or refuse this offer. If a worker expresses the wish to opt for telework, the employer may accept or refuse this request.

The change to telework as such, because it only modifies the way in which work is performed, does not affect the teleworker's employment status.

A worker's refusal to opt for telework is not, as such, a reason for terminating the employment relationship or changing the terms and conditions of employment of that worker.

If telework is not part of the initial job description, the decision to move to telework is reversible by individual and/or collective agreement. The reversibility could imply returning to work at the employer's premises at the worker's or at the employer's request. The modalities of this reversibility are established by individual and/or collective agreement.

D.   EMPLOYMENT CONDITIONS

Regarding employment conditions, teleworkers benefit from the same rights, guaranteed by applicable legislation and collective agreements, as comparable workers at the employer's premises. However, in order to take into account the particularities of telework, specific complementary collective and/or individual agreements may be necessary.

E.   DATA PROTECTION

The employer is responsible for taking the appropriate measures, notably with regard to software, to ensure the protection of data used and processed by the teleworker for professional purposes.

The employer informs the teleworker of all relevant legislation and company rules concerning data protection.

It is the teleworker's responsibility to comply with these rules.

The employer informs the teleworker in particular of:

- Any restrictions on the use of IT equipment or tools such as the internet;
- Sanctions in the case of non-compliance.

F.   PRIVACY

The employer respects the privacy of the teleworker.

If any kind of monitoring system is put in place, it needs to be proportionate to the objective and introduced in accordance with Directive 90/270 on visual display units.[4]

G.   EQUIPMENT

All questions concerning work equipment, liability and costs are clearly defined before starting telework.

As a general rule, the employer is responsible for providing, installing and maintaining the equipment necessary for regular telework unless the teleworker uses his/her own equipment.

If telework is performed on a regular basis, the employer compensates or covers the costs directly caused by the work, in particular those relating to communication.

The employer provides the teleworker with an appropriate technical support facility.

The employer has the liability, in accordance with national legislation and collective agreements, regarding costs for loss and damage to the equipment and data used by the teleworker.

The teleworker takes good care of the equipment provided to him/her and does not collect or distribute illegal material via the internet.

H.   HEALTH AND SAFETY

The employer is responsible for the protection of the occupational health and safety of the teleworker in accordance with Directive 89/391[5] and relevant daughter directives, national legislation and collective agreements.

The employer informs the teleworker of the company's policy on occupational health and safety, in particular requirements on visual display units. The teleworker applies these safety policies correctly.

In order to verify that the applicable health and safety provisions are correctly applied, the employer, workers' representatives and/or relevant authorities have access to the telework location, within the limits of national legislation and collective agreements. If the teleworker is working at home, such access is subject to prior notification and his/her agreement.

The teleworker is entitled to request inspection visits.

---

4. Council Directive of 29 May 1990 on the minimum safety and health requirements for work with display screening equipment within the meaning of Art.16(1) of Directive 89/391/EEC.
5. Directive of 12 June 1989 on the introduction of measures to encourage improvements in the safety and health of workers at work.

I. Organization of Work

Within the framework of applicable legislation, collective agreements and company rules, the teleworker manages the organization of his/her working time.

The workload and performance standards of the teleworker are equivalent to those of comparable workers at the employer's premises.

The employer ensures that measures are taken to prevent the teleworker being isolated from the rest of the working community in the company, such as giving him/her the opportunity to meet with colleagues on a regular basis, and access to company information.

J. Training

Teleworkers have the same access to training and career development opportunities as comparable workers at the employer's premises and are subject to the same appraisal policies as these other workers.

Teleworkers receive appropriate training targeted at the technical equipment at their disposal and at the characteristics of this form of work organization. The teleworker's supervisor and his/her direct colleagues may also need training for this form of work and its management.

K. Collective Rights Issues

Teleworkers have the same collective rights as workers at the employer's premises. There are no obstacles to communicating with workers' representatives.

The same conditions for participating in and standing for elections to bodies representing workers or providing worker representation apply to them.

Teleworkers are included in calculations for determining thresholds for bodies with worker representation in accordance with European and national law, collective agreements or practices. The establishment to which the teleworker will be attached for the purpose of exercising his/her collective rights is specified from the outset.

Workers' representatives are informed and consulted about the introduction of telework in accordance with European and national legislation, collective agreements and practices.

L. Implementation and Follow Up

In the context of Article 139 of the Treaty, this European framework agreement shall be implemented by the members of BUSINESSEUROPE/UEAPME, CEEP and ETUC (and the EUROCADRES/CEC liaison committee) in accordance with the procedures and practices specific to management and labour in the Member States.

This implementation will be carried out within three years after the date of signature of this agreement.

Member organizations will report on the implementation of this agreement to an ad hoc group set up by the signatory parties, under the responsibility of the social dialogue committee. This ad hoc group will prepare a joint report on the actions of implementation taken. This report will be prepared within four years after the date of signature of this agreement.

In case of questions on the content of this agreement, member organizations involved can separately or jointly refer to the signatory parties.

The signatory parties shall review the agreement five years after the date of signature if requested by one of the signatory parties.

The non-binding agreement rightly insists on equal treatment of teleworkers regarding wages and working conditions, training, organization of work and collective rights issues. They should benefit from the same advantages as comparable workers at the employer's premises. This, however, means that the teleworkers need to perform in the country where the employer is located, which may not be the case for all teleworkers. In implementing the agreement, this aspect should be taken into account.

Chapter 3

Implementation of The European Framework Agreement on Telework

Report by the European Social Partners, Adopted by the Social Dialogue Committee on 28 June 2006

I. FOREWORD

On 16 July 2002 the European social partners ETUC (and the EUROCADRES/CEC liaison committee), BUSINESSEUROPE, UEAPME and CEEP signed a framework agreement on telework. This agreement was innovative in many regards, and opened up new perspectives for the European social dialogue as practised for the previous twenty years.

The European social partners chose for the first time to implement their European framework agreement using their own means, under the procedures and practices specific to social partners and Member States, as provided for in Article 139, paragraph 2 of the EC Treaty.

The agreement recalls that teleworkers enjoy the general protection afforded to employees. Hence, the intention was to define a general framework for the use of telework in such a way as to meet the needs of employers and workers. The agreement identifies the key areas requiring adaptation or particular attention when people work away from the employer's premises, for instance data protection, privacy, health and safety, organization of work, training, etc.

At national level, members of the signatory parties agreed on the instruments and procedures for implementation. They also disseminated, explained and transposed the European text in their national context between 2002 and 2006.

Blanpain et al., European Framework, Agreements and Telework, pp. 41–74.
©2007, Kluwer Law International BV, The Netherlands.

This report describes a large number of initiatives which have enabled the agreement to be implemented in virtually every country in the European Union and EFTA. The acceding countries have also started to give thought to how to implement the agreement. It marks an innovative stage in the process of underpinning the autonomy of the European social dialogue.

This agreement has also opened the way to other European framework agreements of the same type. These are now being implemented.

In their content, the autonomous European framework agreements concluded so far on telework and stress at work reflect the diversity of themes they address. The European social dialogue is made richer by these differences, as it is by the range of implementing instruments chosen by the social partners in each Member State. As part of their joint work programme for 2006-2008, the European social partners have decided to develop further their shared understanding of these instruments and how they can have a positive impact at various levels of social dialogue.

For ETUC	For BUSINESSEU-ROPE/UEAPME		For CEEP
John Monks	Philippe de Buck	Hans Werner Müller	Rainer Plassmann
General Secretary	Secretary General BUSINESSEUROPE	Secretary General UEAPME	Secretary General Secretary General

II.   INTRODUCTION

On 16 July 2002, ETUC, BUSINESSEUROPE/UEAPME and CEEP signed a framework agreement on telework. The negotiations began following an official consultation of the European social partners by the European Commission on the modernization of employment relations. They lasted eight months. For the first time ETUC, BUSINESSEUROPE/UEAPME and CEEP aimed at concluding an EU framework agreement to be implemented directly by their members, in accordance with the procedures and practices specific to management and labour in the Member States as defined in Article 139 of the EC Treaty.

The agreement recalls that teleworkers benefit from the same legal protection as employees working at the employer's premises, and defines a general framework for using telework at the workplace, in a way which corresponds to employers' and workers' needs. It concentrates on the aspects which are specific to working at a distance from the employer's premises and highlights key areas requiring adaptation or specific attention, such as employment conditions, data protection, privacy, equipment, health and safety, work organization, training, and collective rights.

Telework is defined as a form of organizing and/or performing work, using information technology, where work, which could also be performed at the employer's premises, is carried out away from those premises on a regular basis. The agreement concerns teleworkers with an employment contract and does not deal with self-employed telework. Neither does it concern employees of call centres who are performing their work at the premises of the call centre employing them. The EU framework agreement deals both with workers who are directly recruited as teleworkers and those who wish to opt for this form of work organization during the course of their employment relationship. It highlights that when telework is not part of the initial job description, the change to telework is voluntary both for the employer and the employee.

Implementation had to be carried out within three years after the date of signature of the agreement – July 2005. An ad hoc group working under the responsibility of the Social Dialogue Committee was set up by the signatory parties to prepare a joint report on the actions of implementation taken. The present joint implementation report was adopted by the European Social Dialogue Committee on 28 June 2006 and transmitted to the EU Commission in September 2006.

When the EU framework agreement on telework was concluded, the EU had only 15 members. However, social partners from the ten countries who joined the EU in May 2004, as well as Romania and Bulgaria, were invited to implement the agreement.

By June 2006, joint national implementation reports had been received from 23 EU Member States and EEA countries. Final joint reports have not yet been received from Cyprus, Estonia, Lithuania and Slovakia. The joint implementation process has not yet started in Bulgaria and Romania, but social partners in these countries are reflecting on how to join in the implementation process.

The number of teleworkers affected by the agreement was estimated at 4.5 million employees in 2002 (Dublin Foundation, 2002). There are no comparable cross-border data to measure its development since then. It is generally considered that telework is more widespread in some sectors of activity, such as in telecommunications, and for qualified workers. Moreover, the importance of telework varies greatly from one country to another. Some estimates indicate a rate close to 8 per cent of the working population in the Netherlands or the UK, around 5 per cent in Spain, Germany and France, and just above 2 per cent in the Czech Republic or Hungary, while telework seems to be less developed in the new Member States.

III. DISSEMINATION ACTIVITIES

The implementation process started in all countries with the translation of the EU framework agreement, followed by dissemination activities.

A. TRANSLATION OF THE EU FRAMEWORK AGREEMENT

The EU framework agreement was negotiated and drafted in English, which is the only original version adopted by the signatory parties. The first step taken in the implementation process in several countries was to agree on the translation of the EU framework agreement in the national language(s) of each country concerned.

This important first step was sometimes carried out as a purely technical exercise. In other instances it overlapped with negotiations and gave rise to difficult discussions revealing sensitive points in the national implementation.

The social partners of some countries such as Greece, the Netherlands or Spain decided to annex the jointly agreed translation to their agreement/recommendations. The locations where translations are made available are listed in the annex of the report.

B.   NATIONAL DISSEMINATION ACTIVITIES

Once the translation process was completed, the second step taken by the social partners in most countries was to carry out information and dissemination activities vis-à-vis their affiliates, in order to make the EU framework agreement known to employers and workers in their respective countries. These dissemination and information campaigns were sometimes carried out jointly and sometimes separately by employers and trade unions.

In, for example, the Czech Republic and Greece, social partners informed their respective members through their internal newsletters. Similar dissemination activities took place in Finland, the UK, Germany or Latvia. They concerned both the EU and the national agreements and included articles in newsletters, organization of special seminars and conferences, internet information, etc. In addition, Spanish social partners organized seminars and agreed to publish different studies on telework in their country. Dutch employers made a brochure entitled 'Telework, something for you?' to promote good practices in companies with regard to the introduction of telework. They also decided to engage at the highest decision-making level in a Foundation called the Telework Forum, which aims at stimulating telework in the Netherlands. Dutch trade unions have also developed a range of activities to promote the take up of telework as an issue in collective bargaining. In Sweden, dissemination activities have taken place both at national and sectoral level, with the aim of informing employers of the provisions of the framework agreement so as to serve as guidance when concluding an individual agreement on telework. In Denmark, the trade union LO prepared a 'paper of understanding' for use by their members in collective bargaining. In Latvia, further information activities targeting a wider audience (society at large as well as public authorities) are planned for the future.

In some countries employers and trade unions decided to make the promotion of telework an important priority, and engaged in initiatives which have a high political value and visibility in their countries. In Germany, for example, the Chairman of the trade union confederation DGB and the President of the German employers' confederation BDA issued a joint statement on 16 July 2002 to welcome the EU framework agreement as a good example of successful social dialogue between employers and trade unions at European level. They have publicly called for, and encouraged, initiatives by the social partners and in companies to implement the principles of the EU framework agreement on telework.

Telework is seen by social partners as a way of facilitating the integration of some disadvantaged groups on the labour market, such as disabled people in

Ireland. It is also seen as a tool to overcome mobility problems or maintain employment in regions facing difficulties. These topical issues were part of the motives which induced the Czech social partners to seek the support of different ministries in order to achieve greater co-ordination in the promotion of telework.

It is also the reason why Spanish trade unions and employers have been setting the implementation of the EU and Spanish agreements on telework as a priority for the social partners' negotiations since 2003.

C.   TRANSNATIONAL DISSEMINATION ACTIVITIES

When implementing a European framework agreement simultaneously in several different countries, it is useful to learn from each other. German social partners therefore took the initiative to organize, in 2003, in co-operation with the Danish, Austrian and French employer confederations, a transnational conference on telework and the practical application of European framework agreements.

Cross-industry European social partners also engaged in dissemination activities during the implementation period, notably when participating in conferences and seminars, where they explained the rationale and the content of the framework agreement on telework to different types of audiences. They also jointly and separately conducted promotion activities for the implementation of the text towards their members, for example the ETUC widely disseminated its own interpretation guide on the agreement.

A further example of joint European social partner promotional activities included the series of joint seminars aimed at facilitating the full integration of the social partners of the new Member States into the EU social dialogue. This took place from 2002 to 2006 as part of a project benefiting from EU financial support. Implementation of the EU framework agreement on telework was discussed as part of the joint texts negotiated in the EU social dialogue, and telework was identified as an issue on which discussions between national social partners should be engaged. This had a direct effect on the kick off of negotiations in several countries, for example in Latvia.

The agreement also had an impact on European sectoral social dialogue activities. Various sectoral social partners echoed the cross-sectoral agreement, notably the local and regional governments and electricity social dialogue committees. The locations where activities at this level are reported are listed in the annex of the report.

D.   THE CHOICE OF INSTRUMENTS: RANGING FROM SOCIAL PARTNER AGREEMENTS TO TRIPARTITE ACTIVITIES

By June 2006, the EU framework agreement had been implemented in the majority of EU Member States and EEA countries. Implementation was under way, but not fully completed, in a number of countries, including Austria, Czech Republic and Slovenia. Social partners from Bulgaria and Romania had expressed an interest in following the telework agreement in view of their forthcoming accession to the EU, but had not yet started their work.

The tools and procedures of implementation chosen by social partners varied in accordance with national practices. They included, for example, social partner agreements in Spain or collective agreements in France, and other joint texts negotiated by the social partners, such as the joint recommendation prepared in the Dutch Labour Foundation. In some cases implementation involved public authorities, as was the case for the guidelines prepared in the UK. In other cases the agreement led to changes in national legislation, for example to clarify the extent to which labour law covers the situation of telework.

The choice of the tools and procedures of implementation was made jointly by employers and trade unions, and was often the occasion of in-depth and sometimes difficult discussions between them. The difficulty of the exercise was sometimes linked to issues of substance, of procedure, or of the status of the implementation tool. This was probably due to the fact that it was the first time ever that the national social partners were asked to find a consensus on how to implement an EU framework agreement through their own means.

A further challenge to the national social partners was to develop a common understanding of what the joint approach to telework meant for both employers and workers in each country concerned, and to reach a consensus on contentious aspects in light of the EU agreement. For example, within the National Labour Council in Belgium, social partners conducted extensive preparatory work to help them fully grasp the phenomenon, including interviews of social partners from the sectors most concerned to understand why telework had been introduced and for what purposes. In Finland and Norway social partners made a thorough analysis of their national labour legislation and existing collective agreements before coming to the joint conclusion that no legislative amendment was necessary. In Slovenia, these discussions are not finalized yet and social partners still have to decide whether the framework agreement will be implemented through amendments to the Labour Relations Act or through sectoral collective agreements.

It is worth noting that the implementation of the EU framework agreement through social partners' own means was seen as an opportunity to boost bilateral social partner discussions at national, sectoral and company levels in some countries. For example, French, Polish, Italian and UK social partners explicitly welcomed the possibility to mirror at national level the bipartite commitment achieved at EU level. Similarly, the promotion of the EU agreement was set as a priority of the general bilateral agreement concluded by Czech social partners in November 2004.

As can be seen below, the implementation of the EU framework agreement has been carried out in different ways across Europe. For the purpose of this report, the results have been grouped into two broad categories: collective agreements or other bilateral social partner agreements on the one hand, and legislation or other types of tripartite activities on the other hand.

3. Implementation of the European Framework Agreement on Telework

E.   SOCIAL PARTNER AGREEMENTS

Depending on the way industrial relations systems are organized in Member States the implementation of the EU framework agreement has in some cases been ensured through a general social partner agreement, which does not have the same legal status as a collective agreement. However, in some cases highlighted below, such as in Spain or Sweden, the social partner agreement reached at national level has prompted the signature of collective agreements at sectoral or company levels. The way in which these different implementation instruments are combined depends on the national industrial relations systems.

On 23 May 2005, in Finland, a social partner agreement was adopted, together with guidelines to negotiators at local level, by the representative organizations of both the public and the private sectors. The agreement recommends to take over the key principles of the EU agreement in employment contracts as from 23 May 2005, and to take account of telework when conducting collective bargaining. The guidelines to negotiators take both the EU agreement and the existing Finnish legislation into account. They are a response to the need for guidance of local players identified by the national level social partners during their preparatory work. No sectoral agreement on telework has been adopted following the EU framework agreement, as most of them are still valid until the end of September 2007.

Since 2003, the Spanish national agreements on collective bargaining have incorporated the EU framework agreement on telework into the Spanish labour relations system. These agreements serve as guidelines for collective agreement negotiators throughout the country, set priorities for negotiations at other levels, and foresee a bipartite commission in charge of the follow up. The first Spanish national agreement on collective bargaining which mentioned the EU framework agreement on telework was concluded in 2003, was extended in 2004 and has been renewed since then. So far, ten different collective agreements on telework exist at sectoral, regional and company levels in Spain. Half of them were concluded after 2002 and they take account of the EU framework agreement either through similar negotiated provisions or by referring directly to the original text of the EU agreement. They concern the chemicals industry, the daily press sector, the region of Valencia, and the companies Telefonica de España, Telefonica Moviles España and Ibermatica. Moreover, in the region of Catalonia, social partners have agreed to promote collective bargaining at sectoral and company levels on telework and to promote legislative changes if needed. Public authorities have not taken into account the transposition of the EU framework in Spain. The action guide of the Spanish labour inspectorate mentions the EU framework agreement and refers to it when detailing the different aspects of the labour relationship between the teleworker and his/her employer.

On 12 April 2006, Latvian social partners concluded a social partner agreement committing the parties to implementing the EU framework agreement on telework.

In September 2003 the EU framework agreement on telework was implemented by a recommendation of the Labour Foundation in the Netherlands. This recommendation, which is the instrument the national social partners use to promote dialogue and agreement on issues concerning working conditions in collective bargaining at company or sectoral level and/or with works councils and individual workers, is addressed to companies and sectoral social partners. The text of this recommendation includes a reference to the agreement of the European social partners, a description of the development of telework in the Netherlands in qualitative and quantitative terms, and a description of the main elements to consider with respect to agreements on telework in collective bargaining and/or in dialogue with works councils and individual workers. The main elements highlighted are the definition of telework, its voluntary character, and the principle of equality of teleworkers and other workers with respect to working conditions as well as training and career development opportunities. Social partners agreed to annex to their recommendation the full text of the European agreement, a description of the relevant Dutch legislation with respect to telework, and some examples of provisions on telework in existing collective agreements.

In Germany a recommendation on telework has been concluded by social partners of the chemicals industry. This recommendation takes over the key elements to pay attention to when introducing telework that are described in the EU framework agreement.

Swedish social partners reached agreement on common guidelines regarding the implementation of the EU framework agreement on telework on 28 May 2003. The document states that the EU text should serve as a guideline when telework agreements are reached in Sweden and that due consideration should be given to the key elements highlighted by the EU framework agreement. As a consequence, addenda have been made to collective agreements in certain branches of industry. In other cases, the matter has been discussed between social partners and employers have taken the responsibility of informing their members of the provisions of the EU framework agreement so that they serve as guidance when concluding an individual agreement on telework.

'Guidelines for telework' were also adopted in Norway in December 2005, which give concrete recommendations to social partners' members when introducing telework. This instrument is considered to be the most appropriate by both sides for a full implementation of the EU framework agreement because of its flexibility and wider impact area.

In Poland negotiations on a national social partner agreement implementing the EU framework agreement are still in process. Social partners intend to finalize both a national agreement (for the first time ever) and a document listing amendments to integrate telework in the Labour Code, which is being revised by public authorities and should be finalized in Autumn 2006. The draft national social partner agreement implements all provisions of the EU framework agreement, and promotes an implementation of telework at company level through collective bargaining, as far as possible.

The implementation process has not been finalized in Austria either. The social partners are now trying to agree on a common social partner recommendation to be implemented at company level, most probably by the end of 2006. In the meantime, guidelines of the implementation of the EU agreement had already been adopted by Austrian employers in July 2005, which they published on the internet. These guidelines are both addressed to employers and employees. They contain the text of the agreement and comment on its provisions in the light of the existing Austrian regulations, giving concrete guidance to enterprises for the introduction of telework.

F.   NATIONAL, SECTORAL AND COMPANY LEVEL COLLECTIVE AGREEMENTS

In Belgium, France, Italy, Luxembourg, Greece, Iceland, Denmark and Sweden, social partners chose to implement the EU framework agreement through national or sectoral collective agreements, with the choice between national or sectoral collective agreements reflecting the features of the national industrial relations systems.

It should also be noted when the provisions of the EU framework agreement on telework are integrated at the occasion of general bargaining rounds in the country or sector concerned, the bargaining periods are determined by the ending period of pre-existing agreements. When these come to an end after the timeframe foreseen for the implementation of the EU agreement, some delays can be encountered in reaching the full effect of implementation of the EU agreement.

In Belgium, a national collective agreement (CNT No. 85) was adopted on 9 November 2005. The CNT No. 85 details how this new collective agreement relates to the existing rules on work conditions or employment contracts in Belgium. Compared to the EU framework agreement, it also specifies in more details the content of the written individual agreement between the teleworker and his/her employer, the consequences of the absence of such a written agreement, the method of calculation of the costs linked to the equipment, and the consequences of equipment breakdowns. In line with the preamble of the EU text which foresees that the EU agreement can be complemented or adapted in order to take into account of the specific needs of the countries concerned, the Belgian agreement also foresees that the implementation modalities of the agreement may be detailed through sectoral, company or individual agreements.

A similar approach has been taken in France, with the adoption on 19 July 2005 of a cross-industry national collective agreement. The provisions of the cross-industry national agreement can be completed and/or adapted through agreements at sectoral or company levels. In the absence of such decentralized agreements, the national agreement applies – an *erga omnes* extension was initiated at the joint request of social partners. The extension decree was published on 9 June 2006 in the Official Journal. The French agreement translates in the French context the provisions of the EU agreement, while detailing further some aspects such as the scope of the notion of teleworker, the possibility for teleworkers to apply for vacant jobs at the employer's premises, and the aspects on which equal treatment between teleworkers and workers at the employer's premises must be ensured.

The same adaptation is foreseen in Italy. On 9 June 2004, the Italian social partners agreed on an interconfederal agreement at national level to transpose the EU framework agreement on telework. This agreement is binding for almost the entire private sector and for local public services in Italy. There again, the provisions of the cross-industry national agreement can be completed and/or adapted through agreements at sectoral or company levels. The national collective agreement therefore inspires agreements at other levels but it also takes into account agreements on telework which were concluded before, notably at sectoral level, for example in the textile industry (28 May 2004), telecommunications sector, electricity, chemicals industry, paper and graphic sector, ceramic industry and for SMEs. An agreement pre-existed also in the services sector (concluded in 2001), which was renewed in July 2004, taking into account the provisions on the national cross-industry agreement on telework.

In Luxembourg, a national collective agreement was adopted on 21 February 2006. This agreement, concluded for a period of three years, implies modifications in Luxemburg's laws on work contracts and health and safety. The agreement mirrors the EU framework agreement and goes beyond on some aspects, such as the information to be given in writing to teleworkers before starting their job, and the way in which a worker can opt for telework and return to his or her previous form of work by introducing, within certain limits, an 'adaptation period' during which he or she has the right to return to work at the employer's premises.

The Greek national collective agreement implementing the EU framework agreement was signed on 12 April 2006, with the Greek translation of the EU agreement annexed.

The Icelandic collective framework agreement was signed on 5 May 2006. It serves as binding guidelines for the provisions on telework in individual employment contracts and foresees the establishment of a joint committee to deal with potential conflicts of interpretation.

In the state sector in Denmark and Sweden, the EU framework agreement on telework was implemented during the general collective bargaining rounds for the state sector employees in 2005. The new collective agreements build upon existing agreements or guidelines on telework agreed for the state sector in both countries. Also in the Danish local and regional public sector, a collective agreement had existed since 1997 which matched the requirements of the EU framework agreement. Concerning the central government sector in Sweden, a collective agreement was reached on 15 December 2005, which recognizes a role of guidelines to the EU framework agreement.

In the Danish private sector, the social partners for industrial activities amended a pre-existing collective agreement in Autumn 2005 to implement the EU framework agreement. Following on the EU agreement, the retail and wholesale trade sectors also concluded new sectoral collective agreements on telework. In order to ensure a total coverage of the private sector, the Danish confederation of employers, DA, and trade unions are currently negotiating an agreement which will implement the European framework in sectors and workplaces not yet covered.

In a company in the German telecommunications sector, social partners agreed on a collective regime which takes into account the different telework forms that exist in the sector, i.e. alternating telework and mobile telework.

G.   STANDARD COMPANY AND SECTOR AGREEMENT MODELS

In Germany, social partners provide, either jointly or separately, models of collective agreements for further use in bargaining at sector, company and/or establishment level.

Regimes for telework at establishment or company level are usually enshrined in works agreements, group agreements or company agreements. They are usually more specific than the European framework agreement and go beyond its provisions. A wide range of agreements also exist across a variety of sectors, ranging from banks, the chemicals industry, the metal industry, the telecommunications sector and skilled crafts, through to the public sector. Some of these agreements were concluded before the European framework agreement and are in line with it. Others have been prompted by the European framework agreement.

Works council agreements also exist in Germany, for example in the metal industry. The agreement existing in the metal industry entails provisions which are in line with the EU framework agreement and concern in particular the definition of telework, its voluntary nature, the way in which data and information protection is ensured, the employer's responsibility for the installation, maintenance and availability of equipment and communication tools, health and safety, working time, career development and training measures, and the participation to establishment and department meetings as well as in the works council. Similarly, in order to ease the conclusion of company level collective agreements on telework, the German confederation for local administrations and companies working in the public sector published for its members a model for a service or company agreement. The aim is to enable social partners in administrations and public sector companies to make suitable arrangements for introducing and managing telework. All of the key elements of the EU framework agreement are reflected in the standard text proposed, with some additional details. The model, for example, proposes that the division of working time between the employer's premises and the teleworker's home should be agreed to meet individual needs. In individual agreements, a suitable range of times should be agreed when the alternating teleworker can be personally contacted. Surveys have shown that local administrations and companies have overwhelmingly put in place telework arrangements via a service or company agreement. Individual contractual arrangements are only in place in the smallest organizations with little need for telework.

H.   GUIDES AND CODES OF GOOD PRACTICE

A joint guide on telework was produced by social partners in the UK in August 2003. This guide was the result of discussions between the national level social partners in the UK on the way to best implement and promote the EU framework agreement. There is no formal system of cross-sector collective bargaining at national level in the UK. The guide has been designed to provide employers, employees and other parties with information, advice and guidance on telework, an issue where employers and trade unions share a common appreciation and understanding of the value of this form of flexible working.

The stated aim of the UK guide is to 'provide a useful checklist of issues to consider when implementing teleworking and explain how the text of the European agreement might best operate in the context of the UK labour market'. As such, it expands on the EU framework agreement, with extensive use of quotations from the original agreement, helpful practical advice on implementation, and information on UK-specific legislation such as the right to request flexible working. The guide also follows the same structure and covers the same issues as the framework agreement. UK social partners believe that their guide has served as a useful checklist to help explain the issues surrounding telework, which is a growing phenomenon in the UK. They received feedback which suggests that many employers and employees have benefited from the guidance.

This guide has been developed with the full support of public authorities. The production costs for the UK guide were met by the UK's Department of Trade & Industry and the UK Government helped in the dissemination of the document.

In Ireland, social partners representing the private sector engaged in the revision of their pre-existing code of practice on e-working (a synonym of telework). Their new 'code of practice on teleworking', which was finalised on 15 December 2004, takes account of the EU framework agreement and implements it. The code of practice highlights key elements to consider when introducing telework and advises employers to draw up a written policy which specifies how telework arrangements will operate in the company. In order to help with drawing up such a policy, concrete guidance with practical examples, a sample telework agreement, and an overview of the minimum legal entitlements for Irish employees are set out in the code.

It should be noted that in a few countries the joint implementation of the EU framework agreement has been preceded by unilateral activities. For example, in Norway, guidelines were developed by the main employer organizations in Norway. Once finalized, trade unions were invited to adopt them, which they all agreed to do. These guidelines were adopted in December 2005. In Latvia too, employers released guidelines for implementation of the EU agreement for their members, following which Latvian social partners negotiated a set of common guidelines on the implementation of telework with the Ministry of Welfare and members of the Latvian Parliament.

I. IMPLEMENTATION THROUGH NATIONAL LEGISLATION

Social partners decided in some cases to call on public authorities to implement the EU framework agreement through legislation. Either they asked to fully integrate the text in national laws or to act on some precise aspects which they considered as falling outside the social partners' remit.

The first solution has notably been chosen in the Czech Republic, where, after several months of negotiations, social partners decided that the EU framework agreement on telework would be best implemented through the new Labour Code. The new Labour Code should enter into force on 1 January 2007. In the new Article 317, the possibility to agree a new form of work organization is foreseen, which includes telework. Teleworkers enjoy the same rights and duties as employees working at their employer's premises.

In Poland too, social partners wish to take advantage of the current revision of the Labour Code. They intend to introduce jointly agreed amendments to the new Labour Code with the effect of integrating telework in the legislation on the terms negotiated by social partners in their bipartite agreement.

In Hungary, the provisions of the EU framework agreement on telework were introduced into the Labour Code and apply since May 2004 to the public and private sector. This method of implementation has been proposed by the government and social partners agreed to it. In this revision of Hungarian labour law, the EU framework agreement and the amendments proposed by the Hungarian social partners have been taken into account, thereby ensuring the implementation of the EU framework agreement. The discussions on the draft Labour Code have taken place within the National Interest Reconciliation Council which is the usual body for tripartite discussions in Hungary. The main points of debate between social partners were the definition of telework, the bearing of the costs related to telework, the responsibility for compensation in case of damages to the equipment, and the definition of working time. It should also be noted that in order to promote telework, in 2004 the Government set up a specific Telework Council.

In Portugal, the transposition of the EU framework agreement on telework was made by law (Law 99/2003 from 27 August 2003, Arts 233-243 of the Labour Code). Social partners disagreed on the opportunity to implement the EU framework agreement through legislation at national level. Nevertheless, the Government took the decision to integrate the provisions of the EU framework agreement through a revision of the Labour Code in 2003. Trade unions wish to enter negotiations with employers on two further issues, namely the organization of work in call centres and the status of self-employed teleworkers. However, employers are not in favour of doing so since these two forms of telework were not covered by the EU agreement.

In Belgium and Luxembourg, in addition to their respective national collective agreements, social partners called on public authorities to act on some aspects which they considered as falling outside the remit of social partners' exclusive competences. In their Opinion (avis n° 1.528), adopted on 9 November 2005, Belgian social partners asked the Government to propose a number of legislative changes in order for the new collective agreement on telework to be harmoniously integrated in the pre-existing regulations. These changes concerned, for example, the recognition of the fact that telework is exercised in the framework of a normal work relation and is not a separate legal status (there exists in Belgium a special status for workers working at home), and how to distinguish work accidents from private accidents. In Luxembourg, social partners called on public authorities to review existing rules of the social security affiliation and tax regime of cross-border workers, in order not to hamper the development of telework. These rules being defined to a large extent at European level, social partners asked their Government to convince their European partners to modify the existing EU regulations on these aspects.

Obstacles to the development of telework due to taxation were also discussed in the UK. The UK guide on telework recalls that a measure introduced in the UK Budget in 2003 enables employers to meet some or all of the incidental household costs incurred by employees who work at home (heating, electricity, etc.) without it giving rise to a tax charge for the employee.

J. OTHER TRIPARTITE ACTIVITIES

Finally, in some countries, social partners called upon the public authorities to help ensure a common understanding of the challenges created by telework, which led to a range of different tripartite activities.

As mentioned above, the Latvian social partners negotiated a set of guidelines on the implementation of telework with the Ministry of Welfare and members of the Latvian Parliament.

In the UK, the Government financed the publication of the joint social partners' guide on telework. In Malta, ground work is under way by the Maltese social partners and the Government to review the existing status of teleworkers in the Labour Code and to tackle cultural and mentality obstacles to the development of telework.

IV. KEY ISSUES IN THE IMPLEMENTATION

In terms of content, the key features of the follow up and implementation of the EU framework agreement on telework in the 27 European countries concerned can be summarized as follows. They are presented in accordance with the structure of the EU agreement.

A. DEFINITION AND SCOPE

> ## 2. DEFINITION AND SCOPE
>
> Telework is a form of organizing and/or performing work, using information technology, in the context of an employment contract/relationship, where work, which could also be performed at the employer's premises, is carried out away from those premises on a regular basis.
>
> This agreement covers teleworkers. A teleworker is any person carrying out telework as defined above.

The EU framework agreement on telework defines telework as 'a form of organising and/or performing work, using information technology, in the context of an employment contract/relationship, where work, which could also be performed at the employer's premises, is carried out away from those premises on a regular basis'. Social partners in most countries adopted this definition or a very similar one, as for example in the recommendation on telework adopted by German social partners in the chemical or the Irish code of practice on telework from 2004. In a Spanish collective agreement for the daily press adopted on 22 July 2005, social partners welcomed the clarity of this definition as it eliminates pre-existing uncertainties on the employee status of the teleworker.

In some countries, the EU definition and scope of the agreeement were changed. For example, the Hungarian legal provisions define a teleworker as someone who communicates the result of his/her work via electronic devices.

Social partners themselves have sometimes changed the EU definition of teleworker. In France, for example, the notion of teleworker includes 'nomad workers'. In Italy, two different types of telework are defined: the teleworker working from home and the teleworker working at a distance. The Irish code of practice stipulates explicitly that the notion of teleworker is synonymous with e-worker and that the code also applies to telecommuters and mobile e-workers. In a company in the telecommunications sector in Germany, the collective regime agreed by social partners takes into account the different telework forms that exist in the sector, i.e. alterning telework and mobile telework.

B. VOLUNTARY CHARACTER

> ## 3. VOLUNTARY CHARACTER
>
> Telework is voluntary for the worker and the employer concerned. Teleworking may be required as part of a worker's initial job description or it may subsequently be engaged in as a voluntary arrangement.
>
> In both cases, the employer provides the teleworker with relevant written information in accordance with Directive 91/533/EEC, including information on

applicable collective agreements, description of the work to be performed, etc. The specificities of telework normally require additional written information on matters such as the department of the undertaking to which the teleworker is attached, his/her immediate superior or other persons to whom she or he can address questions of a professional or personal nature, reporting arrangements, etc.

If telework is not part of the initial job description, and the employer makes an offer of telework, the worker may accept or refuse this offer. If a worker expresses the wish to opt for telework, the employer may accept or refuse this request.

The change to telework as such, because it only modifies the way in which work is performed, does not affect the teleworker's employment status.

A worker refusal to opt for telework is not, as such, a reason for terminating the employment relationship or changing the terms and conditions of employment of that worker.

If telework is not part of the initial job description, the decision to move to telework is reversible by individual and/or collective agreement. The reversibility could imply returning to work at the employer's premises at the worker's or at the employer's request. The modalities of this reversibility are established by individual and/or collective agreement.

The voluntary character of telework is affirmed clearly by the EU framework agreement when it states that 'telework is voluntary for the worker and the employer concerned'. This principle is reaffirmed in all social partners' transposition measures across Europe.

The provision of the EU framework agreement has even been used by the Spanish Supreme Court in a case from 11 April 2005 as an interpretation criterion to highlight the importance of the worker's willingness to opt for telework, if telework is not part of the initial job description.

Two situations are envisaged: 'teleworking may be required as a part of a worker's initial job description or it may be engaged in as a voluntary arrangement subsequently'. All implementation tools mention this distinction as it has important consequences and the possibility for the worker to return to or get a job at the employer's premises.

In both cases, the EU framework agreement foresees the obligation for the employer to provide the teleworker with relevant written information in accordance with Directive 91/533/EEC, including information on applicable collective agreements, description of the work to be performed, etc. The EU framework agreement also states that the specificities of telework normally require additional written information on matters such as the department of the undertaking to which the teleworker is attached, his/her immediate superior or other persons to whom he or she can address questions of professional or personal nature, reporting arrangements, etc.

These indications have been followed in all countries. In some of them, it is specifically stated that this implies an addendum to the work contract (France, Belgium, and Poland). The UK guide on telework recalls the obligation for employers to provide the worker with a written statement of particulars within two months of commencement for teleworkers recruited as such, and within one month for teleworkers subsequently changing work organization.

In some countries, social partners have been even more specific. This is, for example, the case in Belgium. The Belgian national collective agreement, CCT No. 85, from 9 November 2005, foresees in Article 6 that the individual agreement, to be concluded before starting telework, must contain in writing the following:

- The frequency of telework and possibly the days on which telework is done, and if needed the days and/or hours where the worker is present in the enterprise.
- The periods of time during which the teleworker can be contacted and by which means.
- When the teleworker can ask for technical support.
- The way in which the employer covers the costs linked to the equipment and breakdowns.
- The conditions in which a teleworker can return to working at the employer's premises, the notice period and/or the duration of the telework and its renewal modalities.

It also stipulates that in case there is no written agreement on those points, the teleworker has the right to work at the employer's premises.

Also, in Luxembourg, social partners have listed in great detail the mandatory written information to be provided to teleworkers. In addition to what is foreseen at EU level, Article 4 of the national collective agreement states that it should be mentioned in writing:

- The place from which the teleworker performs the work.
- A detailed description of the tasks to be accomplished in a way which allows the teleworker to compare him/herself to similar workers working at the employer's premises.
- The classification of the worker in the classification grid of the collective agreement.
- Days and hours where the teleworker can be contacted by the employer.
- The exact description of the equipment provided and installed by the employer.
- Information concerning the insurances contracted by the employer to guarantee the equipment in case of fire, flooding, theft, etc.

Finally, in the Polish draft social partner agreement, it is mentioned that a written document should entail information on the work system and schedule, the form and manner of reporting for work, the form and manner of explaining absence from work, the work arrangements, including the form and manner of assigning tasks and reviewing their fulfilment, and the rules for sending the teleworker on a business trip and refunding business trip expenses.

Detailing further the consequences of the voluntary character of telework, the EU framework agreement states that:

> If telework is not part of the initial job description, and the employer makes an offer of telework, the worker may accept or refuse this offer. If a worker expresses the wish to opt for telework, the employer may accept or refuse this request. The passage of telework as such, because it only modifies the way in which work is performed, does not affect the teleworker's employment status. A worker's refusal to opt for telework is not, as such, a reason for terminating the employment relationship or changing the terms and conditions of employment of that worker.

On this point, the UK joint guide on telework recalls the UK legislation regarding the right for employees to request flexible working for parents with disabled children or children under six, and the corresponding duty for employers to give serious consideration to such requests (p.8). The Italian national collective agreement mentions one exception to the above-mentioned principles, in the case where telework is the only way to perform a particular job (Article 2 of the national collective agreement). This exception aims at securing the possibility for the employer, in a process of re-organization, to assign the worker to a similar post in the enterprise even if the execution of the tasks requires teleworking.

The next issue mentioned by the EU framework agreement is the reversibility of the choice of telework by individual and/or collective agreement. This applies in case telework is not a part of the initial job description:

> The decision to pass to telework is reversible. The reversibility could imply returning to work at the employer's premises at the worker's or at the employer's request. The modalities of this reversibility are established by individual and/or collective agreement.

In some countries, the conditions in which a worker who opted for telework can return to his/her previous form of work organization has gone beyond what was foreseen in the EU framework agreement.

The provisions of the French national cross-industry agreement can be completed and/or adapted through agreements at sectoral or company levels. Certain provisions apply directly to lower level agreements without the possibility to be amended; others foresee a greater flexibility for social partners at other levels. For example, the principle of reversibility from telework to working at the employer's premises is obligatory. However, the modalities of application of this principle can be adapted at sector or company level. In the case of a change to telework, the French collective agreement foresees in Article 2 that an adaptation period should be created during which the worker and the employer can unilaterally end the telework arrangements. The period of notice should be defined in advance. A job, in accordance with the worker's qualifications and at the employer's premises, shall be proposed to the worker. After the end of this adaptation period, returning to work at the employer's premises is subject to an agreement between the employer and the teleworker.

3. Implementation of the European Framework Agreement on Telework

In Poland, the draft national social partner agreement foresees an adaptation period of three months, during which unilateral termination of telework is possible.

A similar adaptation period, of 3 to 12 months, is foreseen in the Luxembourg national collective agreement (Article 5 of the national collective agreement). The exact length of the adaptation period must be defined in agreement between both parties. A unilateral decision to opt out of telework cannot occur within the two first weeks. The exact ways to put an end to the adaptation period as well as the notice period are regulated in all details in the national collective agreement. After the adaptation period, the return to work at the employer's premises requires an agreement between the employer and the teleworker (Article 17 of the national collective agreement). The teleworker is informed in priority of the job opportunities within the enterprise which correspond to his/her qualifications. In the case of such a return, the national collective agreement entails a list of information to be delivered without delay to the worker and notably his/her location of work, working hours and working conditions.

The Danish collective agreement for the local and regional public sector foresees that individual agreements with teleworkers can only be agreed in the framework of a local collective agreement. Furthermore, if the agreement is terminated the employee has a right to return to the same job or, in the event that this is not possible, to another job with the same or similar specifications.

Irish social partners have agreed in their code of practice that where telework is entered into voluntarily there should be provision for suspending or terminating the telework arrangement and returning to previous employment at the previous location, at the employer's or the employee's request. The modalities/procedure for returning from telework, including adequate notice, should be agreed between the parties, i.e. the employer and the teleworker, or by collective agreement at the outset.

The UK guide on telework recalls that reversibility is subject to agreement between the employer and the teleworker (p.9). The circumstances in which a decision to telework cannot be reversed (for example, no space at the employer's premises or costs of reversal too high) should be spelled out at the beginning, either in collective or individual agreements.

Specific arrangements had not been foreseen at EU level for workers for whom telework is part of the initial job description but who wish to work at the employer's premises. However, some implementation measures in Member States did so. For example, in case telework is part of the initial job description, the French social partners have granted the teleworker wishing to work at the employer's premises the possibility to apply to any vacant post and with a priority to get the job (Article 3 of the national collective agreement).

In the Luxembourg national collective agreement a special article is devoted to regulating this question (Article 16 of the national collective agreement). It states that the change from telework to working at the employer's premises requires agreement between the employer and the worker. The worker for whom telework is part of the initial job description but who wishes to work at the employer's premises is informed in priority of the vacant posts within the enterprise which correspond to his/her qualifications.

C.   EMPLOYMENT CONDITIONS

---

4. EMPLOYMENT CONDITIONS

Regarding employment conditions, teleworkers benefit from the same rights, guaranteed by applicable legislation and collective agreements, as comparable workers at the employer's premises. However, in order to take into account the particularities of telework, specific complementary collective and/or individual agreements may be necessary.

This principle has been translated as it stands in all countries. This is, for example, the case in the labour foundation's recommendation on telework agreed upon in 2003 in the Netherlands, or in the Swedish social partner agreement on common guidelines also adopted in 2003. The Irish code of practice recommends that any changes to normal work practices or to the application of the employee's terms and conditions due to telework be agreed from the outset in a collective or individual agreement.

Social partners in some countries give further details on the aspects to be taken into account when following this principle. The French national collective agreement, for example, states that the workload, production norms and result criteria set for the teleworker must be equivalent to those set for similar workers working at the employer's premises. These notions and principles are rarely used in collective agreements in France.

Going beyond the EU framework agreement, the national collective agreement in Luxembourg foresees that when a change to telework implies the loss of a pre-existing benefit in kind for the worker or implies that the worker will no longer be able to make use of this benefit in kind in the same way as comparable workers at the employer's premises, the employer has to grant a compensatory advantage.

Similarly, the legislator has sometimes added to the EU text to specify how to take into account the particularities of telework. The Hungarian Labour Code, for example, foresees specific rules with regard to the right for the employer to enter the location where the work is performed, the way to control working and resting time, etc.

D.   DATA PROTECTION

---

5. DATA PROTECTION

The employer is responsible for taking the appropriate measures, notably with regard to software, to ensure the protection of data used and processed by the teleworker for professional purposes.

The employer informs the teleworker of all relevant legislation and company rules concerning data protection.

> It is the teleworker's responsibility to comply with these rules.
> The employer informs the teleworker in particular of:
>
> - Any restrictions on the use of IT equipment or tools such as the internet;
> - Sanctions in the case of non-compliance.

Social partners in most countries refer to the application to teleworkers of national data protection rules. This is the case in France where the work of the CNIL (National Commission for Informatics and Freedoms) is mentioned. In Italy, the national collective agreement refers to the code on the protection of personal data and the code on confidentiality. In Germany, both legislation and company rules are mentioned in the works agreement of a company in the German metal industry. The Irish code of practice and the UK guide detail the provisions of applicable national and European regulations.

Some national implementation measures entail further provisions. The Polish draft social partner agreement, for example, foresees an obligation for the employer to issue a policy regarding data protection in his/her enterprise and the corresponding responsibility for the employee to respect the rules.

In the collective regime agreed in a company in the German telecommunications sector, it is stipulated that particular attention is to be paid to protection of data and information vis-à-vis third parties. Confidential data and information must be protected in such a way that third parties have no access. Statutory data protection provisions apply, as do the company's central rules for ensuring data protection and data security. The employee is informed in an appropriate manner about statutory and in-house rules governing data protection and data security.

The Irish code of practice lists a number of elements to pay attention to, such as how to deal with secure document waste, locking of the home office/computer, procedures for computer virus checking and password changes, data backups, confidentiality and non-disclosure agreements. The UK guide on telework contains similar provisions and highlights in addition to the above-mentioned elements the potential risks linked to the access to personal data and breaches of integrity.

E. PRIVACY

6. PRIVACY

The employer respects the privacy of the teleworker.

If any kind of monitoring system is put in place, it needs to be proportionate to the objective and introduced in accordance with Directive 90/270 on visual display units.

In most cases, this provision has been taken over *in extenso* in national implementation measures. A right to information on any checking facility is, for example, enshrined in the Irish code of practice. The use of a monitoring system is, however, not specifically regulated by the Hungarian Labour Code.

F.   EQUIPMENT

---

7. EQUIPMENT

All questions concerning work equipment, liability and costs are clearly defined before starting telework.

As a general rule, the employer is responsible for providing, installing and maintaining the equipment necessary for regular telework unless the teleworker uses his/her own equipment.

If telework is performed on a regular basis, the employer compensates or covers the costs directly caused by the work, in particular those relating to communication.

The employer provides the teleworker with an appropriate technical support facility.

The employer has the liability, in accordance with national legislation and collective agreements, regarding costs for loss and damage to the equipment and data used by the teleworker.

The teleworker takes good care of the equipment provided to him/her and does not collect or distribute illegal material via the internet.

The EU framework agreement stipulates that 'all questions concerning work equipment, liability and costs are clearly defined before starting telework'. Social partners in some countries have translated this provision by introducing it in the list of mandatory written information to be given to the teleworker.

'As a general rule, the employer is responsible for providing, installing and maintaining the equipment necessary for regular telework unless the teleworker uses his/her own equipment'. This question is considered an important one as in most countries the rules applicable have been detailed in national instruments.

In several countries, social partners decided that the employer should bear the entire responsibility of the provision, installation and maintenance of the equipment. This is, for example, the case in the Belgian national collective agreement or the specimen of service or company agreement agreed for local administrations and public sector companies in Germany. Specific rules are very often foreseen in case the teleworker uses his/her own equipment.

However, the Hungarian Labour Code, which takes into account an amendment of national social partners, is more nuanced. The responsibility for providing the equipment and communication facilities are subject to an agreement between the employer and the employee. Only if there is no agreement shall the employer bear this responsibility.

Some countries detail more precisely the responsibilities of both sides. For example, the French national collective agreement from July 2005 foresees that, if the teleworker works from home, the responsibility of the employer to provide, install and maintain the equipment is subject to the conformity of the electricity and work space at the worker's home (Article 7 of the national collective agreement). In the German collective regime of a company in the telecommunication sector it is stated that, in the case of telework from the worker's home, private office furniture which meets health and safety requirements can be used with the worker assuming the costs and risks. However, for the social partners in Luxembourg, the employer bears also the responsibility of controlling the conformity of the electricity and work space of the teleworker (Article 11 of the national collective agreement). A similar provision is entailed in the Irish code of practice, which recalls that an employer is obliged by law to undertake a health and safety risk assessment to ensure that the teleworker's workstation complies with all legislation. This is linked to health and safety questions and has been in some instances dealt with in relation to s.8 on health and safety in the EU framework agreement. In the Polish draft social partner agreement, the conditions under which the teleworker uses their own equipment are narrowly regulated. It is foreseen that the employer and the teleworker may agree that the teleworker will use their own equipment. However, in such a case, the teleworker is entitled to a lump sum, the amount and payment procedure for which should be agreed beforehand between the two parties. Furthermore, parties may agree that the employer covers the costs for installation, repairs and maintenance.

Another important question concerns who bears the costs related to communication, for example internet connection. In most Member States, it was decided that the employer should compensate or cover the costs directly caused by the work, in particular those relating to communication, in accordance with the EU framework agreement.

However, the Belgian national collective agreement, CCT 85, from 9 November 2005, is quite detailed on this aspect. It stipulates in its Article 9 that the costs borne by the employer are calculated before the start of telework proportionately to the amount of telework done or following an allocation rule to be determined by the parties to the agreement.

The implementation of the provision according to which 'the employer provides the teleworker with an appropriate technical support facility' has not led to any controversy and has been integrated as such in all implementation instruments.

The EU framework agreement foresees that 'the employer has the liability, in accordance with national legislation and collective agreements, regarding costs for loss and damage to the equipment and data used by the teleworker'. In most countries, social partners explicitly made reference to the duty of the worker to inform the employer immediately in the case of problems with the equipment. This is also linked to the last provision under this section of the EU framework agreement which states that 'the teleworker takes good care of the equipment provided to him/her and does not collect or distribute illegal material via the internet'.

In Belgium, the national collective agreement from November 2005 also regulated the respective responsibilities of the employer and the teleworker in the case of an equipment breakdown. In its Article 13, it stipulates that in the case of such a breakdown, the teleworker must inform the employer immediately and that the teleworker is paid during that period. Specific arrangements can be foreseen, such as the replacement of the equipment or a temporary assignment at the employer's premises.

G. HEALTH AND SAFETY

---

8. HEALTH AND SAFETY

The employer is responsible for the protection of the occupational health and safety of the teleworker in accordance with Directive 89/391 and relevant daughter directives, national legislation and collective agreements.

The employer informs the teleworker of the company's policy on occupational health and safety, in particular requirements on visual display units. The teleworker applies these safety policies correctly.

In order to verify that the applicable health and safety provisions are correctly applied, the employer, workers' representatives and/or relevant authorities have access to the telework location, within the limits of national legislation and collective agreements. If the teleworker is working at home, such access is subject to prior notification and his/her agreement.

The teleworker is entitled to request inspection visits.

As for data protection (s.5), national implementation measures recall in most cases that the general rules on health and safety are applicable to teleworkers. The UK guide and the Irish code of practice, for example, make reference to the applicable national and European regulations. In these two countries employers are obliged by law to undertake a health and safety risk assessment to ensure that a teleworker's workstation complies with all legislation. The UK guide on telework gives further details on the hazards that can arise from electrical equipment and visual display units, as well as on the special protection due to new or expectant mothers (p.17).

Limitations to the application of health and safety rules are also mentioned. The UK guide recalls that the employer is responsible for the safety of the equipment they supply but that teleworkers' domestic electrical system is their own responsibility. The Hungarian Labour Code stipulates that the general health and safety rules apply to teleworkers in the case where their equipment is owned by the employer. The Polish draft social partner agreement foresees that the teleworker must receive health and safety training before starting teleworking, in particular on the use of visual displays. However, general health and safety rules do not apply to the workplace of the teleworker if it is situated at home.

H. ORGANIZATION OF WORK

---

9. ORGANIZATION OF WORK

Within the framework of applicable legislation, collective agreements and company rules, the teleworker manages the organization of his/her working time.

The workload and performance standards of the teleworker are equivalent to those of comparable workers at the employer's premises.

The employer ensures that measures are taken to prevent the teleworker being isolated from the rest of the working community in the company, such as giving him/her the opportunity to meet with colleagues on a regular basis, and access to company information.

The EU framework agreement states that 'within the framework of applicable legislation, collective agreements and company rules, the teleworker manages the organisation of his/her working time'. The issue of working time has been explicitly dealt with in all countries. Most countries referred to the application of the existing legislation covering workers, as for instance in Italy or Ireland. Some social partners have also detailed particular aspects. The Irish code of practice mentions, for example, the obligation to include mechanisms to avoid unfair extra workload on those working at home or left back at the office. The Luxembourg national collective agreement stipulates that employer and worker must agree on the way to take account of overtime.

The EU framework agreement adds: 'The workload and performance standards of the teleworker are equivalent to those of comparable workers at the employer's premises'. In the UK guide on telework, it is explained that direct productivity comparisons should acknowledge potential for extra administration requirements of office-based workers such as answering telephones, generalized procedural requirements, etc. Feedback on performance is very important for distant workers. Mechanisms for the delivery of feedback should also be clearly defined. In France, the national collective agreement mentions in particular the fact that teleworkers should have similar evaluation meetings as workers at the employer's premises.

A great number of implementation instruments mention the need to pay attention not to isolate the teleworker from his colleagues at the employer's premises. This is done in accordance with the provisions of the EU framework agreement, i.e.:

> The employer ensures that measures are taken preventing the teleworker from being isolated from the rest of the working community in the company, such as giving him/her the opportunity to meet with colleagues on a regular basis and access to company information.

The works agreement in a company active in the German metal sector mentions in addition a need to ensure participation in establishment and department meetings. The UK guide gives examples of innovative organizational practices, such as establishing 'social club facilities', 'soft seating areas' for informal conversations, and 'hot desking'.

I. TRAINING

---

10. TRAINING

Teleworkers have the same access to training and career development opportunities as comparable workers at the employer's premises and are subject to the same appraisal policies as these other workers.

Teleworkers receive appropriate training targeted at the technical equipment at their disposal and at the characteristics of this form of work organization. The teleworker's supervisor and his/her direct colleagues may also need training for this form of work and its management.

In most countries, the provisions of the EU framework agreement on training have been taken over without adding further details. The implemented provisions foresee that teleworkers have the same access to training and career development opportunities as comparable workers at the employer's premises, and are subject to the same appraisal policies as these other workers. They receive appropriate training targeted at the technical equipment at their disposal and at the characteristics of this form of work organization. Moreover it is mentioned that the teleworker's supervisor and his/her direct colleagues may also need training for this form of work and its management.

However, the UK guide on telework lists in addition to the above the core areas in which the teleworker may need training, such as job-related skills, generic skills in IT and communication methods, as well as self-management skills including training in time management. The specimen of service or company agreement developed by social partners for the local administration and public sector companies in Germany, as well as the collective regime agreed by social partners in a company in the German telecommunications sector, specify that the teleworker cannot be put at a disadvantage regarding his/her participation to training compared with his/her colleagues working at the employer's premises.

J. COLLECTIVE RIGHTS ISSUES

---

11. COLLECTIVE RIGHTS ISSUES

Teleworkers have the same collective rights as workers at the employer's premises. There are no obstacles to communicating with workers' representatives.

> The same conditions for participating in and standing for elections to bodies representing workers or providing worker representation apply to them.
>
> Teleworkers are included in calculations for determining thresholds for bodies with worker representation in accordance with European and national law, collective agreements or practices. The establishment to which the teleworker will be attached for the purpose of exercising his/her collective rights is specified from the outset.
>
> Workers' representatives are informed and consulted on the introduction of telework in accordance with European and national legislations, collective agreements and practices.

All implementation instruments recognize the fact that teleworkers have the same collective rights as workers at the employer's premises and that no obstacles can be put to communicating with workers' representatives. They also recognize that the same conditions for participating in and standing for elections to bodies representing workers or providing workers' representation apply to teleworkers.

The other provisions of the EU framework agreement concerning the inclusion of teleworkers in calculations for determining thresholds for bodies with worker representation in accordance with European and national law, collective agreements or practices, and the fact that the establishment to which the teleworker will be attached for the purpose of exercising his/her collective rights is specified from the outset, were also implemented.

Finally, it is generally agreed that workers' representatives must be informed and consulted on the introduction of telework in accordance with European and national legislation, collective agreements and practices.

K. IMPLEMENTATION AND FOLLOW UP

---

12. IMPLEMENTATION AND FOLLOW UP

In the context of Article 139 of the Treaty, this European framework agreement shall be implemented by the members of BUSINESSEUROPE/UEAPME, CEEP and ETUC (and the EUROCADRES/CEC liaison committee) in accordance with the procedures and practices specific to management and labour in the Member States.

This implementation will be carried out within three years after the date of signature of this agreement.

Member organizations will report on the implementation of this agreement to an ad hoc group set up by the signatory parties, under the responsibility of the social dialogue committee. This ad hoc group will prepare a joint report on the actions of implementation taken. This report will be prepared within four years after the date of signature of this agreement.

In case of questions on the content of this agreement, member organizations involved can separately or jointly refer to the signatory parties.

> The signatory parties shall review the agreement five years after the date of signature if requested by one of the signatory parties.

This section refers to the fact that the European social partners have agreed that, for the first time, an EU framework agreement signed by ETUC, BUSINESSEU-ROPE/UEAPME and CEEP would be implemented directly by their members, in accordance with the procedure defined in Article 139 of the EU Treaty. It foresees an implementation period of three years and specifies the reporting procedure, the procedure in case of questions on the content of the agreement, and the possibility to review the framework agreement after five years if so requested by one of the signatory parties.

This section did not require as such an implementation by the national social partners. Nevertheless, the Italian and French collective agreements mention their commitment to report in time to the European social partners on the actions they took to implement the EU framework agreement on telework.

In several countries, the procedure to follow in case of questions or disagreement regarding the interpretation of the EU text was specified. The Italian social partners recalled the possibility given by the EU framework agreement to address queries, jointly or not, to EU level social partners on interpretation. In Iceland, a joint committee was established to deal with conflicts that may arise from the agreement, including conflicts in interpretation that shall be resolved in coherence with the EU framework agreement. The Danish collective agreements on telework are, as are all other collective agreements in Denmark, subject to arbitration.

Finally, in almost all countries, reference is made to the fact that telework is a developing phenomenon, the precise assessment of which is difficult to make after such a short period of time since the adoption of the EU framework agreement.

V.   CONCLUSION

To sum up, ETUC, BUSINESSEUROPE, UEAPME and CEEP consider that the present report clearly demonstrates the wealth of social partner initiatives in the EU framework agreement on telework.

It illustrates the commitment of the national social partners to back up the commitments made on their behalf in the European social dialogue. Many of the social partners across Europe have shown that they can successfully come to grips with an important issue for the future in autonomous negotiations.

The reporting exercise shows the heterogeneity both in reporting and implementation. This is partly due to the fact that it is the first time that member organizations have had to do this. It is also partly due to the novelty of the issue itself and partly due to the diversity of industrial relations systems. However, some challenges had to be overcome, for example the translation of the EU framework agreement and the development of a common understanding on the nature of the autonomous EU framework agreement.

These elements will feed into the discussions European social partners will have, according to their work programme 2006-2008, in order to further develop their common understanding of these instruments and how they can have a positive impact at the various levels of social dialogue.

The report also shows that the EU social dialogue can be a source of development of innovative social dialogue practices across Europe.

VI.   ANNEX

FRAMEWORK AGREEMENT ON TELEWORK

1. GENERAL CONSIDERATIONS

IN THE CONTEXT of the European employment strategy, the European Council invited the social partners to negotiate agreements modernizing the organization of work, including flexible working arrangements, with the aim of making undertakings productive and competitive and achieving the necessary balance between flexibility and security.

The European Commission, in its second stage consultation of social partners on modernizing and improving employment relations, invited the social partners to start negotiations on telework. On 20 September 2001, ETUC (and the liaison committee EUROCADRES/CEC), BUSINESSEUROPE/UEAPME and CEEP announced their intention to start negotiations aimed at an agreement to be implemented by the members of the signatory parties in the Member States and in the countries of the European Economic Area. Through them, they wished to contribute to preparing the transition to a knowledge-based economy and society as agreed by the European Council in Lisbon.

Telework covers a wide and fast evolving spectrum of circumstances and practices.

For that reason, social partners have chosen a definition of telework that permits to cover various forms of regular telework.

The social partners see telework both as a way for companies and public service organizations to modernize work organization, and as a way for workers to reconcile work and social life and giving them greater autonomy in the accomplishment of their tasks. If Europe wants to make the most out of the information society, it must encourage this new form of work organization in such a way, that flexibility and security go together and the quality of jobs is enhanced, and that the chances of disabled people on the labour market are increased.

This voluntary agreement aims at establishing a general framework at the European level to be implemented by the members of the signatory parties in accordance with the national procedures and practices specific to management and labour. The signatory parties also invite their member organizations in candidate countries to implement this agreement.

Implementation of this agreement does not constitute valid grounds to reduce the general level of protection afforded to workers in the field of this agreement. When implementing this agreement, the members of the signatory parties avoid unnecessary burdens on SMEs.

This agreement does not prejudice the right of social partners to conclude, at the appropriate level, including European level, agreements adapting and/or complementing this agreement in a manner which will take note of the specific needs of the social partners concerned.

2. DEFINITION AND SCOPE

TELEWORK is a form of organizing and/or performing work, using information technology, in the context of an employment contract/relationship, where work, which could also be performed at the employer's premises, is carried out away from those premises on a regular basis.

This agreement covers teleworkers. A teleworker is any person carrying out telework as defined above.

3. VOLUNTARY CHARACTER

TELEWORK is voluntary for the worker and the employer concerned. Teleworking may be required as part of a worker's initial job description or it may subsequently be engaged in as a voluntary arrangement.

In both cases, the employer provides the teleworker with relevant written information in accordance with Directive 91/533/EEC, including information on applicable collective agreements, description of the work to be performed, etc. The specificities of telework normally require additional written information on matters such as the department of the undertaking to which the teleworker is attached, his/her immediate superior or other persons to whom he or she can address questions of professional or personal nature, reporting arrangements, etc.

If telework is not part of the initial job description, and the employer makes an offer of telework, the worker may accept or refuse this offer. If a worker expresses the wish to opt for telework, the employer may accept or refuse this request.

The change to telework as such, because it only modifies the way in which work is performed, does not affect the teleworker's employment status.

A worker's refusal to opt for telework is not, as such, a reason for terminating the employment relationship or changing the terms and conditions of employment of that worker.

If telework is not part of the initial job description, the decision to move to telework is reversible by individual and/or collective agreement. The reversibility could imply returning to work at the employer's premises at the worker's or at the employer's request. The modalities of this reversibility are established by individual and/or collective agreement.

4. EMPLOYMENT CONDITIONS

REGARDING employment conditions, teleworkers benefit from the same rights, guaranteed by applicable legislation and collective agreements, as comparable workers at the employer's premises. However, in order to take into account the particularities of telework, specific complementary collective and/or individual agreements may be necessary.

5. DATA PROTECTION

THE EMPLOYER is responsible for taking the appropriate measures, notably with regard to software, to ensure the protection of data used and processed by the teleworker for professional purposes.

The employer informs the teleworker of all relevant legislation and company rules concerning data protection.

It is the teleworker's responsibility to comply with these rules.

The employer informs the teleworker in particular of:

→ Any restrictions on the use of IT equipment or tools such as the internet;
→ Sanctions in the case of non-compliance.

6. PRIVACY

THE EMPLOYER respects the privacy of the teleworker.

If any kind of monitoring system is put in place, it needs to be proportionate to the objective and introduced in accordance with Directive 90/270 on visual display units.

7. EQUIPMENT

ALL QUESTIONS concerning work equipment, liability and costs are clearly defined before starting telework.

As a general rule, the employer is responsible for providing, installing and maintaining the equipment necessary for regular telework unless the teleworker uses his/her own equipment.

If telework is performed on a regular basis, the employer compensates or covers the costs directly caused by the work, in particular those relating to communication.

The employer provides the teleworker with an appropriate technical support facility.

The employer has the liability, in accordance with national legislation and collective agreements, regarding costs for loss and damage to the equipment and data used by the teleworker .

The teleworker takes good care of the equipment provided to him/her and does not collect or distribute illegal material via the internet.

8. HEALTH AND SAFETY

THE EMPLOYER is responsible for the protection of the occupational health and safety of the teleworker in accordance with Directive 89/391 and relevant daughter directives, national legislation and collective agreements.

The employer informs the teleworker of the company's policy on occupational health and safety, in particular requirements on visual display units. The teleworker applies these safety policies correctly.

In order to verify that the applicable health and safety provisions are correctly applied, the employer, workers' representatives and/or relevant authorities have access to the telework location, within the limits of national legislation and collective agreements. If the teleworker is working at home, such access is subject to prior notification and his/her agreement.

The teleworker is entitled to request inspection visits.

9. ORGANIZATION OF WORK

WITHIN the framework of applicable legislation, collective agreements and company rules, the teleworker manages the organization of his/her working time.

The workload and performance standards of the teleworker are equivalent to those of comparable workers at the employer's premises.

The employer ensures that measures are taken to prevent the teleworker being isolated from the rest of the working community in the company, such as giving him/her the opportunity to meet with colleagues on a regular basis and access to company information.

10. TRAINING

TELEWORKERS have the same access to training and career development opportunities as comparable workers at the employer's premises and are subject to the same appraisal policies as these other workers.

Teleworkers receive appropriate training targeted at the technical equipment at their disposal and at the characteristics of this form of work organization. The teleworker's supervisor and his/her direct colleagues may also need training for this form of work and its management.

11. COLLECTIVE RIGHTS ISSUES

TELEWORKERS have the same collective rights as workers at the employer's premises. There are no obstacles to communicating with workers' representatives.

The same conditions for participating in and standing for elections to bodies representing workers or providing worker representation apply to them.

Teleworkers are included in calculations for determining thresholds for bodies with worker representation in accordance with European and national law, collective agreements or practices. The establishment to which the teleworker will be attached for the purpose of exercising his/her collective rights is specified from the outset.

Workers' representatives are informed and consulted on the introduction of telework in accordance with European and national legislations, collective agreements and practices.

12. IMPLEMENTATION AND FOLLOW UP

IN THE CONTEXT of Article 139 of the Treaty, this European framework agreement shall be implemented by the members of BUSINESSEUROPE/UEAPME, CEEP and ETUC (and the EUROCADRES/CEC liaison committee) in accordance with the procedures and practices specific to management and labour in the Member States.

This implementation will be carried out within three years after the date of signature of this agreement.

Member organizations will report on the implementation of this agreement to an ad hoc group set up by the signatory parties, under the responsibility of the social dialogue committee. This ad hoc group will prepare a joint report on the actions of implementation taken. This report will be prepared within four years after the date of signature of this agreement.

In case of questions on the content of this agreement, member organizations involved can separately or jointly refer to the signatory parties.

The signatory parties shall review the agreement five years after the date of signature if requested by one of the signatory parties.

16 July 2002

VII. WHERE TO FIND OUT MORE

More details on national and sectoral implementation measures can be found by consulting the dedicated websites of the European social partners. In particular, national joint social partners' implementation reports from the following countries can be consulted:

- Austria
- Belgium
- Czech Republic
- Denmark
- Finland
- France
- Germany
- Greece
- Hungary
- Iceland
- Ireland
- Italy
- Latvia
- Luxembourg
- Malta
- Netherlands
- Norway

- Poland
- Portugal
- Slovenia
- Spain
- Sweden
- United Kingdom

Further information can also be found at:

- **Employers' Resource Centre**:
  <www.unice.org/erc>
  (accessed 12 December 2006)
- **ETUC European Resource Centre**
  <www.resourceetuc.com>
  (accessed 12 December 2006)

Part II
National Reports

Chapter 4
Australia

Emma Keating and Di van den Broek

I. INTRODUCTION

While the concept of working from home has been around almost since the concept of work itself, over recent decades telework has emerged as a distinct phenomenon in the Australian labour market. Telework as a 'flexible work practice' (FWP) is regularly flagged as a vehicle through which employees, especially women, can successfully balance the competing demands of work and family. Indeed, conceptions of telework in the media, policy papers and some academic writing often unequivocally equate this mode of work with a host of employee advantages, including an improved work/life balance, better quality of working life, reduced travelling time, and positive impacts on family life.[1] While some writers dispute

---

1. See Y. Baruch, 'The Status of Research on Teleworking and an Agenda for Future Research' (2001) *International Journal of Management Reviews*, 3 (2), 119; L. Duxbury and C. Higgins, 'Telework: A Primer for the Millennium Introduction' (2002) in *The New World of Work: Challenges and Opportunities*, C. Cooper and R. Burke (eds) (Oxford, Blackwell Publishers Inc.); Australian Telework Advisory Committee, *Telework for Australian Employees and Businesses: Maximising the Economic and Social Benefits of Flexible Working Practices* (Commonwealth of Australia, Barton, ACT, Department of Communications and Information Technology and Department of Employment and Workplace Relations, 2006); D. Bailey and B. Kurland, 'A Review of Telework Research: Findings, New Directions, and Lessons for the Study of Modern Work' (2002) *Journal of Organizational Behaviour*, Vol. 23, 383–400.

Blanpain et al., European Framework, Agreements and Telework, pp. 77–92.
©2007, Kluwer Law International BV, The Netherlands.

the ability of telework to advance work/life balance (WLB),[2] this short report noting the state of telework in Australia highlights that such positive impacts can be possible if steered by sound legislative policy. As Tremblay argues:

> There is an astonishingly important amount of normative management literature prescribing 'how to manage telework and teleworkers', but there is little documented research on . . . risks or issues related to the gender dimension.[3]

Unfortunately, sound legislative policy does not accurately describe the present situation for teleworkers in Australia. Building on Pittard's work, this report argues that telework is largely treated as a *'managerial prerogative'*, rather than, *'valid work'* in many Australian organizations.[4] Presently, this treatment of telework as a 'privilege' rather than a 'right'[5] is endorsed by a lack of formal telework-specific regulation, reliance on existing legal mechanisms, and emphasis on enterprise level workplace agreements to determine conditions of work organization, as is explored in this report.

Recently, increasing the extent of telework in Australia has formed part of the Federal Government's agenda. For instance, the establishment of the Australian Telework Advisory Committee (ATAC) as part of the Government's Information, Communication and Technology (ICT) election policy, *Connecting an Innovative Australia*, signals a strong association between telework and the pursuit of what is often termed 'the information economy'. During 2005, ATAC released four consultation papers which provide an overview of Australian and international telework developments. A final report was released in February 2006 reporting the findings of policy consultations.

Despite the existence of numerous studies of telework since the 1970s, commonly used definitions are often all encompassing, incorporating employees, subcontractors and people who establish their own business from home. This report incorporates teleworkers as those who:

> regularly work 40 percent or more of their hours (two days of regular five day working week or pro rata for part time employees) from outside the usual workplace (the home) using telecommunications technology linked to their employers system.[6]

---

2. See C. Diamond, 'Telework and Family Responsibilities: Experiences in Public and Private Spheres' (2003) *Labour and Industry*, Vol. 13, Issue 1, 39–54; M. Travis, 'Equality in the Virtual Workplace' (2003) *Berkeley Journal of Employment and Labour Law*, Vol. 24, Issue 2, 283.
3. D.G. Tremblay, 'Balancing Work and Family with Telework? Organizational Issues and Challenges for Women and Managers' (2002) *Women in Management Review*, Vol. 17, Issue 3, 157.
4. M. Pittard, 'Rethinking Place of Work: Federal Labour Law Framework for Contemporary Home-Based Work and its Prospects in Australia' (2005) *Law in Context*, Vol. 23, Issue 1, 148.
5. For further analysis of 'rights' and 'privilege' dichotomy, see E. Keating, 'Telework as 'Valid Work' or 'Managerial Prerogative' Options for Policy Reform in Australia through a Rights Versus Privilege Framework' (2006), Honours Thesis, University of Sydney, 27 October.
6. As in C. Diamond and G. Lafferty, 'Telework: Issues for Research, Policy and Regulation' (2000) *Labour and Industry*, Vol. 11, Issue 1, 125.

Thus, teleworkers have the legal status of 'employee' (not a self-employed contractor), which requires telework to occur on a regular, rather than ad hoc basis, primarily from the employee's own home.

II.   THE POTENTIAL FUTURE OF WORK

While the concept of working from home is not a new phenomenon, its contemporary successor, telework, has developed in distinctive ways over the past three decades. The teleworker has become a powerful icon in post fordist, post industrial and post modern conceptions of work and is dominant in discussions of the 'new information age'. Popular 'futurologists' writing in this context equated the widespread mass adoption of telework in the future with the end of the modern hierarchal industrial organization. According to *Huws*, the 'electronic home worker is a highly charged and powerful symbol that promises full participation in the international traffic of ideas and information and enclosure in the protective sanctuary of the home'.[7]

During the 1980s, telework began to move beyond its presentation as a revolutionary catalyst of social change in the information society and became part of the wider call for 'flexibility' in the workplace.[8] Telework had been redefined in terms of contemporary organizational restructuring and 'flexible, client oriented production'.[9] In this view, telework is seen as simply one alternative mode of work or flexible working arrangement'.[10] As desires for flexibility led to the restructuring of organizations to make them leaner and better able to respond quickly to market changes, telework simply became one option to reduce an employer's overhead costs and increase organizational adaptability.[11] Here, the expansion of teleworking seemed to fall into two main categories – a more autonomous and flexible method of work organization in post industrial society versus an exploitative arrangement which is the inevitable consequence of competitive pressures in an increasingly globalized economy.[12]

This shift towards telework as an exploitative mechanism was often associated with those workers possessing 'more easily replaceable skills and a much weaker labour market position', rather than prior notions of knowledge workers. For instance, Stanworth argued:

> There is a growing body of evidence that employers are in some cases reducing the terms and conditions of teleworkers, and tending to treat work at home

---

7. U. Huws, 'Telework: Projections' (2003) in *The Making of a Cybertariat Virtual Work in a Real World,* U. Huws (ed.) (New York, Monthly Review Press), p. 87.
8. Baruch (2001), n. 1 above, Vol. 3, Issue 2, p. 113.
9. P. Jackson and J. van der Wielen, *Teleworking: International Perspectives. From Telecommuting to the Virtual Organisation* (London, Routledge, 1998), p. 12.
10. Baruch (2001), n. 1 above, Vol. 3, Issue 2, 115.
11. Huws (2003), n. 7 above, pp. 96–97.
12. G. Lafferty, R. Hall, B. Harley and G. Whitehouse, 'Homeworking in Australia: An Assessment of Current Trends' (1997) *Australian Bulletin of Labour,* Vol. 23, Issue 2, 143.

as a privilege granted to employees, without the reciprocity of relationships emphasized in the HRM literature.[13]

Indeed, recent studies by Felstead *et al.* (2002) highlight the treatment of telework as a 'privilege'. Here, 'having the opportunity to choose where to work represents another perk for already occupying an advantaged position in the labour market'.[14]

The fact is, however, that the predicted outcomes of telework remain unrealized, despite technical innovation and employee desire to participate in telework. In many cases, the assumptions underpinning optimistic predictions overlook important factors influencing the take up of telework, most significantly the legislative framework and how this influences the fundamental power relations at the heart of the employment relationship.

Further, the re-occurring barriers to the adoption of telework identified in the literature appear to be cultural, rather than structural in nature. That is, the main impediments to telework seem to be driven by cultural and social perceptions, such as employer values and attitudes, rather than information technology limitations. According to ATAC, 'impediments are attitudinal, educational and management related' and 'the single most important barrier to greater take up of telework is the "traditional view" attitude of managers and employees'.[15] Other empirical data, such as the Toshiba Mobility and Mistrust report, claims that, of managers who did not support teleworking arrangements, 65 per cent cited difficulties relating to the proper supervision of remote working employees as the single most important impediment to telework adoption.[16] Additionally, Di Martino and Wirth[17] observed that 'organisational and cultural factors seem to be the major obstacle to a more rapid and extensive adoption of telework', namely 'problems of managerial control and supervision'. Other studies support such claims, with managerial culture resistance and lack of managerial interest widely reported to be the main barriers to telework adoption.[18]

III.   TELEWORK AND WORK/LIFE BALANCE

Given its focus on flexibility, telework is widely perceived as a highly attractive work option, particularly for women in attaining an effective WLB.[19] For

---

13. C. Stanworth, *Telework and Human Resource Management* (London, Institution of Electrical Engineers, IEE, 1996), pp. 2, 3.
14. A. Felstead, N. Jewson, A. Phizacklea and S. Waters, 'The Option to Work at Home: Another Privilege for a Favoured Few? (2002) *New Technology, Work and Employment*, Vol. 17, Issue 3, 204.
15. Australian Telework Advisory Committee (2006), n. 1 above, pp. 5, 26.
16. Sweeney Research, *Mobility and Mistrust* (Toshiba (Australia) Information Systems Division, 2004).
17. V. Di Martino and L. Wirth, 'Telework: A New Way of Working and Living' (1990) *International Labour Review*, Vol. 129, Issue 5, 535.
18. Duxbury and Higgins (2002), n. 1 above, p. 164.
19. See Australian Telework Advisory Committee (2006), n. 1 above; Bailey and Kurland (2002), n. 1 above, Vol. 23, 388.

example, it is claimed that 'for many, telework's flexibility is a key factor in their search for practical ways to reconcile their family responsibilities or styles of life with earning an income'.[20] According to ATAC, 'consultations indicated that from an employee's point of view, telework is primarily driven by a desire to achieve an improved work life balance'.[21] Additionally, the flexibility around telework is thought to be particularly appealing to women because they tend to be the family caregivers, hence, are more likely to require strategies to 'balance the conflicting demands of motherhood and professional life'.[22]

Existing research and academic analysis suggests that telework is treated as a privilege in Australia. Certainly, some Australian studies suggest an employee's bargaining power and status in an organization may significantly influence both their ability to access teleworking and the quality of teleworking arrangement offered. According to Gray and Tudball, 'profit maximizing (or cost minimizing) behaviour of employers means they are likely to differentiate between employees in the extent to which family friendly practices are made available'.[23] Further, Earle claims that business case arguments always have more traction in relation to high skilled occupations and industries where training and replacement costs are high and recruitment and retention benefits are easier to quantify.[24] This argument has been reiterated by other empirical studies which have demonstrated that despite both job types deemed suitable for teleworking, clerical workers may face greater opposition from management to their requests to work at home.[25] These studies all infer that 'consideration of such factors as job suitability often masks issues of status and power that are densely intertwined with occupation'.[26]

Research highlights that the majority of telework arrangements occur on an informal basis, with little mention of teleworking found in formal organizational policies or formalized industrial instruments.[27] Additionally, when telework clauses are formalized, they are often 'enabling' rather than conferring any rights on employees to undertake home-based work or any obligations on employers to

---

20. Di Martino and Wirth (1990), n. 17 above, Vol. 129, Issue 5, 533.
21. Australian Telework Advisory Committee (2006), n. 1 above, p. 20.
22. *ibid.*, p. 21.
23. M. Gray and J. Tudball, 'Access to Family-Friendly Work Practices: Differences Within and Between Australian Workplaces' (2002) *Family Matters*, Australian Institute of Family Studies, No. 61, Autumn, 31.
24. J. Earle, 'Family Friendly Workplaces: A Tale of Two Sectors' (2002) *Family Matters*, Australian Institute of Family Studies, No. 61, Autumn, 13.
25. Including Huws *et al.*, 1990; Mokhtarian *et al.*, 1998; Olson & Primps, 1984; Tomaskovic-Devey & Risman, 1993; as in Bailey and Kurland (2002), n. 1 above, Vol. 23, 383–400.
26. Bailey and Kurland (2002), n. 1 above, Vol. 23, p. 386.
27. Australian Telework Advisory Committee (2006), n. 1 above; HILDA, 2003 as in Australian Telework Advisory Committee, 'Telework in Australia' (2005), Paper II, p. 12; ACIRRT as in Australian Telework Advisory Committee, 'Telework in Australia' (2005), p. 11; M. Pittard, 'Rethinking Place of Work: Federal Labour Law Framework for Contemporary Home-Based Work and its Prospects in Australia' (2005) *Law in Context*, Vol. 23, Issue 1, 148.

provide or agree to home-based work. As such 'the ability to undertake home-based work remains a management prerogative in Australia today'.[28]

Further, judicial interpretation of anti-discrimination laws in relation to tele-work also suggests that one's ability to access telework is considered a privilege in Australia. For instance, in the *Schou* case elaborated upon later, the Supreme Court ruled:

> The Act (Sex Discrimination Act 1984) forbids discrimination. It does not compel the *bestowing of special advantage*. The unreasonable refusal to extend a benefit to an individual or individuals where that benefit is, with good reason, not available to others is not discrimination.[29]

Such a ruling reinforces the status problem of telework, presenting it as special treatment as opposed to a right or legitimate working option in Australia.

IV. TELEWORK: AUSTRALIAN STATISTICS

In Australia, while teleworkers remain a minority group compared to the labour force as a whole, the prevalence of teleworking has increased from a small base over the past decade. After taking into account a range of definitions, employees who regularly work from home in Australia using ICTs range between 8–15 per cent of the workforce. Australian Bureau of Statistics (ABS) data estimated that there were approximately 438,000 workers who worked from home on the day of the 2001 census, constituting 5.3 per cent of Australia's working population; while the 2000 'Locations of Work Survey' showed that 1 million employed Australians (11 per cent) had an arrangement with their employer to work from home and 62 per cent of these were employees. Further, an ABS Social Trends survey found that of the 1.8 million home workers, 692,600 persons who worked only or mainly from home and a further 287,700 had an arrangement with an employer to work from home. This report showed that 58 per cent of these were employees and most incorporate teleworkers, with 64 per cent using information technology.[30] Additionally, the Household Income and Labour Dynamics in Australia (HILDA) Wave 3 survey found that 17 per cent of total Australian employees had worked some hours from home in 2003.[31] Further, according to the National Telework Survey conducted by the Labour and Industry Research Unit at the University of Queensland, 15 per cent of Australian organizations employed some 'regular' teleworkers (those teleworking at least 40 per cent of their working time), while 44 per cent of employed people

---

28. Pittard (2005), n. 27 above, Vol. 23, Issue 1, 148, 177.
29. Emphasis added; Schou [2001] 3 VR 655, 661.
30. Australian Bureau of Statistics, *Australian Social Trends* (2002), Commonwealth of Australia, 4102.0, p. 144.
31. HILDA, 2003 as in Australian Telework Advisory Committee, 'Telework in Australia' (2005), Paper II, p. 12.

had teleworked at some time.[32] Despite definitional disparities, these studies reveal an increasing trend toward telework in Australia.

More recent findings support such growth trends. For instance, figures from the 2006 'Locations of Work Survey' reveal that 24 per cent of people did at least some work from their own home, compared with 20 per cent in 2000. Additionally, 81 per cent of people used information technology at home in their job,[33] revealing a trend toward telework rather than more traditional modes of homeworking. While 7.7 per cent of employed people worked only or mainly at home,[34] only 1.5 per cent of 'employees' worked mainly at home during the reference week. However, 42 per cent of respondents had worked in two or more location types in their main job.[35] This suggests that employees who work from home tend to balance time between both office and home locations.

Australian data on telework reflects similar occupational segregation and gender patterns that exist in the wider workforce. For example, the 'Persons Employed at Home' survey revealed that 47.3 per cent of males accounted for home-based workers who were managers, administrators and professionals; while the majority of women (55.2 per cent) fell into the clerks category.[36] Such disparities are confirmed by recent data showing that the most common male occupational groups of those who worked mainly from home were managers and administrators (36 per cent) and professionals (31 per cent); while women dominated the advanced and intermediate clerical, sales, and service workers categories.[37] Similarly, those men who worked some hours at home were concentrated in the categories of professionals (31 per cent), managers and administrators (24 per cent), and associate professionals (15 per cent); while most common groups for women were professionals (38 per cent), advanced clerical and service workers (15 per cent), intermediate clerical and service workers (13 per cent), associate professionals (13 per cent), and managers and administrators (13 per cent).[38] These statistics indicate the impact of gendered occupational segregation that affects the ability of women to effectively bargain for the option to telework in the current Australian context.

In Australia, such gender disparities appear to extend beyond the public sphere of work and into the private sphere of unpaid work in the home. This trend was

---

32. University of Queensland, Unisys Australia Ltd and the Queensland Department of Employment, Training and Industrial Relations, 'The Management of Telework: An Employment and Industrial Relations Model for Australian Industry' (2002) Final Report, June 2002.
33. Australian Bureau of Statistics, *Locations of Work Survey, November 2005* (2006), 6275.0, pp. 4, 5.
34. Australian Bureau of Statistics (2006), n. 33 above, p. 7.
35. Australian Bureau of Statistics (2006), n. 33 above, p. 4.
36. ABS (1995), as in G. Lafferty, R. Hall, B. Harley and G. Whitehouse, 'Homeworking in Australia: An Assessment of Current Trends' (1997) *Australian Bulletin of Labour*, Vol. 23, Issue 2, 151–52.
37. ABS, (2006: 6).
38. Australian Bureau of Statistics (2006), n. 33 above, p. 5.

recognized publicly during the Work and Family Provisions Test Case 2005 when it was stated that:

> There is very little evidence of a gender redistribution of family work. It appears that mothers adjust their jobs and personal lives to accommodate family commitments more than men do.[39]

Australian data also indicates that balancing childcare with work responsibilities is predominately a female concern. For example, of the 17 per cent of respondents who cited childcare responsibilities as a reason for working from home, a significantly greater proportion of women cited childcare responsibilities (24 per cent) than men (1.8 percent).[40] Further, more recent data shows that this gender imbalance has persisted over the last decade. That is, for persons who worked any hours at home, 9.2 per cent of females compared to 2.2 per cent of males cited childcare/family reasons for working at home.[41] Similarly, for persons who worked mainly at home 14.2 per cent of females compared to 2.1 per cent of males cited childcare/family reasons.[42] The utilization of teleworking to balance work/family life mostly by women is highlighted by other statistics. Women working from home were more likely to have children aged under 15 years than women working in other locations (42 per cent compared to 30 per cent), while 35 per cent of male home workers and 32 per cent of male workers had children under 15 years.[43] Again, this confirms that women appear to be those most in need of flexible work practices, such as teleworking.

Research highlights the potential for teleworking employees in Australia to have reduced access to employment benefits that are made available to more traditionally organized employees. Lafferty (1997) found conditions in 1995 had worsened since the equivalent 1992 survey, showing increasing numbers of home workers had become marginalized with low union membership, high levels of casualization, and low levels of access to industrial benefits. His work presents the 'worst practice' examples of home working where informal arrangements can lead to the creation of a substantial periphery of home workers characterized by insecurity and poor pay and conditions.[44] More recently ABS data showed that employee home workers are less likely to access employment benefits than other employees. For instance, in 2000, 80 per cent of employees working from home in their main job had access to workers' compensation, compared with 93 per cent of all employees.[45] While 84 per cent of all employees had superannuation coverage

---

39. Family Provisions Test Case 2005 (2005) 143 IR 245 at [63].
40. ABS (1995), as in G. Lafferty, R. Hall, B. Harley and G. Whitehouse, 'Homeworking in Australia: An Assessment of Current Trends' (1997) *Australian Bulletin of Labour*, Vol. 23, Issue 2, 148–49.
41. Australian Bureau of Statistics (2006), n. 33 above, p. 21.
42. Australian Bureau of Statistics (2006), n. 33 above, p. 26.
43. Australian Bureau of Statistics, *Australian Social Trends* (2002), Commonwealth of Australia, 4102.0, pp. 142–3.
44. G. Lafferty, R. Hall, B. Harley and G. Whitehouse, 'Homeworking in Australia: An Assessment of Current Trends' (1997) *Australian Bulletin of Labour*, Vol. 23, Issue 2, 154.
45. ABS, 2001: 6361.0 as in Australian Bureau of Statistics, *Australian Social Trends* (2002), Commonwealth of Australia, 4102.0, p. 144.

provided by their current employer, only 74 per cent of employees working from home shared this entitlement.[46] Further, in 2000, 59 per cent of employees working from home had access to either paid sick leave or paid holiday leave, compared with 71 per cent of all employees.[47] Such statistics indicate that the experience of Australian home workers (many of whom are increasingly teleworkers) may lead to a more contingent workforce.

V. REGULATING TELEWORK

While telework in Australia is increasing, it still forms only a small proportion of FWPs offered in organizations. According to the annual Work/life Initiatives 2006 Report, while 78 per cent of organizations had increased the range of FWPs during 2005, telecommuting (14 per cent) and working from home on an ad hoc basis (22 per cent) were found to be options still only available in a small number of organizations.[48] Similarly, telework appears only to feature in a small minority of organizational policies that do exist. The 2004 Toshiba Australia report found that of the 26 per cent of companies that had formal written policies on FWPs, only 21 per cent of these included uniform guidelines on working away from the office.[49] The Sensis Insights survey revealed that 87 per cent of teleworking small to medium enterprises (SMEs) use informal arrangements.[50] Further, while large companies (100 + employees) were more than three times as likely as SMEs to have flexible working policies in place, the majority of teleworking was undertaken at an individual level as part of the teleworker's informal arrangements with a manager.[51] Thirty one per cent of respondents said that the policy to which they adhered was either part of their employment contract agreement or a non-contractual, individual agreement.[52] Interestingly, two thirds of people within organizations without a policy indicated they would favour one within their organization, with an equal preference among both managers and employees.[53]

Further, evidence reveals that telework is dealt with relatively informally at an organizational level. The incidence of teleworking in formal enterprise agreements and registered industrial instruments remains relatively low, illustrating that this type of work tends to be organized informally at an individual level. According to the Australian Centre for Industrial Relations Research and Training (ACIRRT), in 2003 there were working from home provisions in just 2.2 per cent of collective agreements and less than 1 percent of Australian Workplace Agreements (AWAs),

---

46. *ibid.*
47. *ibid.*
48. Managing WLB, 'Work/Life Initiatives: The Way Ahead Report on the Year 2006 Survey' (2006), Executive Summary.
49. Sweeney Research, *Mobility and Mistrust* (Toshiba (Australia) Information Systems Division, 2004), p. 7.
50. Sensis Insights, *Teleworking Report* (Telstra Corporation Limited, June 2005).
51. Sweeney Research (2004), n. 49 above.
52. Sweeney Research (2004), n. 49 above, p. 21.
53. Sweeney Research (2004), n. 49 above, p. 22.

suggesting that employers deal with working from home informally.[54] These findings were echoed in the HILDA survey findings, showing only one third of employees who work from home have a formal teleworking arrangement with their employer.[55]

In addition, the small amount of formal clauses providing for telework in registered Australian industrial instruments are 'enabling' only and do not confer any rights on employees to undertake home-based work or any obligations on employers to provide or agree to home-based work.[56] Through her analysis of clauses relating to home work and telework in Australian awards and collective agreements, Pittard concluded that 'a common thread of awards, certified agreements and policies making provision for home based work is the retention by management of the right to decide whether work may be performed at home'.[57] Her research illustrates that even when teleworking arrangements are more formalized, an employee's ability to access this practice remains within the discretion of the employer. That is, telework in Australia 'is not a right which an employee can exercise unilaterally but rather is a matter for arrangement and agreement'.[58]

VI. IMPEDIMENTS TO TELEWORKING AS A RIGHT

Given the discussion above, it is apparent that telework in Australian organizations is perceived as a special privilege awarded to a 'trusted' employee. The Toshiba Australia survey found that executives primarily consider flexible working to be an employee perk, rather than a viable and long-term business strategy,[59] and case study evidence has revealed that the privilege of telework is linked to increased productivity on the basis of perceived gratitude. For example, in several case studies managers exhibited evidence of an expectation that teleworkers would make an extra effort in return for the privilege of teleworking and many teleworkers seemed comfortable with this arrangement, often giving extra unpaid time in return for the ability to save on commuting time.[60] Additionally, there was some evidence of an unspoken expectation by management that extra hours would be completed but also that teleworkers be available during 'normal' business hours.[61] Further, some managers stated that the continuation of the privilege of telework was conditional on performance.[62]

54. Australian Telework Advisory Committee, 'Telework in Australia' (2005), Paper II, p. 11.
55. HILDA, 2003 as in Australian Telework Advisory Committee, 'Telework in Australia' (2005), Paper II, p. 12.
56. Pittard (2005), n. 27 above, Vol. 23, Issue 1, 177.
57. Pittard (2005), n. 27 above, Vol. 23, Issue 1, 164.
58. *Ibid.*
59. Sweeney Research (2004), n. 49 above, p. 16.
60. G. Whitehouse, C. Diamond and G. Lafferty, 'Assessing the Benefits of Telework: Australian Case Study Evidence' (2002) *New Zealand Journal of Industrial Relations*, Vol. 27, Issue 3, 260.
61. *Ibid.*
62. Whitehouse, Diamond and Lafferty (2002), n. 60 above, Vol. 27, Issue 3, 266.

4. Australia

Barriers to the increased adoption of telework at an organizational level appear to be driven by cultural perceptions underpinned by traditional assumptions, rather than a lack of technical feasibility. That is, ATAC findings suggest that technology is not seen as a primary barrier to telework adoption,[63] and this proposition is supported by data from the Toshiba Australia survey, showing that 63 per cent of managers and 57 per cent of employees did not consider technology a reason why FWPs were not implemented.[64] In contrast, 'cultural resistance' has been found to be a significant factor impairing telework adoption. For instance, the Work/Life Initiatives 2006 Report concludes that:

> these options have been discussed in business literature for two decades, and technology that enables employees to work from home has been available for ten years now, so this low uptake indicates that these options involve cultural issues which organisations have not yet addressed adequately.[65]

Further, evidence points to managerial resistance as a driving force behind other organizational barriers that are implicitly disguised as other issues (including trust and control) often viewed as integral to operations. For example, it is often noted that if telework is to be successful, a considerable degree of trust is essential.[66] However, in Australian organizations a lack of trust between managers and their employees seems to be impairing an employee's ability to partake in telework. Several case study analyses found that some teleworkers with families often believed supervisors and co-workers were suspicious of their work habits and therefore did not make full use of the flexibility available from teleworking.[67] Additionally, one of the greatest hurdles to teleworking was the anxiety of line managers supervising teleworkers. According to Diamond, 'anxious managers tended to sabotage telework as a legitimate flexible work option, for example, by treating it as a privilege which could be revoked at any time'.[68] In relation to managerial 'control', Australian based studies reflect and reinforce the argument by Felstead et al. that managers have difficulty releasing traditional assumptions of 'visibility' and 'presence'.[69] Such an inability to overcome focus of managerial control is problematic for telework participation. For instance, difficulty in monitoring and supervising employees was perceived as the main obstacle in the Toshiba Australia Survey, where managers (65 per cent) and employees (59 per cent) reported that the main barrier to implementation of flexible working was the

---

63. Australian Telework Advisory Committee (2006), n. 1 above.
64. Sweeney Research (2004), n. 49 above, p. 7.
65. Managing WLB (2006), n. 48 above.
66. Whitehouse, Diamond and Lafferty (2002), n. 60 above, Vol. 27, Issue 3, 266.
67. Whitehouse, Diamond and Lafferty (2002), n. 60 above, Vol. 27, Issue 3, 262.
68. C. Diamond, G. Lafferty and G. Whitehouse, 'Submission to the Australian Telework Advisory Committee (ATAC)' (2005), 27 May 2005, 3.
69. See A. Felstead, N. Jewson and S. Waters, 'Managerial Control of Employees Working at Home' (2003) *British Journal of Industrial Relations*, Vol. 41, Issue 2, 241–64; and A. Felstead, N. Jewson and S. Walters, *Changing Places of Work*, (Hampshire, Palgrave MacMillan, 2005).

difficulty in managing and supervising employees.[70] These findings were reiterated more recently in the Work/Life Balance Report, showing that a key challenge in 60 per cent of organizations were leaders who did not have the competence to manage the demands of business and staff with work/life issues.[71]

Such perceptions could be addressed through employer education. On a positive note, the Work/life Balance Report found that since 2004 fewer organizations (45 per cent compared with 54 per cent) perceived lack of data was preventing managers from building a good business case for work/life programmes.[72] However, organizations do not appear to have extensive support networks outside their industry that can provide information on flexible workplace policies. Nearly a quarter of enterprises intimated they look to industry associations for guidance on flexible working policies and procedures. Only nine per cent indicated government legislation or directives provided assistance, while 11 per cent looked to trade unions for advice.[73] The fact that organizations lack resources and advice on best-practice policy, implementation and management of flexible workers suggests that organizations may not be deliberately mistrustful of staff. Rather, many organizations do not have the awareness and resources to set up boundaries and a culture supporting flexible working.[74]

VII.   LEGISLATIVE ASSESSMENTS AND CONCLUSION

At present the regulation of telework fits within existing legal frameworks in Australia, rather than existing as an independent and unique issue requiring specific legislation. However, Harris (2003) argues, as others have done elsewhere, that taking work into the home environment 'challenges and changes the responsibilities of employers accustomed to traditional employment relationships shaped by paying for work time that is distinguishable from non work time'.[75] Indeed, by making the underlying assumptions shaping current labour law obsolete, telework challenges the existing regulatory labour law system in Australia, bringing into question the applicability of existing employment laws.

With an absence of specific legislation to deal with issues associated with telework, the current federal legislative framework emphasizes the role of enterprise level agreement making in creating family friendly working conditions.[76] However, the incidence of teleworking clauses in formal agreements remains low and most clauses are 'subject to the employer's approval and is not a right given to

70. Sweeney Research (2004), n. 49 above, pp. 33–36.
71. Managing WLB (2006), n. 48 above.
72. Managing WLB (2006), n. 48 above.
73. Sweeney Research (2004), n. 49 above, pp. 21–22.
74. *ibid.*
75. L. Harris, 'Home-based Teleworking and the Employment Relationship: Managerial Challenges and Dilemmas' (2003) *Personnel Review*, Vol. 32, Issue 4, 434.
76. Earle (2002), n. 24 above, No. 61, Autumn, 13.

employees'.[77] This failure in providing any formal regulation of telework supporting its use as a family friendly policy undermines cotemporary claims made under
recent 'Workchoices' reforms that 'bargaining at workplace level is particularly
suited to tailoring working arrangements in ways that assist employees to balance
work and family responsibilities'.[78] Instead, it seems that current policy makers'
beliefs that FWPs are ideally negotiated at workplace level are flawed. Additionally, according to the family friendly agreement clauses database, only 85 federal
certified agreements currently provide for working from home provisions that
incorporate teleworking, compared with 233 clauses allowing for part-time
work.[79] This reveals a regulatory system that prioritizes enterprise level agreements and fails to accommodate the use of teleworking as a valid family friendly
option for the majority of employees that are in need of this flexibility.

Similarly, Australian anti-discrimination legislation is primarily reactive and
does not pose any positive duty on employers to provide FWPs, such as telework.[80]
Further, interpretation of discrimination and equal employment opportunity laws
propels the conception of telework as an advantage bestowed upon an employee
rather than a legitimate form of work organization. For instance, in *Schou v.
Victoria*, Ms Schou brought an indirect discrimination claim on the ground of parental status, under the Sex Discrimination Act 1984, when the State failed to honour
a telework agreement for home-based work two days per week with Ms Schou.
Here, despite agreeing that Ms Schou could work from home on a part-time basis
while her son was ill, the employer failed to supply her with a modem so this arrangement could be enacted. Due to her family obligations and her employer's inflexibil-
ity, Ms Schou was forced to end her 16 year career as a Hansard legislative reporter as
her short-term circumstance did not permit full-time attendance at the workplace.[81]

Initially, VCAT found in Ms Schou's favour ruling that the cost alternative
arrangement (teleworking via employer-provided modem) was reasonable.
However, this ruling was overturned by the Supreme Court on appeal. The
Court stated:

> 'The Act forbids discrimination. It does not compel the *bestowing of special
> advantage*. The unreasonable refusal to extend a benefit to an individual or
> individuals where that benefit is, with good reason, not available to others is
> not discrimination'.[82]

---

77. Pittard (2005), n. 27 above, Vol. 23, Issue 1, 163, 177.
78. Department of Employment and Workplace Relations, *Work Choices and Australian Families*
    (Commonwealth of Australia, 2006), Fact Sheet 26.
79. Family Friendly Clauses Online Database (Commonwealth of Australia, 2003). Available at
    <http://ffac.dewr.gov.au/Main/Search.aspx>.
80. B. Smith and J. Riley, 'Family Friendly Work Practices and the Law' (2004) *Sydney Law Review*,
    Vol. 26, 394.
81. B. Gaze, 'Judicial Interpretation of Anti Discrimination Legislation' (2002) *Melbourne Univer-
    sity Law Review*, Vol. 18.
82. Schou [2001] 3 VR 655, 661.

This decision rests on the assertion that what was sought was an advantage over others, rather than treatment which aimed to improve equality by taking account of a person's different situation.[83]

Interestingly, though, it appears that if teleworking was generally available to other employees in the workplace, Ms Schou's treatment may well have been considered discriminatory.[84] For instance, J. Harper said:

> The section does not turn to the denial by an employer of a favour to the employee into discrimination, although if the favour is generally available to other employees, its denial to one, could conceivably . . . amount to an offence against the Act.[85]

The *Schou* case raises serious questions about the ability of current Australian employment and anti-discrimination legislation to address gender inequalities in relation to FWPs, such as teleworking. Indeed, Ms Schou's experience highlights the 'strange gulf between the legal and human realities of working life'.[86] For instance, the employer's unwillingness to be flexible for a short time to see the child grow out of his ailment robbed Ms Schou of her career, and the law appeared incapable of remedying her loss.[87] Further, such a decision reveals that current policy rhetoric perceiving telework arrangements as a valid solution to achieving work/family balance for working parents (particularly working mothers) in the current legislative context are flawed.

Di Martino and Wirth have recognized telework's potential as 'an instrument for improving the living and employment conditions of workers as well as for assisting enterprises and organisations to improve their productivity and efficiency'. However, they warn that 'the price of this convenience should not include reduced social protection'.[88] That is, telework policy should support beneficial employment conditions that emphasize equal rights between teleworkers and non-teleworking employees. Regardless of the social rationales discussed above, in the current Australian political context a clear case for government intervention to support and accelerate the availability of telework has been identified through ATAC's final report to the Government. Despite the flaws raised earlier, this report identifies a legitimate place for government intervention and offers some useful solutions to encourage the increased use of teleworking in Australia. It recommends government support of telework through management training, building technological capacity, creating a telework online resource centre, promoting telework in the Australian Public Service, and greatly promoting the benefits of telework for employers.[89]

---

83. Gaze (2002), n. 81 above, Vol. 18.
84. Smith and Riley (2004), n. 80 above, Vol. 26, 414.
85. *State of Victoria v. Schou* [2001] 3 VR 655 at para.658.
86. J. Murray, 'Work and Care: New Legal Mechanisms for Adaptation' (2005) *Labour and Industry*, Vol. 15, Issue 3, 82.
87. Smith and Riley (2004), n. 80 above, Vol. 26, 425.
88. Di Martino and Wirth (1990), n. 17 above, 529, 554.
89. Australian Telework Advisory Committee (2006), n. 1 above, pp. 8–10, 55.

4. Australia

However, it should be noted that 'options for law reform in an era of neo-liberal labour policy are limited',[90] and without policy change based on critical advice[91] teleworking in its current context is likely to increase labour market inequalities between genders. This point is highlighted by Murray who argues that 'the sharp end of worker disadvantage rests with the existing legal mechanisms governing employment'.[92]

The principal objectives of the Workplace Relations Act (WRA) include the provision of a framework that:

> promotes the economic prosperity and welfare of the people of Australia . . . by encouraging . . . a flexible and fair labour market . . . assisting employees to balance their work and family responsibilities effectively through the development of *mutually beneficial* work practices with employers.[93]

Further, the propositions outlined below address the principal objectives of the Equal Employment for Women in the Workplace Act 1999, including the promotion of:

> the principle that employment for women should be dealt with on the basis of merit; and to promote, amongst employers, the elimination of discrimination against, and the provision of equal opportunity for, women in relation to employment matters; and to foster workplace consultation between employers and employees on issues concerning equal opportunity for women in relation to employment.[94]

Formal telework regulation and policies outlined herein assist in the achievement of the abovementioned legislative objectives of both the WRA and the Equal Employment for Women in the Workplace Act 1999. However, Australian telework is mostly regulated informally at an organizational level in Australia with access primarily dependent on one's recognized bargaining power, and there is an absence of existing employment laws that effectively support teleworking. To protect disadvantaged groups and individuals within the labour market, legislative change is required to move from a 'privilege' to a more 'rights' based approach.

Indeed, the Schou litigation suggests that little will be achieved for women workers wishing to accommodate their work and family lives through the legal mechanism of Australian discrimination laws.[95]

In an Australian context the 'right to request part time work', recently added to industrial awards as a result of the Family Provisions Test Case,[96] means that

---

90. McCallum (2005), as in J. Murray, 'Introduction' (2005) *Law in Context*, Vol. 23, Issue 1, 11.
91. C. Diamond, G. Lafferty and G. Whitehouse, 'Submission to the Australian Telework Advisory Committee (ATAC)' (2005), 27 May 2005, 3.
92. Murray (2005), n. 86 above, Vol. 15, Issue 3, 82.
93. Pt 1, ss. 3, 3 (a) and 3 (l), Workplace Relations Act 1996, Vol. 1, *emphasis added*.
94. Equal Employment Opportunity for Women in the Workplace Act 1999, s. 3.
95. Knowles (2004), as in J. Murray, 'Work and Care: New Legal Mechanisms for Adaptation' (2005) *Labour and Industry*, Vol. 15, Issue 3, 74.
96. Family Provisions Test Case 2005 (2005) 143 IR 245.

employers can only refuse a request 'on reasonable grounds related to the effect on the workplace or employers business'. A wider application of such a provision could force employers bound by industrial instruments to treat telework as a valid right that may be requested by the employee. There would also be an obligation imposed on an employer to give due consideration and to identify the grounds for refusal.[97] Further, such a provision would satisfy Pittard's claim that:

> provisions in awards and certified agreements should be adjusted to ensure that reasonable requests to undertake part of the employees work at home are not capriciously or arbitrarily refused, or refused for no good or objectively sound reason.[98]

Certainly, legislative change would need to also address employer concerns. For instance, organizations lack resources and advice on best practice policy, implementation and management of flexible workers, and many organizations do not have the awareness and resources to establish firm cultures that support flexible working.[99] Certainly the Government could consider widening the role of the ATAC as an educator,

Several submissions to ATAC call for public sector teleworking to act as an exemplar to employers, and ATAC's final report also recommends the promotion and support of telework in the Australian Public Service (APS).[100] Of course, such initiatives would lead to exposure and establish best practices, and could be used to encourage social change in wider society through successful experiences in the public sector. However, as noted by Toshiba Australia, 'industry and government have a united role to play in overcoming these barriers'.[101] Therefore, while public sector initiatives may be useful, employer driven policies are central to overcome cultural impediments. While such policies should exhibit 'high road' approaches, they also need to be driven by business case arguments, to attract the profit maximizing behaviour of firms.

As has been shown, existing Australian policy mechanisms create problems for the successful use of teleworking as a WLB practice for many Australian working families. Only through legislative change and supportive cultural developments might there be a situation where telework is available as a genuine WLB option for the majority of Australian workers engaged in suitable employment.

97. Pittard (2005), n. 27 above, Vol. 23, Issue 1, 170.
98. *ibid.*
99. Sweeney Research (2004), n. 49 above, pp. 21–22.
100. Australian Telework Advisory Committee (2006), n. 1 above, p. 40.
101. Toshiba (Australia) Pty Ltd, 'Submission to the Australian Telework Advisory Committee on Teleworking' (2005), 27 May 2005.

Chapter 5

Belgium

Roger Blanpain

I. INTRODUCTION AND BACKGROUND

A. TELEWORK ON THE MOVE

Telework in Belgium is on the move. More than 54 per cent of Belgian employees consider telework at home as a possibility; moreover they believe that work at home would be more productive than work at the standard workplace. In doing so, Belgium scores the highest in an inquiry organized in 15 EU countries,[1] well above Italy, Spain, the UK with 48 per cent, Finland with 43 per cent and Germany with only 28 per cent. One out of five Belgians is against the increase in telework.

So, telework seems to be 'in'. Nevertheless, only 1 out of 10 employees in Belgium actually engages in one or another form of telework. So there is room for more.

Not that official support is lacking. The Belgian Government in its 2006 action plan wants to encourage telework, a.o. for civil servants via organizational and regulatory changes. Social partners concluded the inter-industry wide collective agreement No. 95 of 9 November 2005 concerning telework, implementing the European Voluntary Framework of 2002. That agreement is agreed upon in the

---

1. A study by Manpower involving 12,000 respondents, 18-65 years of age. In Belgium 992 respondents, especially white collar workers and supervisory personnel (cadres), were involved.

Blanpain et al., European Framework, Agreements and Telework, pp. 93–106.
©2007, Kluwer Law International BV, The Netherlands.

National Labour Council and will, once extended by Royal Decree, be binding for the whole private sector. In the Flemish Government a directive on telework was adopted.

So, there is a lot of push. But what is the reality?

The fact is that we are not at all sure about the numbers: are there 10 per cent of employees who engage in telework or more?

This uncertainty is also due to the lack of a uniform notion of 'telework'. Various notions are used. Are we only referring to 'structural' teleworkers who perform at regular times in a place other than the standard workplace? Or do we also include occasional, informal teleworkers, who perform from time to time, also during the weekend, without formal, explicit agreements between employer and employee on the matter.

Should we include only those who perform at home and/or at another place of their choice, or do we also consider those teleworkers who work from a distance in satellite offices or in a telecentre linked to the head office.

Are so-called mobile workers who perform with their own laptop as consultants in the clients' workplace or, for example, commercial travellers, also to be considered as teleworkers?

B. A Diversified Picture

A study of four cases[2] tells us that home telework is mostly occasional, ad hoc and non structural. Informal arrangements prevail: 'tomorrow I will work at home as I want to concentrate, the weather is going to be bad, the kids are ill, there is a transport strike, to avoid a traffic jam'.

Structural telework at home seems rather exceptional. On the contrary, structural telework with clients and in satellite offices are more frequent.

The reasons for this situation are self evident. Telework at home is expensive, especially regarding infrastructure and communication. Moreover, there is a danger of social isolation for the teleworker and a decrease of his/her involvement in the work organization and with the team to which he/she belongs.

Telework at home is thus limited. Full-time telework is rather exceptional. Structural telework, if it occurs, is mostly limited to a maximum of 2 to 3 days a week.

Telework at the premises of the client (consultancy) and for those who want to work closer to home, structural then, in satellite offices or telecentres, is, as indicated, more frequent than structural home work.

The questions, however, remain. What is the difference between structural and occasional telework? Is evening or weekend telework at home ad hoc or structural? The last is not excluded if it occurs regularly.

2. IBM, General Motors, VRT (Flemish TV) and a Flemish Governmental Service – all situated in Belgium. See R. Blanpain, *Telewerk. Arbeidsrecht en praktijk. Internationaal, Europees en Belgisch* (Brugge, Die Keure, 2006), forthcoming.

C. TELEWORK AND HRM

Telework is not an isolated phenomenon. The fact is that telework in all its forms is part and parcel of a global human resources strategy which aims at:

- Giving employees more responsibility in the fostering of their own careers regarding the place and timing of work;
- Evaluating the contribution of the employee on the basis of the results obtained;
- Increasing work satisfaction;
- Providing for a better balance between private life and work;
- Providing a better service for clients;
- Increasing the image of the company;
- Increasing productivity;
- Saving on office space and infrastructure in the standard workplace.

D. FREE AND TRANSPARENT

It is remarkable that telework does not constitute a right for the employee and can also not be unilaterally imposed by the employer. Telework requires the agreement of both parties. In principle, the teleworker is allowed, on short notice, to return to the standard workplace.

Self evidently, someone can be engaged expressly for telework, e.g. to work as a consultant at the premises of the clients or as a commercial traveller.

E. NOT FOR ALL JOBS

Telework fits only certain jobs. As well as the function the used infrastructure and communication equipment come into play.

Typical activities are:

- Collection, inserting and manipulation of information;
- Conceptual work;
- Knowledge intensive activities;
- Planning and organization of projects;
- Policy supportive tasks;
- Consultancy;
- Commercial travelling.

F. NOT FOR EVERY EMPLOYEE

Indeed, not all employees qualify. We can think especially about competencies such as:

- Working independently;
- Result-oriented work;

- Initiative;
- Efficiency; working according to plan;
- Discipline;
- Skills and competence.

Candidates for telework need to motivate and indicate why they qualify for telework.

G. INTEGRATION

It is indicated that teleworkers should stay in close contact with their team and their superiors through sufficient communication, meetings, happy hours, etc.

H. CLEAR ARRANGEMENTS

Indeed, clear arrangements, collective as well as individual, are a must. Telework needs to be a subject of involvement with employee representatives and thoroughly explained to all employees, as well as those who do not participate in telework, like assembly line workers, so that everyone understands what is going on and can have empathy with the teleworkers.

Clear arrangements regarding infrastructure, such as its use, costs, health and safety, and possible visits of the workplace at home by the employer are, self evidently, also more than indicated.

Individual telework agreements will lead to a change in the individual employment contract, by way of an addendum or of a specific telework labour contract. For satellite work or work at the premises of the client, an additional contract is strictly not necessary if the description of the place of work in the basic employment contract is sufficiently flexible.

Adaptation of the work rules – indicating the possibility of telework and specific conditions in the company – is also necessary.

I. PAY

No additional pay is provided for telework.

J. STRUCTURAL AND AD HOC INSURANCE

Here one has to be extremely careful. Quid regarding work accidents which take place at home? Does the insurance cover fire or other damages, e.g. to the laptop of the enterprise if ad hoc telework has been undertaken at home? Also, whether structural or occasional, the necessary proctection – read insurances – has to be provided for.

II. HOME WORK – THE ACT OF 1996

A. GENERALITIES

Traditionally, home workers are manual workers, which as a category have disappeared almost altogether. There are no reliable figures. In 1990, a few hundred were reported in the clothing industry, the leather and textile industry. Those workers are traditionally defined as employees working for remuneration under the authority of an employer, in a place which is not imposed by the employer, but usually in the vicinity of, or in the home of, the worker. The basic criterion distinguishing the home worker from other employees is the fact that he/she more or less chooses for himself the place of work.

The Belgian Cour de Cassation decided in a landmark case (30 November 1992) that the Act of 1978 concerning individual employment contracts did not apply to home workers. So home workers were workers, but their status was not specifically regulated. You had to check each labour law Act in order to find out whether it applied to home workers.

There is no legal definition either of 'teleworker' or 'telework'. We could define telework as work involving the use of telecommunications in a way which is independent from a fixed, traditional location. This may be the home of the worker, a 'telecottage', or any other place. The teleworker may do this work in the capacity of an employee, including as a home worker or as a self-employed worker.

There is no overall statistical data available in Belgium on the number of teleworkers. The number of teleworkers, however, still seems to be relatively small. It is also unknown how many people operate as freelance teleworkers, such as journalists, consultants, etc.

Teleworkers can be fully fledged employees, home workers or self employed, depending on whether work is done in subordination. This is under command and control, thus the authority of the employer. As employee, the teleworker will either be a white-collar worker, eventually a commercial representative, or a temporary worker. The teleworker employee can also be a home worker, but, as mentioned above, traditionally home workers have been mainly manual labourers.

Teleworkers can work part time or full time, engaged with a contract for a fixed period or for an indefinite duration, or even with a contract for replacement. Teleworkers can have one or more employers. If the teleworker is an employee, labour law applies. Home workers are accounted for in a number of thresholds, including social elections for works councils or for closing of enterprises.

If teleworkers are self employed, general rules relating to contracts prevail. Labour law is not applicable.

Teleworkers can be employees and self employed at the same time depending on the nature of their relationship with contractors. Seventy three per cent of employees ('cadres') and 63 per cent of white-collar workers (2000) are willing to work at home, 39 per cent of them for a maximum one day a week and for 25 per cent half time.

According to Article 15 of the Belgian Constitution, 'a person's home (is) inviolable; no search can be made other than in the cases laid down by statute and in the manner prescribed'. This applies to a teleworker's home. It should be noted that the violation is criminally sanctioned. In case of telework outside of the employee's home, e.g. in telecottages or telecentres or in decentralized units, normal rules regarding inspection apply. The labour inspector is entitled to visit them day and night. The labour inspector can visit homes only when the judicial authority grants permission beforehand. Legally there is scope to inspect teleworkers at home. However, in practice, the Belgian labour inspection suffers from a shortage of manpower.

B.   The Act of 6 December 1996

A special Act of 6 December 1996 deals with the employment of home workers, covering traditional home work as well as newer fortes like telework. The Act can be summarized as follows.

The Government starts from the fact that telework, which is expected to grow considerably in the near future, is a form of work at a distance by which use is made of telematics, which can constitute a new variant of home work. This form of work allows for certain tasks of an intellectual nature to be performed by home workers who use a computer which is or is not linked to the central computer of an enterprise. Acknowledging the fact that some pilot projects have already been introduced in Belgium, the Government is of the opinion that it is necessary to ascertain the legal certainty regarding home work in order to be prepared for the day that it expands. The Act only deals with home workers who work under the authority of the employer, i.e. as employees, and not the self employed.

To that end the Act introduces a separate Title VI (Article 119.1-12) dealing with home work in the 1978 Act concerning individual employment contracts. Self-employed teleworkers continue to be covered by general principles of contract law.

1.   Definition

The employment contract for home work is a contract by which an employee, the home worker, undertakes, in return for remuneration, to perform work under an employer's authority, in his/her home or another place chosen by him/her, without being under the supervision or the direct control of the employer. According to the case, the home worker will be either a manual or an intellectual worker (Article 119.1). In case of a mixed situation, where a regular employee is also working at home, he/she will have two legal statuses: his normal status and he will also be covered by the Act of 6 December 1996.

2. Form

The employment contract has to be in writing no later than when the home worker takes up his employment (Article 119.4). In absence of a written contract, the home worker will be able to terminate his employment at any moment without notice or compensation (Article 119.5).

3. Content of the Agreement

The written agreement should mention:

- The identity of the parties;
- The remuneration or the way and criteria for its calculation;
- The payment of expenses related to home work; in absence of such a regulation, expenses will be calculated at a rate of 10 per cent of the remuneration;
- The place(s) chosen by the home worker to work;
- The job description;
- The working time, the work roster or the minimum number of duties (Article 119.4).

4. Conditions

a. *Incapacity of Work, Guaranteed Salary*

The Act guarantees the home worker the following:

- If he/she is receiving a regular wage, a guaranteed salary for the days he/she is incapable of working, for reasons beyond his/her control (Article 119.5).
- In cases of incapacity to work for reasons of illness or accident, with the exception of an act of God, the home worker must;
  - i. Inform his/her employer immediately
  - ii. Send a medical certificate within a period of two days.

Other articles of the Act concern the right to a guaranteed salary if the home worker is not paid on the basis of a regular wage; in that case the salary is in principle equal to that of blue- or white-collars workers: the compensation per day will equal 1/7 of the average weekly income.

b. *Working Time*

The Act confirms that regulations concerning working time and Sunday rest are not applicable to home workers, but the Government can extend those regulations totally or partially to home workers, taking the opinion of social partners into account.

III. THE ACT OF 26 JULY 2006 – TELEWORK

A. SCOPE OF APPLICATION

According to the Act of 26 July 2006, the 1996 Act on home work does not apply to workers which are covered by the collective agreement on telework concluded in the framework of the National Labour Council (see s.IV).

If telework is only performed part time and the worker also performs at 'normal' work premises, the telework will be governed by the collective agreement mentioned above, and the work done at 'normal' premises by the normal rules governing the employee contract, be it as a blue-collar or as a white-collar worker.

B. WORK RULES

The Act of 26 July 2006 also foresees that the work rules in an enterprise can mention the periods during which the employee, on request of the employer, may or may not engage in telework as meant by collective agreement No. 85.

IV. THE COLLECTIVE AGREEMENT NO. 85 OF 9 NOVEMBER 2005

A. PURPOSE

The European Agreement is concluded by the European social partners with the aim of:

- Modernizing the organization of work;
- Providing more autonomy for workers to perform their jobs;
- Providing a better relationship between private and working life;
- Promoting flexibility and security;
- Enhancing the quality of work;
- Improving the chances for the handicapped to become employed.

B. DEFINITIONS AND SCOPE

1. Teleworker

Telework is, according to Article 2 of the Agreement:

- Performed in the framework of a labour contract using information technology;
- Undertaken on a regular basis;
- Carried out at another place other than the employer's premises.

2. Place

a. Home and any other chosen place.
b. A satellite office provided for by the employer. This is a decentralized location, which the employer puts at the disposal of the employee. It falls outside the scope of the collective agreement.
c. Mobile work. This applies to teleworkers for whom mobile work is part and parcel of the performance of their jobs, e.g. commercial travellers, medical representatives, technical workers, those providing services on the premises of the client, such as home nurses. Mobile work also falls outside the scope of the Collective Agreement No. 85.

3. Voluntary Character

Telework is performed on a voluntary basis: both employer and employee have to agree.
 Telework can be part of the original job description or can be agreed upon in the course of the employment contract between employer and employee.
 In other words, if telework is not a part of the original employment contract and the employer offers the possibility of telework, the employee can either accept or refuse the offer.
 If an employee indicates his desire to engage in telework, the employer can also either agree or refuse.

C.   Nature of the Telework Contract

1. No Home Work

The National Labour Council is of the opinion that telework cannot be classified as home work, according to the 1996 Act described above. Its argument to justify this point of view is not clear and is a question of debate in Belgium at the moment.

2. An Employment Contract for White-Collar Workers

The National Labour Council has consequently asked the Belgian legislator to amend the 1978 Act on employment contracts, in order to provide for a specific telework employment contract.

3. White Collar

A white-collar worker performs 'intellectual work', so teleworkers should come under this category. Blue collars, performing mainly manual work, would not qualify.

4. Form: A Written Agreement

a.   Timing

i.   When Hiring
The written agreement has to be concluded prior to the moment the employee starts performing the job.

ii.   In the Course of the Employment Contract
A written addendum has to be made.

b.   Content

The written agreement should at least contain the following:

- The frequency of the telework, eventually the days on which telework will be performed and eventually the days and/or hours of presence in the enterprise;
- The periods during which the teleworker must be reachable and via what means;
- When the teleworker can ask for technical support;
- The rules according to which the employer will compensate costs or will pay for them;
- The conditions and rules regarding a return of the teleworker to the 'normal' workplace and, in case of such a return, the term of notice and/or the duration of working time and its prolongation.

c.   Sanction

In case of a lack of a written agreement, the teleworker has the right, at any moment, to terminate his activities at the standard workplace or return to that 'normal' workplace.

5.   Working Conditions

a.   Equal Treatment

Regarding working conditions, the teleworkers enjoy the same conditions as comparable workers who perform at the standard workplace.

b.   Specific Conditions

Specific conditions can be laid down in collective or individual labour agreements in order to take account of the specificities of telework.

5. Belgium

Thus, it is possible to provide in the telework contract – in case of defect of the infrastructure or in case of an act of God, due to which the teleworkers can not perform their task – specific rules, such as the performance of other activities or partial return to the standard workplace.

c.   Information

Teleworkers are entitled to information about their working conditions and especially regarding complementary conditions, namely:

- The description of the task to be performed in the framework of telework;
- The division of the enterprise to which they are attached;
- The identification of their immediate superior and of other persons to whom they may address questions relating to their job or of a personal nature;
- Arrangements that relate to reporting.

The written agreement or addendum does not necessarily contain all of the working conditions, but can refer to a collective agreement on telework which is concluded at sectoral level, at enterprise level or to the enterprise work rules.

6.   Organization of Telework

a.   Working Time

Teleworkers organize their work themselves within the framework of the prevailing working time schedule in the enterprise.

b.   Workload and Norms of Efficiency

Teleworkers have the same workload and efficiency norms as comparable employees in the standard workplace.

c.   Prevention of Isolation

The employer must take all measures to prevent the teleworker from becoming isolated from the rest of the labour community in the enterprise, namely by offering opportunities for the teleworker to meet colleagues and by organizing access to information regarding the enterprise. The employer is entitled, to that end, to recall the telework at regular intervals.

d.   Equipment

i.   Installation by the Employer Technical Support
The employer is responsible for making available to the teleworker the necessary equipment, and installing and maintaining it.
      The employer provides appropriate technical support facilities to the teleworker.

ii.   Costs

The employer, and he/she alone, compensates or pays for the costs related to the communications which are associated with telework.

If teleworkers use their own equipment, the costs related to telework, namely installation of information programmes, working and maintenance, as well as costs relating to the writing of the costs of the equipment, should entirely be paid by the employer.

The costs to be paid by the employer will be established before the commencement of the telework, pro rata of the work performed as telework, or according to a key agreed upon by the parties.

The costs which occur due to the loss or damage of the equipment or of the data used in the framework of the telework are to be paid by the employer.

iii.   Diligence and Determined Use

Teleworkers should use the equipment put at their disposal by the employer with care. Teleworkers will not gather materials or communicate via the internet in ways which fall outside the performance of their job.

iv.   Breakdown

In case of a breakdown of the equipment or an act of God, as a consequence of which a teleworker can not perform his/her job, he/she will immediately inform the employer. The employer remains, however, obliged to pay the agreed remuneration.

7.   Protection of Data

a.   *Measures for Protection*

The employer should take the necessary measures to protect data which is used by the teleworker.

The employer has to inform the employee about the applicable legal and company rules concerning the protection of data. The teleworker has to live up to these rules.

b.   *Limitations of Using IT Equipment*

The employer informs the teleworker about the limitations of the use of IT equipment or facilities and of the possible sanctions in case he/she does not live up to these limitations. Here, the National Collective Agreement No. 81 of 26 April 2002 on the protection of employees' personal data in respect of monitoring online communication data[3] applies *mutatis mutandis*.

---

3. See R. Blanpain and M. Van Gestel, *Use and Monitoring of E-Mail, Intranet and Internet Facilities at Work*, Studies in Employment and Social Policy (The Hague, Kluwer Law International, 2004), pp.160-191.

5. Belgium

The objective of National Collective Agreement No. 81 is to safeguard the fundamental rights of employees to have their personal privacy respected in the employment context by specifying, while at the same time taking account of what is required for the company's efficient operation, the purposes for which a system for monitoring electronic online communication data may be installed, the conditions of proportionality and transparency with which it must comply, and the rules governing the permissibility of individualizing such data.

8. Health and Safety

a. Policy, Information and Execution

The employer should inform the teleworker of the company policy relating to safety and health in the workplace, especially regarding the requirements relating to display screen equipment.

b. Inspection of the Teleworker's Workplace, Home Included

The competent internal prevention services of the employer have access to the workplace of the teleworker in order to control whether the prevailing rules regarding safety and health have been applied. If telework takes place in a living room, the visit will have to be pre-arranged and the consent of the teleworker obtained.
   The teleworker can request the visit of these health and safety services.

9. Vocational Training and Career Development

a. Equal Treatment

Teleworkers have the same rights as comparable employees in the enterprise regarding vocational training and career development. They enjoy the same evaluation procedures.

b. Vocational Training

Teleworkers receive adequate vocational training regarding the use of technical equipment which is put at their disposal and of the workings of the internet.
   Hierarchical superiors and direct colleagues can also be trained for this form of work and for the management thereof.

10. Collective Rights

a. Rights of Teleworkers

Teleworkers enjoy the same collective rights as other workers. They have the right to communicate with the representatives of the employees and *vice versa*.

b. *Rights of the Representatives of the Employees: Information and*
   Consultation

Employee representatives are informed and consulted concerning the introduction
of telework in the enterprise in the same way as regarding the social consequences
of the introduction of new technologies.

V.   CONCLUSION

The national collective agreement No. 85 translates the European Voluntary
Agreement in an appropriate way.

Two remarks however.

As we discussed in the introduction, is structural home telework *de facto*
rather than exceptional? The Collective Agreement No. 85 excludes form its
scope of application occasional home telework as well as telework in satellites
and telecentres.

It seems to me that the scope of application of the collective agreement is very
narrow, excluding the most important forms of telework, when all teleworkers
need the same or similar protection.

So the question arises, does the agreement have any impact in practice?

Secondly, in Belgium national collective agreements, which are extended by
Royal decree, are hard law and penally sanctioned. This is not so in other EU
Member States, e.g. in the UK or the Scandinavian countries where such extending
mechanisms do not exist.

Are we in this way not heading towards a dual social Europe? And what about
a European level social playing field?

May be voluntary agreements are, after all, not such a good idea.

Chapter 6

Belgium

A discussion on the Collective Bargaining Agreement No. 85 on Telework, Implementing the European Framework Agreement on Telework

Chris Engels

I. INTRODUCTION

The inter-industry wide Collective Bargaining Agreement (CBA) No. 85 of 9 November 2005 on telework implements the Voluntary European Framework Agreement (EFA) on telework which was concluded a little more than three years earlier.

This chapter will discuss just a few topical issues dealing with telework. It will look at the voluntary nature of telework, the organization of it and the application of the principle of equal treatment. Finally, it will briefly touch on the follow-up procedure that the framework agreement refers to.

II. VOLUNTARY CHARACTER OF TELEWORK

A. ENTERING EMPLOYMENT AS A TELEWORKER

The EFA on telework states in point 3:

> Telework is voluntary for the worker and the employer concerned. Teleworking may be required as part of a worker's initial job description or it may be engaged in as a voluntary arrangement subsequently.
>
> . . .

Blanpain et al., European Framework, Agreements and Telework, pp. 107–116.
©2007, Kluwer Law International BV, The Netherlands.

If telework is not part of the initial job description, and the employer makes an offer of telework, the worker may accept or refuse this offer. If a worker expresses the wish to opt for telework, the employer may accept or refuse this request.

It will come as no surprise that a job announced as a teleworking job can require the applicant to work from home, or from outside the company premises. Holding otherwise would mean that one would be outlawing work from home or from other premises chosen by the teleworker.

The Belgian CBA No. 85 on telework merely repeats the principle as stated in the EFA.

B.   Becoming a Teleworker in the Course of the Employment Relationship

The EFA wanted to fully stress the voluntary nature of telework, and clearly indicate that an employer cannot unilaterally require a worker to become a tele-worker:

If telework is not part of the initial job description, and the employer makes an offer of telework, the worker may accept or refuse this offer.

It is equally clear that the teleworker him/herself cannot just decide, without the employer agreeing, that he or she will no longer perform at the company premises or the client's premises, but at home. An employer may thus refuse the employee's request to become a teleworker.

The latter seems to be absolutely clear under Belgian employment law. The employee has no right to unilaterally make a decision as to where he or she would perform his or her job.

With respect to the employer's decision, one has to take into account that quite often the place of employment is not considered to be an essential element of the job – at least when dealing with high level employees fit for teleworking. So the employer, in these circumstances, can reserve itself the contractual right to unilaterally change the place of employment. A modification of the place of employment within just a few miles would in these circumstances not be considered a breach of contract. It would not be considered a constructive discharge.

With respect to telework things seem to be substantially different, however. While the mere geographical place of employment may as such not be essential to the employment contract, it is clear that the decision to change from 'normal' employment at the employer's premises to home work (or telework) involves more than a mere geographic change. It will have a fundamental impact on the general work surroundings of the employee. The emphasis that both the EFA and the Belgian CBA No. 85 put on the voluntary nature of telework stresses this position clearly.

C.   RETURNING BACK TO 'NORMAL' – ENDING TELEWORK

Both the EFA and the Belgian implementing measure include the explicit hypothesis in which telework is not part of the initial job description:

> If telework is not part of the initial job description, the decision to pass to telework is reversible by individual and/or collective agreement.

The modalities of this reversibility can be established by individual and/or collective agreement, so the EFA holds.

The implementing Belgian CBA No. 85 refers to the conditions for reversal only when describing the items that need to be addressed in the individual written agreement for telework, prior to engaging in this kind of work. The Belgian measure therefore imposes an additional requirement. The conditions for the reversal and terms of notice have to be part of an individual agreement.

Given the hierarchy of the sources of Belgian labour and employment law,[1] such conditions could also be set by collective bargaining agreement. CBA No. 85 seems to impose an additional condition, namely the necessity to conclude an individual agreement even if a CBA already exists with respect to the issues concerned. It is debatable whether this provision is enforceable at all, since an employer cannot reserve the right to unilaterally modify an essential condition of employment (see s.III below). The CBAs or individual agreements that are concluded in execution of CBA No. 85 and contain the modalities to end telework are presumably null and void.

The sanction for not concluding an individual agreement is not that far reaching. If no individual agreement is concluded, the worker concerned has the right to work at the employer's premises. The application of CBA No. 85 to home workers who were previously covered by the Act of July 3, 1978, ss.119.1 e.s., is rather far reaching in this respect. If the individual agreement of the home worker who is not covered by CBA No. 85 does not contain the mandatory provisions, the home worker can terminate the employment contract at any time, without respecting any term of notice or paying any indemnity in lieu.[2] If the home worker is a teleworker and thus no longer covered by Article 119.5 of the Act on contracts of employment, he or she will have the opportunity to return to work at the employer's premises.

D.   FORMAL ASPECTS

The EFA refers to Directive 91/533/EEC[3] and determines that in accordance with this directive, the employer has to provide the teleworker with the relevant

---

1. Art.51, Act on Collective Bargaining Agreements and Joint Committee, 5 December 1968.
2. Art.119.5, Act on Contracts of Employment, 3 July 1978.
3. Council Directive 91/533/EEC of 14 October 1991 on an Employer's Obligation to Inform Employees of the Conditions Applicable to the Contract or Employment Relationship.

information, including information on applicable collective agreements, description of the work to be performed, etc. Since telework is special, it will require additional written information on matters such as the department of the undertaking to which the teleworker is attached, his/her immediate superior or other persons to whom he or she can address questions of a professional or a personal nature, reporting arrangements, etc.

CBA No. 85 contains the same references.[4] In a comment in Article 7 it is stated that not all employment conditions have to be described *in extenso*, but that a further reference to other documents, such as collective bargaining agreements on telework either at sector or company level or company work rules, may suffice.

Article 6 of CBA No. 85 adds to the list of issues to be mentioned:

- The frequency of the telework and the days when it will be performed, and the days and hours of presence in the company workplace, if any;
- The periods in which the teleworker must be accessible and the ways this can be done;
- When the teleworker can rely on technical support;
- Rules for cost reimbursement; and
- The conditions of return to the employer's premises.

The EFA merely requires the information to be provided. The Belgian implementing measure is clearly more formalistic in its approach. It requires the signature of an agreement – either an initial employment contract if telework is part of the original job description or an annex to an existing employment contract.

The contract needs to be entered into prior to the start of the telework. The reference to Directive 91/533/EEC in the EFA reflects a more lenient approach at European level. The directive does not require the information to be provided prior to the start of the employment. CBA No. 85 is therefore much more stringent in this respect. However, sanctions in case of non compliance are, as already stated, minimal.

E. REFUSAL TO GET INTO TELEWORK

The EFA explicitly mentions that a worker's refusal to accept telework as proposed by the employer is, as such, not a reason for terminating the employment relationship or changing the terms and conditions of employment of that worker. CBA No. 85 does not mention this explicitly.

However, it seems clear that when telework should be entirely voluntary and an employer can thus not force one of its workers to accept telework, the refusal should not be the sole reason for the termination. Given the fact that teleworkers are considered white-collar workers under Belgian law, the question is whether a termination for a refusal to accept telework could be considered as an abusive termination by the employer, entitling the employee concerned to damages. While

---

4. Art.7, CBA No. 85.

one may expect courts to award damages in egregious cases, this should not always be so. Imagine a situation in which an employer – following proper consultation – decided to reorganize its financial department or IT department so that it could save space and costs at the company premises. All those working in those departments should become teleworkers. It seems that such a decision can validly be taken by an employer and constitutes a sufficient organizational or economic reason to avoid any claims of an abusive dismissal by an employee who would not be willing to convert to telework.

III. ORGANIZATION OF WORK

The EFA grants the teleworker the right to organize the organization of his or her working time within the limits of what the rules applicable in the company hold.

In the advice accompanying the text of CBA No. 85, the National Labour Council explicitly states that the provisions from the Act of March 16, 1971 dealing with working time are fully applicable to teleworkers covered by CBA No. 5. This is, however, not entirely correct. By an omnibus Act of July 26, 2006, the legislator has enacted – with immediate effect – that a number of the provisions of the Act on employment contracts dealing with home workers are no longer applicable to those workers covered by CBA No. 85, regardless of whether CBA No. 85 is rendered generally binding by Royal Decree. However, teleworkers working from their home remain home workers, also within the definition of the home worker in Article 119.1 of the Act of July 3, 1978 on employment contracts. The Act of March 16, 1971 excludes 'home workers' as such from its principal provisions, without any further definition of the concept and without any reference to any other legal text. This therefore means that those home workers still covered by the provisions of the Act on contracts of employment, as well as the teleworkers covered by CBA No. 85 and working from their home, are not subject to the provisions of the Act of March 16, 1971, contrary to the statement made by the National Labour Council in the advice that accompanies CBA No. 85.[5]

The company work rules can indicate the periods during which teleworkers can perform telework at the request of the employer.[6] There does not seem to be any such obligation. However, it is allowed to mention these periods in the company work rules.

The EFA further reiterates the premise that the workload and the performance standards of the teleworker and other comparable workers should be the same (see s.IV below regarding equal treatment).

Recognizing a danger of isolation, the EFA puts an obligation on the employer to take measures to prevent the teleworker from being isolated from the rest of the

---

5. Advice No. 1528, session of Wednesday 9 November 2005, Execution of the European Voluntary Framework Agreement of 16 July 2002 on telework, p. 5.
6. Art.245, Act of July 26, 2006.

workforce. The teleworker should be granted the opportunity to meet with colleagues on a regular basis and to have access to company information.

CBA No. 85 reiterates these principles, and adds that in order to prevent isolation the employer may call the teleworker back to the company at certain points in time.

It is questionable whether this latter provision is enforceable at all. It is clear that it is contained in a CBA only. Even if and when rendered generally binding by Royal Decree, such a CBA is, in terms of hierarchy of sources in labour and employment law, ranks below a Parliamentary Act such as the Act on contracts of employment. The latter Act holds that an employer may not reserve itself the right to unilaterally modify an essential element of the contract of employment.[7] In the present context it seems that working at company premises or at a self chosen location is – by definition – considered to be an essential element of the contract of employment, since CBA No. 85 clearly does not allow telework to be imposed on any of its employees without their (explicit) consent. If and when essential, the employer cannot be granted the right to unilaterally modify it.

IV.   EQUAL TREATMENT

A.   PRINCIPLE OF EQUAL TREATMENT

'Regarding employment conditions', so the EFA states, 'teleworkers benefit form the same rights, guaranteed by applicable legislation and collective agreements, as comparable workers at the employers premises. However, in order to take into account the particularities of telework, specific complementary collective and/or individual agreements may be necessary'.[8] The same wording can be found in CBA No. 85.[9]

While wanting to insist on an absolute necessity not to discriminate those who are engaging in telework in the sense of CBA No. 85, it is clear that both texts at the same time also recognize the particular nature of telework.

Furthermore, both the EFA and CBA No. 85 make reference to an obligation of equal treatment with respect to:

- Workload and performance standards (see above);
- Access to training and career development opportunities;[10]
- Same appraisal policies;[11]
- Collective rights, including the right to communicate with their representatives.[12]

---

7. Art.25, Act on Contracts of Employment, 3 July 1978.
8. European framework agreement, Point 4.
9. Art.7, CBA No. 85.
10. European framework agreement, Point 10; Art.16, CBA No. 85.
11. *Ibid.*
12. European framework agreement, Point 11; Art.17, CBA No. 85.

Even though it is not expressly mentioned, it seems obvious that a teleworker cannot be discriminated against, either directly or indirectly.

The principle of non-discrimination and equal treatment is certainly an undisputed one. At the same time it is clear, however – and this is also explicitly recognized by the EFA and CBA No. 85 – that a number of specificities of telework may require treatment that is different from that received by ordinary employees.

B.   Difficulties in Making a Comparison

1.   'Regular' as a Concept

The first difficulty one encounters is to know who is and who is not covered by the EFA, and even more importantly CBA No. 85. Telework is defined by the EFA as:

> A form of organizing and/or performing work, using information technology, in the context of an employment contract/relationship, where work, which could also be performed at the employers premises is carried out away from those premises on a regular basis.
>
> A teleworker is then a worker carrying out the described telework.

CBA No. 85 is a bit more specific than the EFA. Where the latter referred to work that is carried out on a regular basis outside the company premises, the CBA adds: 'on a regular basis and not occasionally'.

What does the term regular (and by contrast the term occasional) mean? Does it include regular telework but for a very small part of the working week?

Does regular mean 'at regular intervals'? Or does it include the situation in which someone would telework from home one day a week, but without any regularity, meaning that once a week he/she would work at home on Monday; another week working, then 2 days? Can the weekly duration of the telework vary? For instance, 1 week 1 day, another week 2 days. . . .

In other words, when does the very general term 'regular' turn into the legal concept of 'regular' as used in a binding collective bargaining agreement, the violations of which will carry criminal sanctions once the CBA is rendered generally binding? The answer is certainly not clear at present.

2.   A Comparable Worker at the Employer's Location or Premises

The concept of employer – and thus also the employer's location – can have different meanings. Is the CBA referring to the employer as a legal entity? Or as a technical unit of operation – as used in social election matters dealing with elections for works council representatives? Or could the employer concept also cover the notion of a site or establishment?

Up to now it seemed undisputed that an employer could have different pay scales for workers engaged in equal work, but working at different sites. Labour market shortages, etc. can easily explain differences in pay.

Can such differences – based mainly on geographical distance – still be invoked to justify a difference in pay between comparable workers, one of which is working at the employer's headquarters and the other one remotely from his/her own home?

They should. However, on the basis of the terminology of CBA No. 85 it can be doubted, since the CBA merely states that teleworkers should have the same rights as comparable workers working at the employer's premises. Furthermore, one could equally ask the question whether it is justifiable to treat a teleworker working from his/her own house, who commutes to the employer's premises only once every three weeks, the same way as a worker from whom the employer demands a presence in the office every day. What if the latter is commuting every day for over three hours?

And to whom should a teleworker be compared if the employer has, for example, a location (headquarters) in Brussels, but also a satellite office in Hasselt, if employees with comparable jobs at these two locations do not earn the same?

The most comparable worker for any comparison is, of course, the worker him/herself. Would you be allowed to compare the work done by a teleworker to the work done by the same worker at the company premises?

It will be up to case law to come up with the appropriate comparators. It will equally be up to the courts to determine which differences between the teleworker and the company location worker can still justify a difference in treatment. It seems that mere geographical distance should as such not be excluded as a justifying factor.

C.   UNEQUAL TREATMENT AS PROVIDED BY CBA No. 85

CBA No. 85 installs itself a different treatment for home workers with respect to a number of issues.

1.   Appropriate Initial Training

Teleworkers receive appropriate training targeted at technical equipment and the characteristics of this specific form of work organization.[13]

While this may seem absolutely logical, there seems to be no similar provision with respect to ordinary workers or home workers who do not make use of information technologies.

---

13. European framework agreement, Point 10; Art.16, CBA No. 85.

2. Equipment

The EFA clearly states that as a general rule the employer is responsible for providing, installing and maintaining the equipment necessary for regular telework, unless the teleworker uses his/her own equipment.[14] It continues, stating in a rather awkward form,[15] that 'if telework is performed on a regular basis, the employer compensates or covers the costs directly caused by the work, in particular those relating to communication'.[16]

CBA No. 85 does not refer to a general rule, but merely states that the employer is responsible for putting the appropriate equipment at the disposal of the worker and for maintaining it.[17]

By imposing this, the CBA deviates from the rules applicable to workers in general, and from those applicable to home workers. The Act on contracts of employment contains a provision similar to the one contained in the EFA. It foresees as a general rule that the employer will provide the instruments necessary to perform the work, if the circumstances so warrant. However, it clearly adds a provision stating that this applies only if the parties have not agreed differently.[18]

A mobile teleworker who is excluded from the scope of CBA No. 85 will be covered by the general provisions of the Act on contracts of employment. It could therefore be agreed upon between the mobile teleworker and the employer that the teleworker will have to buy his/her own car in order to be able to get to clients and will have to buy his own laptop. With respect to the ordinary teleworker covered by CBA No. 85, no such contractual arrangement can be validly entered into. This difference in treatment is not warranted.

The same holds with respect to the reimbursement of the costs involved in telework. The CBA obliges a reimbursement. With respect to home workers, the Act on contracts of employment only determines that the parties have to come to a contractual arrangement. It is not excluded to agree that no cost reimbursements will occur.

3. Liability

The EFA refers to the national legislative framework when dealing with the issue of liability. It states that the employer has liability in accordance with national legislation and collective agreements regarding costs for loss and damage to equipment and data used by the teleworker.[19]

One would have expected the general rule on employee liability to become applicable in Belgium. Article 18 of the Act on contracts of employment restricts an employee's liability to instances of fraud, serious fault or repetitive minor faults.

---

14. European framework agreement, Point 7.
15. Rather awkward since the CBA is only applicable to *regular* teleworkers.
16. European framework agreement, Point 7.
17. Art.9, CBA No. 85.
18. 18 Art.20, 1°, Act on Contracts of Employment, July 3 1978.
19. European framework agreement, Point 7.

While CBA No. 85 states that a teleworker will handle the equipment with care,[20] it seems to further severely limit the worker's liability. Article 11 of CBA No. 85 holds that costs for the loss or damage by the teleworker of equipment and data are to be carried by the employer. This seems to be a limitation of liability which may lead to irresponsibility. It comes as a surprise that this is part of a CBA approved by the employers' federations.

V.   FOLLOW UP

The EFA provides for implementation by the members of the signatory parties in accordance with the procedures and practices in the different Member States.[21]

The implementation needed to happen within 3 years following July 16 2002.

With the conclusion of CBA No. 85 on November 9 2005, the Belgian social partners were almost on time.

The social partners also launched an appeal to the legislator in order to modify certain legal provisions which obviously they did not have the power to change. The Belgian legislator enacted the requested provisions on July 26 2006.

The members of the signatory parties have to report back to the latter about what was done at country level. On the basis of these reports, a joint report will be prepared.

---

20. Art.12, CBA No. 85.
21. European framework agreement, Point 12.

Chapter 7

E-Monitoring the Teleworker: Belgian and Dutch Law in an International Perspective

Frank Hendrickx

I. INTRODUCTION

The Telework Agreement defines telework as:

> A form of organising and/or performing work, using information technology, in the context of an employment contract/relationship, where work, which could also be performed at the employers premises, is carried out away from those premises on a regular basis.[1]

With regard to the issue of privacy and data protection, two relevant aspects of the concept may be pointed out. In the first place, the use of information technology forms a constitutive part of the concept. This makes it more likely that the monitoring of a teleworker is considered to be more appropriate when arranged through information technology. A second relevant item of the definition concerns the fact that the work is carried out away from the employer's regular premises. If this implies that the work is performed in the employee's own private house, evident privacy issues will be raised as regards monitoring (e.g. the use of video

---

1. Art.2, Telework Agreement.

Blanpain et al., European Framework, Agreements and Telework, pp. 117–156.
©2007, Kluwer Law International BV, The Netherlands.

surveillance, and what needs to be done about the employer's wish to visit the teleworker's workplace). If it concerns mobile forms of telework (which are not undertaken, or not exclusively, in the employee's home), the employer may have additional concerns with regard to locating the teleworker. Related to the use of information, communication and technology (ICT) in a professional context and remote workplace, the issue of private facilities for the employee will also be raised.

In this chapter, the focus will be on the issue of electronic monitoring in the workplace. It is indeed quite explainable that telework gives rise to the use of ICT facilities by the teleworker, so that monitoring of the teleworker through, for example, internet, e-mail or video surveillance is put into the discussion. In doing so, an overview will be given of relevant employment privacy instruments and principles under international and European law, as well as under Belgian and Dutch law. Furthermore, a synthesis will try to give guidance on main themes regarding electronic monitoring, on the basis of the laws and principles provided in that regard.

II. THE REFERENCE IN THE TELEWORK AGREEMENT TO PRIVACY AND DATA PROTECTION

In providing employee privacy and data protection principles, one should refer to the Telework Agreement first. Indeed, the Telework Agreement provides two sections on this issue:

Article 5. Data protection
The employer is responsible for taking the appropriate measures, notably with regard to software, to ensure the protection of data used and processed by the teleworker for professional purposes.
The employer informs the teleworker of all relevant legislation and company rules concerning data protection.
It is the teleworker's responsibility to comply with these rules.
The employer informs the teleworker in particular of:

- Any restrictions on the use of IT equipment or tools such as the internet,
- Sanctions in the case of non-compliance.

Article 6. Privacy
The employer respects the privacy of the teleworker.
If any kind of monitoring system is put in place, it needs to be proportionate to the objective and introduced in accordance with Directive 90/270 on visual display units.

This contribution is too limited to elaborate extensively on the difference between the notion of data protection on the one hand and privacy on the other. Both concepts are used in the Telework Agreement. It would appear that privacy is a broader term, not only covering data protection issues, but also implying the protection of personal life, the home and correspondence, personal integrity, and

118

individual self-determination. On the other hand, data protection is also broader than the strict privacy concept. If data protection is seen as the protection of information relating to an (identified or identifiable) individual, data of a non-private nature (such as professional data) will also come in its scope.

Article 6 of the Telework Agreement refers to one particular source of Community law. It provides that if any kind of monitoring system is put in place, it needs to be introduced in accordance with Directive 90/270 on visual display units. This reference concerns Council Directive 90/270/EEC of 29 May 1990 on the minimum safety and health requirements for work with display screen equipment (fifth individual directive within the meaning of Article 16.1 of Directive 89/391/EEC).[2]

This reference may seem rather odd at first sight. Indeed, Article 1, 3° of Directive 90/270 provides that it shall not apply to: '(...) "portable" systems not in prolonged use at a workstation' (Article 1, 3°, d). This appears to suggest that the 'distant' teleworker using portable equipment is not envisaged. However, it does not take away that Article 6 of the Telework Agreement recovers the principles of Directive 90/270 for this situation. One might still argue that Article 6 of the Telework Agreement does not imply that all provisions of Directive 90/270 are applicable in case of telework as defined in the Agreement, since the reference to this directive is not made in general terms but only under the rubric of 'privacy'. It leaves the question whether this would mean that only the privacy-relevant aspects of Directive 90/270 would apply in the case of telework.

The most relevant part as far as privacy is concerned is to be found in the Annex of Directive 90/270, which sets minimum requirements. It provides that:

- No quantitative or qualitative checking facility may be used without the knowledge of the workers;[3]
- Systems must provide feedback to workers on their performance.[4]

With this provision, Directive 90/270 does not offer mere isolated principles. The principle of prior information and transparency towards employees forms part of employee privacy protection rules found in most international (and national) legal instruments.

III. FUNDAMENTAL RIGHT TO PRIVACY
      IN A EUROPEAN CONTEXT

The most basic reference in terms of employment privacy is the fundamental right to privacy. In a European context, two essential documents may be mentioned, produced by the two main European international institutions: Council of Europe and European Union (EU). On the one hand, Article 8 of the European Convention

---

2. OJ L 156, 21 June 1990, pp. 14–18.
3. Art.3, b) Annex, Directive 90/270.
4. Art.3, c) Annex, Directive 90/270.

on Human Rights (1950) protects the right to privacy, while on the other hand the Charter on Fundamental Rights of the European Union (2000) provides for both the right to respect for one's private and family life, and the protection of personal data.

The relevance of these instruments could be questioned in a private employer–employee context. However, the legal doctrine and cases of the past ten years have shown that employees are capable of invoking privacy rights on the basis of international human rights standards vis-à-vis their employer.[5]

A. EUROPEAN CONVENTION ON HUMAN RIGHTS

The European Convention's relevance lies not only in its enforceable character, with a supervising court in Strasbourg. It is at the same time rather instructive on the principles that should govern a balance between privacy and other rights.

Article 8 of the European Convention on Human Rights reads as follows:

1. Everyone has the right to respect for his private and family life, his home and his correspondence.
2. There shall be no interference by a public authority with the exercise of this right except such as is in accordance with the law and is necessary in a democratic society in the interests of national security, public safety, or the economic well-being of the country, for the prevention of disorder or crime, for the protection of health or morals, or for the protection of the rights and freedoms of others.

This provision suggests that privacy should be protected along the lines of its second paragraph.[6] A privacy case could then be dealt with as follows:

1. *Legitimate purposes (legitimacy)*: the right to privacy is a fundamental right and may only be interfered with for the protection of other legitimate interests or for legitimate purposes. The interests named in Article 8 are national security, public safety, economic well-being of the country, disorder, crime, health, morals, and rights and freedoms of others. Not necessarily all, but some of these rights or interests opposing the right to privacy might be relevant within employment relationships. Certainly 'rights and freedoms of others' are recognized, meaning that if the employer has a legitimate reason to interfere with an employee's privacy, this has to be approved.
2. *Described by law (transparency)*: the Convention provides that 'there shall be no interference by a public authority with the exercise of this right except such as is in accordance with the law'. The meaning of this

---

5. See S. Nouwt, *Reasonable Expectations of Privacy* (The Hague, TMC Asser Institute, 2005), p. 363.
6. F. Hendrickx, *Privacy en Arbeidsrecht* (Bruges, die Keure, 1999), p. 358.

wording for employee–employer relationships is that any interference with the employee's right to privacy should be in accordance with a clear and accessible norm. In this sense, it requires a sufficient degree of transparency.

3. *Necessary and proportionate (proportionality)*: the words 'necessary in a democratic society' are the emanation of the proportionality principle or the 'least-means' principle.[7] 'Necessary' means 'proportionate to the legitimate aim pursued'.[8] It is believed that it is not a requirement of 'indispensable', but stronger than mere 'acceptable' or 'reasonable'.[9] Further, the expression 'in a democratic society' used in the wording implies that the necessity has to be interpreted against the background of democracy, implying a climate of broad mindedness and tolerance.[10]

The main reference with regard to the case law of the European Court of Human Rights in the area of workplace privacy is *Halford v. United Kingdom*, dating from 25 June 1997. In its judgment, the court made it clear that the protection of 'private life' enshrined in Article 8 does not exclude the professional life as a worker and is not limited to life within the home. In this case, in which the telephone calls of Assistant Chief Constable, Ms Halford, were being intercepted by a superior, the court stated that 'it is clear from its case-law that telephone calls made from business premises as well as from the home may be covered by the notions of "private life" and "correspondence" within the meaning of Article 8' of the European Convention on Human Rights.

The court also followed that 'there is no evidence of any warning having been given to Ms Halford, as a user of the internal telecommunications system operated at the Merseyside police headquarters, that calls made on that system would be liable to interception'. She would, the court considers, have had a reasonable expectation of privacy for such calls, the expectation for which was, moreover, reinforced by a number of factors.

From this case it can be concluded that prior information or a warning with regard to telephone monitoring may be a requirement of compliance with Article 8 of the European Convention. Furthermore, it does not seem to follow

---

7. M.A. Eissen, 'The Principle of Proportionality in the Case-Law of the European Court of Human Rights' (1993) in *The European System for the Protection of Human Rights*, R. St J. Macdonald, F. Matscher and H. Petzold (eds) (Dordrecht, Nijhoff), pp. 125–146.
8. *Handyside v. UK*, Judgment of the European Court of Human Rights, 7 December 1976, Series A, No. 24; *Dudgeon v. UK*, Judgment of the European Court of Human Rights, 23 September 1981, Series A, No. 45.
9. M. Delmas-Marty and C. Chodkiewicz (eds), *The European Convention for the Protection of Human Rights: International Protection Versus National Restrictions* (Dordrecht, Nijhoff, 1992), p. 326.
10. K. Rimanque, 'Noodzakelijkheid in Een Democratische Samenleving – Een Begrenzing van Beperkingen Aan Grondrechten' ('Necessity in a Democratic Society – A Limit to Limitations of Fundamental Rights') (1983) in *Liber Amicorum Frédérick Dumon*, II (Antwerpen, Kluwer, 1983), p. 1224.

from this case that employers are not able to monitor telephone calls made from the workplace.

B.   CHARTER ON FUNDAMENTAL RIGHTS

The Charter of Fundamental Rights of the European Union seems to follow the main lines of the ECHR and the case law based upon it. It contains two relevant provisions:

> Article 7. Respect for private and family life.
> Everyone has the right to respect for his or her private and family life, home and communications.
> Article 8. Protection of personal data.
> 1. Everyone has the right to the protection of personal data concerning him or her.
> 2. Such data must be processed fairly for specified purposes and on the basis of the consent of the person concerned or some other legitimate basis laid down by law.
> Everyone has the right of access to data which has been collected concerning him or her, and the right to have it rectified.
> 3. Compliance with these rules shall be subject to control by an independent authority.

It is widely accepted that the Nice Charter, albeit drafted 'as if' binding, did not go much further than the status of a political declaration. This rather political and non-binding status of the Charter of Fundamental Rights also suggested that its effect on the legal position of workers would be rather limited and indirect.[11] Nevertheless, some impact could have been anticipated on the basis of the European Court of Justice's (ECJ's) case law in applying general principles of Community law. A wider meaning than merely political can be found in the Advocate-General's Opinion in the *Bectu* case.[12]

IV.   EUROPEAN AND INTERNATIONAL REGULATION OF WORKER DATA PROTECTION

On a European level, various legal instruments have come into existence with regard to employment privacy and data protection. The most important instruments dealing with data protection of employees in particular are those drafted within the Council of Europe and the EU. However, seen the relevant character of the instrument, also the International Labour Organisation (ILO) on worker data protection should be mentioned.

---

11. L. Betten, 'The EU Charter on Fundamental Rights: A Trojan Horse or a Mouse?' [2001] I.J.C.L.L.I.R., 157.
12. Case C-173/99, Opinion of 8 February 2001.

7. E-Monitoring the Teleworker

A. COUNCIL OF EUROPE CONVENTIONS AND RECOMMENDATIONS

The Council of Europe adopted a specific convention with regard to personal data protection on 28 January 1981. It was a concern of the Member States of the Council of Europe to bring more unity in the national legal systems to protect the human rights on a higher level throughout Europe. To date, it is still the world's only binding international legal instrument in this field, open to signature by any country, including countries which are not members of the Council of Europe.

The convention defines a number of principles for the fair and lawful collection and use of data. Notably, data can only be collected for a specific purpose and should not be used for any other reason. Data must be accurate, adequate for this purpose and stored only for as long as is necessary. The convention also establishes the right of access to and rectification of data for the person concerned (data subject), and requires special protection for data of a sensitive nature, for example on religion, political beliefs, genetics, or medical information.[13]

The desirability of adapting these data protection principles to the particular requirements of the employment sector has led to the adoption of Recommendation No. R (89)2 on the Protection of Personal Data Used For Employment Purposes. This recommendation was adopted by the Committee of Ministers on 18 January 1989 at the 423rd meeting of the Ministers Deputies.[14]

The Recommendation R (89)2 provides, among other things, that:

- Employers should, in advance, fully inform or consult their employees or the representatives of the latter about the introduction or adaptation of automated systems for the collection and use of personal data of employees. This principle also applies to the introduction or adaptation of technical devices designed to monitor the movements or productivity of employees.
- Personal data collected by employers for employment purposes should be relevant and not excessive, bearing in mind the type of employment as well as the evolving information needs of the employer. In the course of a recruitment procedure, the data collected should be limited to that which is necessary to evaluate the suitability of prospective candidates and their career potential. In the course of such a procedure, personal data should be obtained solely from the individual concerned. Subject to provisions of domestic law, sources other than the individual may only be consulted with his/her consent or if he/she has been informed in advance of this possibility.
- Recourse to tests, analyses and similar procedures designed to assess the character or personality of the individual should not take place without his/her consent or unless domestic law provides other appropriate safeguards. If he/she so wishes, he/she should be informed of the results of these tests.

---

13. <www.coe.fr/dataprotection/eintro.htm> (accessed 13 December 2006).
14. <www.coe.fr/dataprotection/rec/r(89)2e.htm> (accessed 13 December 2006).

- Personal data collected for employment purposes should only be used by employers for such purposes.
- In accordance with domestic law and practice or the terms of collective agreements, personal data may be communicated to employees' representatives in so far as such data is necessary to allow them to represent the interests of the employees.
- Information concerning personal data held by the employer should be made available either to the employee concerned directly or through the intermediary of his representatives, or brought to his notice through other appropriate means.
- Each employee should, on request, be enabled to have access to all personal data held by his employer which concern him/her and, as the case may be, to have such data rectified or erased where they are held contrary to the principles set out in this Recommendation. In the case of judgmental data, each employee should have the right, in accordance with domestic law, to contest the judgment.

B. EUROPEAN DIRECTIVES

The international developments have also led to the adoption of a specific instrument within the framework of the European Union, namely the European Directive 95/46/EC of 24 October 1995 regarding[15] data protection.

It must be noted that the directive has not been written only for labour relations or human resources (HR) data. The directive applies to any operation or set of operations which is performed upon personal data (i.e. 'processing' of data). Such operations include collection, storage, disclosure, etc. The directive applies to data that is processed by automated means (e.g. a computer database of customers) and to data that is part of, or intended to be part of, a non automated 'filing system' in which information is accessible according to specific criteria (i.e. traditional paper files, such as a card file with details of clients, ordered according to the alphabetic order of their names). Clearly, the European directive will apply to HR data processing activities and therefore also protects workers' privacy.

Data controllers (companies, employers) are required to observe several principles. These principles not only aim at protecting the data subjects, but are a statement of good business practices which contribute to reliable and efficient data processing. Some examples of obligations imposed by the directive:[16]

- Data processing is only allowed for limited purposes.
- Data should be processed fairly and lawfully and should be collected for specified purposes and used accordingly. The purpose of the processing should be explicit and should be legitimate.

---

15. OJ L 281/31, 23 November 1995.
16. <www.europa.eu.int/comm/internal_market/en/media/dataprot/backinfo/info.htm#int>

- Data should be adequate, relevant and not excessive in relation to the purpose for which it is processed.
- Data should be accurate and where necessary kept up to date.
- Data controllers are required to take any reasonable step to ensure the rectification or erasure of inaccurate data.
- Data should be kept in a form which permits identification of individuals for no longer than it is necessary.

Furthermore, Directive 97/66/EC of 15 December 1997[17] concerning the processing of personal data and protection of privacy in the telecommunications sector has in its turn required further consideration with regard to employee monitoring, e.g. as far as the scope of the permissible exceptions to the principles of privacy and confidentiality are concerned (cf. Article 5 of this directive).

Article 5(1) of this Telecommunications Data Protection Directive requires Member States to ensure via national regulations the confidentiality of communications by means of a public telecommunications network and publicly available telecommunications services. In particular they are obliged to prohibit listening, tapping, storage or other kinds of interception or surveillance of communications, by others than users, without the consent of the users concerned, except when legally authorized, in accordance with Article 14(1).

The directive permits two exceptions to this principle. Firstly, Article 5(2) provides that Article 5(1) shall not affect any legally authorized recording of communications in the course of lawful business practice for the purpose of providing evidence of a commercial transaction or of any other business communication. Secondly, Article 14(1) allows Member States to adopt legislative measures to restrict the scope of the obligations and rights provided for in Article 5 when such restrictions constitute a necessary measure to safeguard, *inter alia*, the prevention, investigation, detection and prosecution of criminal offences or of unauthorized use of the telecommunications system.

Also relevant is Directive 2002/58/EC of the European Parliament and of the Council concerning the processing of personal data and the protection of privacy in the electronic communications sector (the so-called 'e-Privacy Directive'). This directive applies to the processing of personal data in connection with the provision of publicly available electronic communication networks in the Community. The provisions of this directive particularize and complement the Data Protection Directive 95/46. This directive emphasizes the issue of confidentiality of communication.

Finally, reference should also be made to Council Directive 90/270/EEC of 29 May 1990 on the minimum safety and health requirements for work with display screen equipment (fifth individual directive within the meaning of Article 16.1 of Directive 89/391/EEC).[18] As indicated before, this directive provides for some

---

17. OJ L 24, 13 January 1998.
18. OJ L 156, 21 June 1990, pp. 14–18.

minimum requirements with regard to monitoring workers in the context of visual display units.

C. WORKING PARTY OPINION 8/2001 ON WORKER DATA PROTECTION

In order to contribute to the uniform application of the national measures adopted under the European Directive 95/46/EC, the so-called 'Article 26 Working Party', established under the directive, has adopted Opinion 8/2001 of 13 September 2001 on the processing of personal data in the employment context.[19] The Working Party is an advisory group composed of representatives of the data protection authorities of the Member States, which acts independently and has the task, *inter alia*, of examining any question covering the application of the national measures adopted under the Data Protection Directive in order to contribute to the uniform application of such measures.

The opinion starts by pointing out that employers and workers must be aware that many activities performed routinely in the employment context entail the processing of personal data of workers, sometimes of very sensitive information. Any collection, use or storage of information about workers by electronic means will almost certainly fall within the scope of the data protection legislation. This is also the case for employers monitoring workers' e-mail or internet access. Monitoring e-mail involves the processing of personal data. The processing of sound and image data in the employment context falls within the scope of the data protection legislation, and video surveillance of workers is covered by the provisions of the directive and the national laws transposing it.

The opinion then continues by establishing fundamental data protection principles that employers, when processing workers' personal data, should always bear in mind. These principles are:

- *Finality*. Data must be collected for a specified, explicit and legitimate purpose and not further processed in a way incompatible with those purposes.
- *Transparency*. At the very minimum, workers need to know what data the employer is collecting about them (directly or from other sources), and what the purposes are of processing operations envisaged or carried out with this data presently or in the future. Transparency is also assured by granting the data subject the right to access his/her personal data and with the data controller's obligation of notifying supervisory authorities as provided in national law.
- *Legitimacy*. The processing of workers' personal data must be legitimate. The directive lists the criteria making the processing legitimate.
- *Proportionality*. The personal data must be adequate, relevant and not excessive in relation to the purposes for which they are collected and/or

---

19. 5062/01/EN/Final, WP 48.

further processed. Assuming that workers have been informed about the processing operation and assuming that such processing activity is legitimate and proportionate, such processing still needs to be fair with the worker.

- *Accuracy and retention of data.* Employment records must be accurate and, where necessary, kept up to date. The employer must take every reasonable step to ensure that data inaccurate or incomplete, having regard to the purposes for which they were collected or further processed, are erased or rectified.
- *Security.* The employer must implement appropriate technical and organizational measures at the workplace to guarantee that the personal data of his/her workers is kept secure. Particular protection should be granted as regards unauthorized disclosure or access.
- *Awareness of the staff.* Staff in charge, or with responsibilities for the processing of personal data of other workers, need to know about data protection and receive proper training. Without adequate training of the staff handling personal data, there can never be appropriate respect for the privacy of workers in the workplace.
- *Consent.* The Working Party has taken the view that, where as a necessary and unavoidable consequence of the employment relationship an employer has to process personal data, it is misleading if it seeks to legitimize this processing through consent. Reliance on consent should be confined to cases where the worker has a genuine free choice and is subsequently able to withdraw the consent without detriment.
- *Workers are data subjects who benefit from the rights conferred by the directive.* The most important of these rights is the right of access.
- *Interaction between labour law and data protection law.* The Working Party would like to point out that data protection law does not operate in isolation from labour law and practice, and labour law and practice does not operate in isolation from data protection law. This interaction is necessary and valuable and should assist the development of solutions that properly protect workers' interests.
- *Surveillance and monitoring.* Data protection requirements apply to the monitoring and surveillance of workers, whether in terms of email use, internet access, video cameras or location data. Any monitoring must be a proportionate response by an employer to the risks it faces, taking into account the legitimate privacy and other interests of workers. Any personal data held or used in the course of monitoring must be adequate, relevant and not excessive for the purpose for which the monitoring is justified. Any monitoring must be carried out in the least intrusive way possible.
- *Transfer of workers' data to third countries.* Article 25 of the directive establishes that transfers of personal data to a third country outside the EU can only take place where the third country ensures an adequate level of protection for the data. The Working Party points out that, whatever the

basis of the transfer, the data processing involved in the transfer must still satisfy the provisions of the directive. The Working Party believes that it is preferable to rely on adequate protection in the country of destination rather than relying on the derogations listed in Article 26 of the directive, for example the workers' consent. Where consent is relied on, it must be unambiguous and freely given. Employers would be ill-advised to rely solely on consent other than in cases where, if consent is subsequently withdrawn, this will not cause problems.

D. COMPLEMENTING WORKING PARTY INSTRUMENTS

The Working Party Opinion 8/2001 has set the general scene of how Directive 95/46 has to be interpreted with regard to more specific employee data protection issues. It was soon realized, however, that complementary guidance was desirable, certainly in the growing field of workplace communication monitoring.

In order to clarify the more general principles of the first opinion, a working document of 29 May 2002 on workplace communications was issued. This working[20] document complements Opinion 8/2001 and also has to be seen in light of the Data Protection Directive 95/46/EC. The document was designed in particular to offer guidance and concrete examples about what constitutes legitimate monitoring activities and the acceptable limits of workers' surveillance by the employer.

For example, the Data Protection Working Party has found that a so-called 'blanket ban on personal use of the Internet by employees does not appear to be reasonable and fails to reflect the degree to which the Internet can assist employees in their daily lives'.[21] However, the working party at the same time has defended the employer's right to determine professional and/or private use of ICT facilities.

Another relevant working party document is the Working Document on the Processing of Personal Data by means of Video Surveillance, issued on 25 November 2002.[22] Although this document considers video surveillance in general, it also touches upon some issues of monitoring in the employment context.

Finally, the Working Party Opinion 2/2006 on Privacy Issues Related to the Provision of E-mail Screening Services of 21 February 2006 also has to be mentioned,[23] but it contains no specific employment related provisions.

---

20. Data Protection Working Party, *Working Document on the Surveillance of Electronic Communications in the Workplace,* 29 May 2002, 5401/01/EN/final, p. 35.
21. Data Protection Working Party, *Working Document on the Surveillance of Electronic Communications in the Workplace*, 29 May 2002, 5401/01/EN/final, p. 2.
22. Data Protection Working Party, *Working Document on the Processing of Personal Data by means of Video Surveillance*, 25 November 2002, 11750/02/EN, p. 23.
23. Working Party Opinion 2/2006 on Privacy Issues Related to the Provision of E-mail Screening Services of 21 February 2006, 451/06, p. 10.

E.   Iɴᴛᴇʀɴᴀᴛɪᴏɴᴀʟ Lᴀʙᴏᴜʀ Oʀɢᴀɴɪᴢᴀᴛɪᴏɴ (ILO)

While various national laws have established binding procedures for the processing of personal data, the ILO found that there was a need to develop data protection provisions which specifically address the use of workers' personal data. The
ILO code of practice concerning the protection of workers' personal data was
drafted to this end and adopted by a Meeting of Experts on Workers' Privacy of
the ILO in 1996.[24] The preamble of the code points out that the purpose thereof is to
provide guidance on the protection of workers' personal data. It does not have
binding force and it is not designed to replace national laws, regulations or
international labour standards or other accepted standards. It should be used in
the development of legislation, regulations, collective bargaining agreements,
work regulations, policies, and other practical measures.

     Some general principles outlined in the code of practice are similar to those
which can be found in other instruments as outlined above. Still, particular specifications are made with regard to the employment relationship. For example, it is
stated that the mere fact that an employment contract is considered or has already
been concluded does not entitle an employer to gather any information that he or
she is interested in. The collection of personal data must be seen as an exception
which needs to be justified.[25] The code also accepts a modification of the initial
processing purposes within certain explicitly addressed limits. According to the
code, it may be compatible with the original collection purposes to use personal
data concerning the qualification or performance of workers in decisions to grant
newly introduced fringe benefits.

V.   EMPLOYEE PRIVACY AND E-MONITORING IN BELGIUM

A.   Gᴇɴᴇʀᴀʟ

The most basic source to be mentioned in Belgium is the constitutional right to
privacy. The right to privacy is protected by Article 22 of the Belgian Constitution
and by Article 8 of the European Convention on Human Rights. The privacy issue
often arises in cases where information regarding (prospective) employees is gathered. Indeed, the right to privacy covers information privacy, but also medical
privacy, communication privacy and personal autonomy or self-determination.
At present, various scholars entered into a doctrinal debate among different states
in Europe regarding the manner in which the constitutional right to privacy should
be protected in private labour relations.[26] The discussion relates to the so-called
doctrine of third applicability ('Drittwirkung') of constitutional rights. Indeed,
while most people would still agree that a worker enjoys privacy protection,

---

24. ILO, *Protection of Workers' Personal Data, An ILO Code of Practice*, (Geneva, ILO, 1997),
     p. 47.
25. Explanation 5.1.
26. cf. F. Hendrickx, *Privacy en Arbeidsrecht* (Bruges, die Keure, 1999), p. 358.

it remains unclear whether he or she may directly invoke the constitution or, alternatively, should rather rely on existing provisions of civil law or employment law, referring to concepts such as 'fairness', 'reasonableness' or 'good faith'. Apart from the theoretical discussions, it must be observed that judges often apply the constitution in employment cases, either directly or indirectly. In a recent case regarding video surveillance, the Cour de Cassation (Belgian Supreme Court) has directly applied Article 22 of the Belgian constitution (right to privacy).[27]

There is no uniform abstract definition of the right to privacy. A concept often used as an alternative for privacy is the notion of 'private life' (vie privée). The right to be left alone[28] can be used to define the right to privacy in Belgium.

In Belgium, both the relationship between an applicant and a prospective employer as well as, partly, the employment relationship itself are governed by civil law, in so far as labour law does not make specific exemptions. Certainly in the pre-employment or pre-contractual situation, which is also indicated as the stage of the formation of the employment contract, most labour laws are absent and, therefore, legal principles arising out of civil law become very important. Issues such as offer and acceptance are regulated by the Belgian Civil Code, as well as the way in which parties should behave in conducting their negotiations.

In 1992 a specific law came into force with regard to the protection of personal privacy in relation to data processing. This is the Law of 8 December 1992 regarding data protection ('LDP'). This law also applies to labour relations. This law has been amended by the Act of 11 December 1998 so as to bring Belgian data protection legislation in line with European Directive 95/46 of 24 October 1995.

In line with the European legal regime, the LDP is applicable to both automatic and manual processing of personal data. Personal data is understood as any information relating to an identified or identifiable 'data subject', an identifiable data subject being someone who can be identified, directly or indirectly, in particular by reference to an identification number or to any factor specific to his identity. It should be noted that there are very few published[29] court cases regarding this act, certainly in the field of the employment relationship. Still, the LDP contains important principles to be taken into account when assessing the information flow from worker to management.

B.   Electronic Monitoring

1.   All Types of Monitoring

There is no single and uniform rule in Belgian law for the legal assessment of electronic monitoring of workers. Under Belgian law this involves the application of different sets of rules.

---

27. Judgment of 27 February 2001 (Nr. P.99.0706.N.).
28. S. D. Warren and L.D. Brandeis, 'The Right to Privacy' [1890] H.L.R., 193–220.
29. In Belgium not all court cases are published.

7. E-Monitoring the Teleworker

Firstly, the assessment should take into account existing employment laws and principles. This seems obvious, as electronic monitoring at work relates to rights and obligations arising from the employment relationship. Secondly, the Law on Data Protection is important. Indeed, electronic monitoring will trigger the applicability of this law, providing guarantees for the employee's privacy in case monitoring involves the processing of personal data, which is most often the case. Furthermore, a legal assessment of monitoring also needs to take account of specific monitoring laws. For example, there is Article 314b of the Belgian Criminal Code as well as Article 109 D and E of the Law of 21 March 1991. These provisions relate to the protection of telecommunication privacy and are fully applicable to electronic monitoring in the workplace, in so far as telecommunication is involved (like telephone conversations or internet use).

It should be noted that both the employment law principles as well as the Law on Data Protection will apply to all types of electronic monitoring of workers. The specific monitoring laws will only play their part if a case comes up under their specific scope of application.

In addition to the legal sources mentioned above, two collective bargaining agreements have to be mentioned, which specifically regulate employment privacy issues. The first is Collective Bargaining Agreement No. 68 of 16 June 1998,[30] which regulates camera surveillance in the workplace. The second is Collective Bargaining Agreement No. 81 on electronic online communication data of 26 April 2002. This collective bargaining agreement covers the issue of internet and e-mail monitoring at work. Both collective bargaining agreements are applicable to the entire private sector in Belgium.

As far as employment and labour laws are concerned, a distinction should be made between rules which govern the individual position of an employee vis-à-vis his employer and rules which concern collective rights of workers.

a. Employers' Monitoring Rights

From a Belgian employment law perspective, it may appear rather unusual to question the employer's monitoring rights. Indeed, in the first place, the kind of information that is normally collected by electronic monitoring often relates to the professional activities of the employees and is, therefore, directly work related. Furthermore, an employer is considered to be entitled to control how employees make use of the time they are at his/her disposal or how they make use of the company's equipment. Furthermore, one may see electronic monitoring of workers as a new and modern way of exercising traditional managerial powers in the company. Indeed, the monitoring of work may be viewed from the employer's

---

30. This CBA has been concluded within the National Labour Council (Conseil National du Travail), which is a public body where the three big country-wide unions are represented on the one hand, and the main employers' organizations on the other. As a general rule, such a national CBA receives a number and force of law by Royal Decree, meaning that it becomes applicable to the entire private sector.

viewpoint as his/her right to manage, direct and monitor the work at the company. It must indeed be pointed out that the employment relationship, which is a subordinate relationship, implies a reduction of the employee's freedom and privacy rights.

One should thus imply the principle that the employer has the right to impose restrictions on the use of computers, internet and, in general, ICT at the workplace, as these instruments are introduced primarily for the performance of the employment agreement and in order to reach the company's goals and purposes. The above would also imply that the employer has the right to draft instructions and communicate policies with regard to the proper (and improper) use of internet and e-mail in the company.

Another argument that is often produced in Belgium in favour of the employer's competencies concerning monitoring of internet and e-mail relates to the fact that the employer is considered to be the 'owner' of the available ICT in the company. The fact that these instruments 'belong' to the employer would also imply the employer's right to prohibit any use or abuse of its proper equipment.[31]

b.   *Collective Rights of Workers*

Electronic monitoring does not only open the debate of individual (privacy) rights. It is also important to pay attention to collective labour law aspects of e-monitoring and of collective rights of workers. In this respect, questions arise with regard to information and consultation rights of workers, their representatives and trade unions.

1. Belgian law does not provide for general collective labour law rules as far as employee data protection is concerned.[32] Nevertheless, legal doctrine points out that the existing provisions of collective labour law may be applied to electronic monitoring.[33]

2. In Belgian business, works councils[34] are important institutions. Therefore, the employer's duty to inform and consult its works council should be examined with regard to electronic monitoring in the workplace.

In this respect, the competencies of the works councils regarding social matters must be addressed. These are laid down in the Law of 10 September 1948 and in Collective Bargaining Agreement No. 9 of 9 March 1972 ('CBA No. 9'). It must be noted that the information duties laid down in CBA No. 9 are interpreted quite

---

31. Cf. Tribunal of Brussels, 14 February 1961, J.T., 223: 'Attendu qu'étant seul titulaire de sa ligne, l'abonné peut en interdire l'usage aux tiers; qu'il est également en droit de n'autoriser l'usage de sa ligne par des tiers que si ceux-ci, dûment avertis de cette condition, consentent à ce que leurs communications soient éventuellement surveillées, notamment à l'aide d'un enregistreur' (in this case it did not concern an employment relationship).
32. Apart from CBA No. 68 (National Labour Council) of 16 June 1998 regarding cameras in the workplace.
33. Cf. For the discussion, see F. Hendrickx, n. 26 above, 92.
34. In Belgium, a works council needs to be installed in companies with at least 100 employees (cf. Art.3.1, Royal Decree 25 May 1999, *Belgian State Gazette*, 30 June 1999).

extensively. Indeed, within the framework of social matters, the employer would not suffice to merely communicate information to the works council. The information must also enable the works council (and its members) to enter into an exchange of views, during which the workers' representatives should be able to formulate suggestions, express their criticism, ask questions, etc. The head of the company must then reply to the remarks of the representatives. In other words, a real discussion must be held in the works council. Furthermore, the law provides that information must be provided before decisions are taken.[35] Nevertheless, the managerial prerogatives remain respected ('management decides').[36]

Works council competencies and information and consultation rights with regard to electronic monitoring may be defended on the basis of the provisions regarding work organization, working conditions and productivity; personnel policies; internal memoranda; and introduction of new technologies.

It is also important to refer to the specific obligations laid down in Collective Bargaining Agreement No. 39 of 13 December 1983 (CBA No. 39) regarding information and consultation concerning the social consequences of the introduction of new technologies. Article 2.1 of CBA No. 39 provides that the employer, who has decided to invest in a new technology that has significant consequences for employment, work organization or working conditions, should provide information regarding the kind of technology envisaged as well as regarding the factors which justify its introduction. The employer must also inform and consult with the works council concerning the social consequences of the introduction of the new technology. In legal doctrine it is argued that the provisions of CBA No. 39 are applicable in cases where technologies are introduced which may have an impact on the employee's working environment, and thus, to a certain extent, also on his privacy.[37] It must be clear, however, that the managerial prerogative on the decision to invest or not in certain technologies remains fully respected.

3. In Belgium, every employer must draft work regulations. Work regulations form part of the working conditions and are regulated by the Law of 8 April 1965 regarding Work Regulations. It concerns a document required by law and this law also determines the content (topics which should be covered) of the work regulations, as well as the procedures of drafting and modification thereof. Work regulations should therefore be distinguished from internal memoranda or company policies, such as internet policies. Indeed, internet policies emanate from the employer's general right to manage and direct the workers and to give orders and instructions which the employees must obey. The content of internet policies is therefore not explicitly regulated by the law.

An important point is the involvement of the workers in the drafting and modification of the work regulations. Indeed, the Law of 8 April 1965 stipulates

---

35. Art.3, CBA No. 9.
36. Art.2, CBA No. 9.
37. R. Blanpain, 'Arbeidsverhoudingen: Overzicht van Maatregelen in Binnen- en Buitenland' in R. Blanpain, a.o, *Nieuwe Technologieën en Arbeidsverhoudingen* (Leuven, Acco, 1982), pp. 9, 73–74.

that the work regulations should be drafted (and modified) by the works council. This implies that the employer cannot unilaterally determine the content of the work regulations. The agreement of the works council is thus necessary. If there is no works council, the employer should make a draft of the work regulations and communicate it to all employees. The employees then have a right to make suggestions and objections which the employer needs to take into account.[38]

The question which often arises is whether the introduction of electronic monitoring (such as control of internet and e-mail) and the development of internet policies require a modification or amendment of the company's work regulations. In this respect, reference is often made to some rubrics which are obligatory in every work regulation, and in particular to Article 6.2 and 6.5 of the Law of 8 April 1965. Furthermore, disciplinary sanctions must also be laid down in the work regulations.

Article 6 of the Law of 8 April 1965 provides that the work regulations have to mention the manner in which the work is controlled/monitored with a view to determining employees' wages (Art.6.2), and the rights and duties of the supervising personnel (Art.6.5). It should be noted that the legal impact of these provisions is often underestimated in daily business practice. However, while there is still some discussion regarding the bearing of Art.6.2 and Art.6.5, it may be argued that those provisions are applicable in cases of electronic monitoring, meaning that the work regulations should be adapted and contain the necessary information.[39]

Furthermore it must be noted that most internet policies contain disciplinary sanctions in case of violation by the employees of the rules laid down herein. According to the Law of 8 April 1965, all disciplinary sanctions in the workplace have to be mentioned in the work regulations. This also counts for discipline relating to the violation by the employees of internet and e-mail policies. Important to note is that the employer can only apply the sanctions mentioned in the work regulations.[40] This means that the sanctions need to be explicitly incorporated in the work regulations. It is not sufficient, for example, to apply wording such as 'appropriate action' or 'such action may take a variety of forms, up to and including termination of employment and or legal action'. It is recommended to describe the sanctions very precisely.[41]

c. Law on Data Protection

The Law on Data Protection (the 'LDP' or the Law of 8 December 1992 as amended by the law of 11 December 1998, see above) is applicable to most forms of electronic monitoring. Whenever the LDP is applicable, the employer's

---

38. Cf. Art.11, Law 8 April 1965.
39. A judgment of the Labour Tribunal of Bruges of 14 March 1996 (*Soc.Kron*, 1997, 26) shows the limitations of Arts 6.2 and 5 of the Law of 8 April 1965 (this case concerned video monitoring).
40. Art.16, Law 8 April 1965.
41. Like e.g. a reprimand, suspension, demotion, dismissal or a fine.

monitoring activities must comply with the rules and principles laid down herein. The LDP has, since 1 September 2001, been brought in conformity with European Directive 95/46 of 24 October 1995. Due to the language used in the directive, the Belgian legislator has almost literally copied all articles with the complete wording of the directive into its national law. Therefore, as far as the LDP is concerned, there is nothing new or specifically to be mentioned with regard to electronic monitoring, compared with the text of the European directive. According to an official (but not binding) opinion of the Belgian Privacy Commission, the monitoring of electronic communication (internet and e-mail) comes under the data protection legislation.[42]

2. Monitoring Involving Telecommunication

Many forms of electronic monitoring involve the monitoring of telecommunication in the workplace. The most obvious examples are the monitoring of telephone communications or e-mail messages. In this regard, reference should be made to specific case law on this issue, to an authoritative opinion of the Belgian Privacy Commission, as well as to specific telecommunication privacy laws.

Self evidently, the general legal framework (see above) remains applicable to these types of monitoring.

On several occasions, case law has taken the general employment law principles (the right of the employer to monitor) as a starting point to assess situations in which employees' communications were monitored by the employer. In some instances it concerned cases where an employee communicated confidential information to third parties (such as competitors) using a company telephone. Although such circumstances must be seen as quite particular, some general principles were nevertheless forwarded in this case law.

In a judgment of 17 May 1985, the Labour Court of Liège stated:[43]

1. Employees should dedicate their complete working time to their assigned tasks and duties, under the authority of the employer.
2. An employee may not shift the working time or the costs of personal phone calls to his or her own benefit.
3. The employer did not give any permission for private conversations via the phone; therefore, the employer is allowed to monitor and tap all incoming and outgoing telephone conversations.

---

42. Opinion 23/93 of 14 December 1993, *Parl. Docs.* Senate 1992–93, No. 843/2, 247; Report of the Commission of Justice, *Parl. Docs.* Senate B.Z. 1991–92, No. 445/2, 57.
43. Labour Court of Liège, 17 May 1985, J.T.T., 472. In this case, a telephone operator passed confidential information to a competitor, run by ex-employees of the company. As far as the evidence was concerned, the court raised some doubts regarding voice recognition. The court pointed out that it was not familiar with the concerned employee's voice and asked for witnesses to testify its authenticity.

4. The employer enjoys the same property rights with regard to telephone lines as with regard to company correspondence. All communication is therefore per se of a professional nature and therefore subject to control.
5. The secrecy of communication has not been violated. Nor have the provisions of the Constitution or the European Convention on Human Rights been violated, as they are not applicable in the case at hand.
6. Employers may use control devices, certainly in cases where they suspect their employees of certain misconduct.

A judgment of the Labour Tribunal of Brussels of 7 February 1990[44] was considering a similar case. An employee was dismissed for serious cause because he passed on confidential information to a competitor of his employer. The Labour Tribunal stated:

1. The employer is allowed to monitor, with all useful means, the incoming and outgoing communication made at the company's premises during working time. This right to monitor may be used to gather evidence or to control the performance of the employment contract by the workers.
2. The fact that employers show a certain tolerance with regard to the private use of the telephone by personnel does not mean that an employer should warn an employee about possible monitoring of their conversations.
3. In the case at hand, the employer prohibited, through an internal note, the use of the phone for private purposes. The note was held to be justified in light of the importance of such a communication tool in the company.
4. In any case, following the Labour Tribunal, it did concern professional communication, which is not covered by the right to privacy as protected by Article 8 of the European Convention on Human Rights.

a. Telecommunication Privacy Laws

1. Even if a privacy issue has been assessed according to existing employment laws and in light of the Law on Data Protection, two specific monitoring laws may still become important. Specific attention should then be paid to the types of monitoring that involve telecommunications of employees. Indeed, there are two telecommunication privacy laws that are applicable to the monitoring of various types of telecommunications, such as telephone conversations, the use of internet, both through surfing or the use of e-mail, the use of intranet, and even video surveillance to the extent that it monitors communication.

In contrast with the aforementioned employment law principles, the telecommunication privacy laws depart from the principle that monitoring is prohibited. This is done, of course, to protect the privacy of the individuals concerned. But in daily business practice, these laws are considered to be too rigid and severe for employers. It should also be noted that it concerns criminal laws, enforced through both fines and imprisonment.

---

44. Labour Tribunal Brussels, 7 February 1990, *Pas.*, II, 88.

Criminal sanctions are imposed on the unlawful registration, interception, monitoring or use of communication or messages. Two legal sources are important, namely the Act of 21 March 1991[45] and Article 314bis of the Criminal Code.

While the Act of 1991 only covers registering or logging of telecommunication messages, Article 314bis of the Criminal Code covers interception or consultation of the content of (tele)communication.

None of these provisions are specifically written for the employment context. Nevertheless, these laws are fully applicable to monitoring by the employer in the workplace. It is important to note, however, that even in cases in which specific criminal laws would not be applicable, monitoring should be in compliance with respect for the right to privacy of the employees and third parties.

2. Both aforementioned laws provide for the same three exceptions to the prohibition of monitoring. These exceptions are laid down in Article 109D of the 1991 Act. So, all three exceptions may be invoked within the framework of Article 314bis of the Criminal Code as well as in the framework of Article 109D of the 1991 Act.

i. Permission by Law

The first exception relates to the permission by the law. Article 109E of the Act of 21 March 1991 indeed provides that the criminal prohibitions laid down in Article 314bis of the Criminal Code and Article 109D of the 1991 Act respectively are not applicable if the law allows or obliges the monitoring of workers.

The difficulty in Belgian law is that there is no law explicitly allowing the employer to monitor an employee's communications. Therefore, it is not yet clear which law the employer could invoke in order to satisfy this exception under criminal law. In this respect it is sometimes argued that an employer could invoke his general right to manage and direct the workplace. Indeed, this right can be based on Article 1134 of the Civil Code (providing that the contract is 'law' for the parties which agreed to it) as well as Article 17 of the Law on Employment Contracts of 3 July 1978 (referring to the right of management to give orders and instructions and obliging the employee to obey the instructions given by the employer). However, some legal authors reject the idea that, without further specification, such general provisions cannot constitute 'permission by the law' in the sense of the criminal law.[46]

ii. Consent

Both Article 314bis of the Criminal Code as well as the Law of 21 March 1991 provide that there is no crime if the employer has obtained the consent from all persons involved in the telecommunication. It must nevertheless be noted in this respect that, if a third party were involved, e.g. a client, the employer

---

45. *Belgian State Gazette*, 27 March 1991.
46. F. Hendrickx, *Privacy en Arbeidsrecht* (Brugge, die Keure, 1999), p. 199; J. Dumortier, 'Internet Op Het Werk: Controlerechten van de Werkgever' (2000) *Or*, 38.

would not only need the consent of the employee, but also the consent of that third party.

It is also important to address the issue of the validity of the employee's consent. Indeed, in Belgium it is often argued that a general clause in the employment contract by which the employee agrees to the monitoring of all his communications in the workplace would not be valid. This idea is based upon the preparatory works ('travaux préparatoires') of Article 314bis of the Criminal Code and the general theories regarding waiver of privacy. Furthermore, it must be noted that there is no useful case law guidance on this particular matter. However, it can be argued that Belgian law does not hinder such employee consent. Indeed, the primary concern of the legislator was to avoid employees signing very broad and general clauses on a routine basis. Therefore, taking into account the conditions of valid consent laid down in the Law of 8 December 1992 (see above), it can be argued that the employee can validly give his or her consent in the individual employment contract (or on another individual basis), as long as such consent is specific and based on sufficient information (informed consent). This would mean that consent should go hand in hand with, for example, clarifications regarding the scope of the monitoring activities, the conditions in which monitoring could take place, the guarantees for the employee's privacy, monitoring and post-monitoring procedures, etc. A reference to a company telecommunications policy may be advised in this respect.

iii. Network Management

Article 109E of the Act of 21 March 1991 also provides that the provisions of Article 109D of this Act, as well as the provisions of Article 314bis of the Criminal Code, are not applicable if the monitoring activities are only performed for the purpose of verifying the smooth operation of the network and in order to guarantee an efficient telecommunication service.

The question arises whether this exception would be applicable to the system manager of the company who manages and verifies a private computer network. The scope and applicability of this exception is currently under debate. There is no case law yet in this regard, but it is very likely that a judge would accept this exception for the case of a system manager.

iv. New Legal Provisions on Telecommunication Privacy

Article 109D of the Act of 21 March 1991 has been replaced by Article 155.3 of the Act of 13 June 2005 on electronic communication.[47] Relevant for the discussion above is Article 124 of the Law on Electronic Communication. It formulates an exception to the rule that communication is protected against disclosure to third parties. However, it also provides that the registration of electronic communication and the related traffic data performed in the framework of a legal business in order to prove a commercial transaction or another business communication is allowed, if the involved parties to the communication are informed before the

---

47. *Belgian State Gazette*, 20 June 2005.

registration takes place. This provision may change, in an employment context, the requirement of consent into a requirement of prior information before monitoring.

b.   *Collective Bargaining Agreement No. 81*

The conclusion of Collective Bargaining Agreement No. 81 (CBA No. 81), with regard to electronic online communication data, has significantly influenced the employer's monitoring rights with regard to internet and e-mail at work. CBA No. 81 has two main parts. The first part is concerned with the conditions in which monitoring of internet or e-mail may be considered to be lawful. The second part deals with procedures that need to be followed in case of individualization of data regarding employee use of internet or e-mail.

With regard to the conditions of monitoring, CBA No. 81 provides that monitoring is only lawful for limited purposes. Summarized, these are: (1) the prevention of severe misbehaviour; (2) the protection of economic, commercial or financial interests; (3) the monitoring of safety and technical operation of IT services; and (4) the monitoring of company policies with regard to internet or e-mail use. Apart from this, the employer also needs to take into account the principle of proportionality. For example, internet monitoring should concern general logging data and not an individualized employee's visited website.

Furthermore, CBA No. 81 provides for procedural guarantees. Before introducing a monitoring system in the company, the employer needs to give information regarding all aspects of employee monitoring. This information is given to the works council, if there is one. The employer also needs to inform the individual employees concerned of all aspects of monitoring activities, like company policy, the purposes of monitoring, whether or not data are kept, whether or not monitoring is permanent, rights and duties, and disciplinary sanctions.

A second element of procedure concerns the rules for the individualization of data (meaning establishing the identity of an employee behind one or more given data). The employer can only link general or global (logging) data with an individual employee if it relates to the purpose of either:

1. The prevention of severe misbehaviour;
2. The protection of economic, commercial or financial interests; or
3. The monitoring of safety and technical operation of IT services.

If the employer's individualized control measures are concerned with the monitoring of company policies with regard to internet or e-mail use, an additional guarantee is put in place. In this case, the employer has to give a prior warning and hold a hearing with the concerned employee before taking a decision that may influence the position of the employee.

c.   *E-mail and Internet Use*

1. Employers are allowed to monitor employees' e-mail and internet, but under strict conditions.

2. According to CBA No. 81, monitoring is only allowed for: (1) the prevention of severe misbehaviour; (2) the protection of economic, commercial or financial interests; (3) the monitoring of safety and technical operation of IT services; or (4) the monitoring of compliance with company policies regarding internet or e-mail use.

3. According to the Opinion of the Belgian Data Protection Commission, the employer needs to take into account the principle of proportionality. This implies that employers first have to apply abstract monitoring. For example, internet monitoring should concern general logging data and not an individualized employee's visited website. As far as the monitoring of e-mail is concerned, the Belgian Privacy Commission is of the opinion that gaining access to the content of e-mail messages is excessive and thus not in compliance with the Law on Data Protection. Therefore, e-mail must in the first place be monitored on the basis of a list of e-mail traffic and not on the basis of the content of e-mails.

Individualized monitoring is, according to CBA No. 81, only possible in limited circumstances. The employer can only link general or global (logging) data with an individual employee if it relates to the purpose of either: (1) the prevention of severe misbehaviour; (2) the protection of economic, commercial or financial interests; or (3) the monitoring of safety and technical operation of IT services. If the employer's individualized control measures are concerned with the monitoring of compliance with company policies regarding internet or e-mail use, an additional guarantee is put in place. In this case, the employer has to give a prior warning and hold a hearing with the concerned employee before taking a decision that may influence the position of the employee.

4. Monitoring also requires respect of other principles, such as transparency, security and a form of employee involvement.

5. Lawful monitoring implies respect for specific telecommunication laws, which are criminally enforced. In general, these laws require the consent of all participants to the communication, not only employees but also possible third parties that are involved (for example, clients of the company).

d.   *Telephone Communications*

In respect of telephone communications, taking into account the case law mentioned earlier, the following may be concluded.

1. From an employment law perspective, the monitoring of telephone communications is in principle allowed if the employer is able to identify a legitimate business interest (work performance, cost control . . .).

2. The specific telecommunication laws, however, strongly limit the employer's monitoring competencies. The employer is not able to lawfully register or monitor a telephone conversation in which he does not actually participate, unless he has received the consent of all communicating parties. The law therefore requires the employer to ask third parties (like clients) for their consent.

In practice, some solutions are found on a more pragmatic basis. For example, employers may ask their employees to register all telephone calls made with clients. This is not a criminal offence in the sense of the aforementioned telecommunication laws. However, it remains unclear what rights (e.g. under tort law or other legal provisions) the third party may invoke in such a case. It is very likely that the LDP provisions have to be respected.

It must be noted that the prohibition of monitoring (without consent) also refers to the mere logging of telephone communications (without accessing the actual message), like registration of the time of communication, the numbers dialled, and so on. Such (criminally enforced) prohibition does not seem to be in line with daily business practices and needs. Practice also shows that employers receive this information via the invoice of the telecom provider (such as Belgacom, British Telecom, Telenet, Orange, etc.).

3. Currently, no difference is made under Belgian law as regards incoming or outgoing telephone calls.

3. Camera Surveillance

As far as camera surveillance is concerned, specific attention must be paid to the relevant case law, as well as to CBA No. 68 of 16 June 1998 regarding camera surveillance at the workplace.

a. Case Law

There are rather few cases involving camera surveillance at the workplace. There is a case at the Labour Tribunal of Brussels of 26 March 1990, where employees were filmed by a video camera without their knowledge.[48] In its judgment the Labour Tribunal stated that it is not permissible to spy on employees with a video camera during their activities, as such forms of control constitute a violation of the privacy to which an employee is entitled during working hours, taking into account that not every control relates to work performance, but that private conversations are also tapped. Such controls, the Tribunal stated, violated Article 16 of the Law on Employment Contracts providing that employers and employers have a duty of mutual respect.

A few years ago, the Belgian Cour de Cassation had a chance to give its opinion on some elements of principle regarding a case in which shop attendants were stealing from their employer. They were caught on the basis of a secret camera installed by the employer. In its judgment of 27 February 2001,[49] the court held that Article 8 of the European Convention on Human Rights (right to privacy) does not prevent that an employer installs a camera in a shop without the knowledge of the workers in order to verify his sincere suspicion of serious wrongdoing or misconduct. Still, the Cour de Cassation has not verified the use of a secret camera in case of theft in light of CBA No. 68 of 16 June 1998, discussed below.

---

48. Labour Tribunal Brussels, 26 March 1990, *Soc Kron*, 154.
49. Judgment of 27 February 2001, No. P.99.0706.N.

Recently, the Cour de Cassation has confirmed that, in criminal matters, results of hidden video surveillance techniques may be used, even if acquired contrary to the provisions of transparency laid down in CBA No. 68.[50]

b. Collective Bargaining Agreement No. 68

Camera surveillance at the workplace is regulated by a specific collective bargaining agreement, namely CBA No. 68 of 16 June 1998. It is applicable to the entire private sector and explicitly states that it must be seen as completing the LDP on the issue of camera monitoring at work.

The lawful purposes of camera surveillance are enumerated in a limiting way. Allowed are the following uses of cameras: the protection of health and safety, the protection of the employer's property, the monitoring of the production process, and the monitoring of employees' work performance.

Thus, in theory, CBA No. 68 does not constitute an obstacle for electronic monitoring, as various uses of cameras may be justified on these grounds.

However, it must be noted that CBA No. 68 also requires that specific procedures should be followed if an employer introduces cameras in the workplace. Indeed, the CBA provides for information to be given to the employees concerned (such as number of cameras, the position of the cameras, the purposes thereof). Furthermore, information and consultation (exchange of views) is required with the workers' representatives, or in their absence, with the workers. Furthermore, if camera surveillance has an impact on the rights and duties of the supervising personnel or is used for the determination of the workers' wages, an amendment of the work regulations is required.

VI. EMPLOYEE PRIVACY AND E-MONITORING IN THE NETHERLANDS

A. GENERAL

Specific regulation in the area of employment privacy is not found in The Netherlands. In this country, the issue is significantly left to case law approaches, flanked with practical or authority-based guidance of the Dutch Data Protection Commission. A form of decentralization can nevertheless be found throughout the role of the works council in the area of personnel policy and data protection.

Either way of dealing with the issue in The Netherlands occurs within the context of constitutional privacy protection and European based, but employment unspecific, data protection legislation. To a certain extent, this stands in competition with the application or implication of general employment law concepts and mechanisms.

---

50. Cass. 2 March 2005, cited in Working Party on Data Protection, *Eighth Annual Report*, pp. 21–22.

7. E-Monitoring the Teleworker

In the Netherlands, the right to privacy receives constitutional protection through Article 10 of the Dutch constitution,[51] stating that everyone has the right to respect for his/her privacy:

1. Everyone shall have the right to respect of his/her privacy, without prejudice to restrictions laid down by or pursuant to an Act of Parliament.
2. Rules to protect privacy shall be laid down by an Act of Parliament in connection with the recording and dissemination of personal data.
3. Rules concerning the rights of persons to be informed regarding data recorded about them and of the use that is made thereof, and to have such data corrected, shall be laid down by an Act of Parliament.

As the Dutch constitution primarily covers the relationship between the State and its citizens, the question arises as to what extent Article 10 of the constitution can have horizontal effect ('Drittwirkung'), particularly in the relationship between employer and employee. While horizontal effect is quite broadly accepted, this matter still seems to keep on an ongoing debate in legal theoretical terms.[52] It would appear that, in practice – and more precisely in the practice of the labour case law – the right to privacy has the ability to receive both direct as well as horizontal effect.

Constitutional protection is complemented with data protection legislation. In the year 2000, the Netherlands adopted a new data protection law, following the duty to implement the European Data Protection Directive 95/46.[53] The new Data Protection Act of 6 July 2000[54] replaced the former Dutch Data Protection Act of 1988.[55] The Data Protection Act applies to employer–employee relationships, although it remains a framework of data protection not specifically designed for this context. It would appear, therefore, that the Dutch data protection legislation does not provide a very strong basis for employees to successfully invoke privacy rights versus their employers. The latter is due to many reasons, but certainly to the extent in which employment lawyers continue to make use of their own traditional and familiar concepts or mechanisms.

Typical in the field of employment privacy is the use of 'open' labour law norms of 'good employership', laid down in Article 7:611 of the Civil Code, requiring the employer to act as a 'good employer'. This concept might be a

---

51. Grondwet Voor het Koninkrijk der Nederlanden, 24 August 1815, *Stb.* 45: last modification 22 June 2000 *Stb.* 294.
52. See for this discussion, J. Boesjes, 'De Horizontale Werking van Grondrechten' [1973] NJB, 911; L.F.M. Verhey, *Horizontale Werking van Grondrechten, in Het Bijzonder van Het Recht op Privacy* (Tjeenk Willink Zwolle, 1992), p. 487; F. Hendrickx, *Privacy en Arbeidsrecht* (Brugge, die Keure, 1999), p. 358.
53. Tweede Kamer, 'Wijziging van Bepalingen met Betrekking tot de Verwerking van Persoonsgegevens' (1998–1999) 26 410 No. 3; L.F.M. Verhey, De EG-richtlijn Bescherming Persoonsgegevens' Uitgangspunten en Hoofdlijnen (1997) NJCM-Bulletin No. 3, pp. 239–256, in particular p. 253 and further.
54. Wet Bescherming Persoonsgegevens, 6 July 2000, *Stb.* 301.
55. Wet Persoonsregistraties, 28 December 1988, *Stb.* 655.

way to give indirectly horizontal effect to the right to privacy of employees.[56] However, the use of this concept of 'good employership', instead of more typical data protection language or fundamental rights mechanisms, leads to criticism in legal doctrine, which argues that labour case law falls short of solutions based upon data protection legislation. This leads again to what has been called a 'concealed existence' of data protection legislation in employment matters.[57] Underlying is the fact that judges believe to reach reasonable similar results with 'good employership' as with data protection laws.[58]

Predictable is the consensus on the analysis. The Dutch legal doctrine often discusses the so-called 'paradox', as employees do invoke privacy rights while at the same time their contract allows authority to be exercised by their employer.[59] It is also argued that information and personal data processing concerning employees is obviously inherent in a workplace setting,[60] whereby it would be too easy to assume that there would be no limitations to the employer's authority here. The analysis is often there also in case law, but synthesis and solution often seem to come on a case-by-case basis and might diverge.

A form of decentralized regulation of privacy issues is to be found in the Dutch Works Council Act of 28 January 1971. With regard to data processing, this act gives an important role to the works council when it comes to the use and processing of personal data of employees by the employer.[61] According to Article 27 of the Works Council Act, the employer needs the works council's consent when he intends to implement, alter or withdraw rules on the processing of personal data of employees.[62] This act provides works councils with a firm position in advising the employer on this issue.[63] For example, the works council receives a role in

---

56. M.A.C. de Wit, *Het Goedwerkgeverschap als Intermediair van Normen in Het Arbeidsrecht* (Kluwer Deventer, 1999), pp. 161–164.

57. M.A.C. de Wit, n. 56 above, p. 358; D.J. Kolk and M. Verbruggen, 'Het Verborgen Bestaan van de Wet Bescherming Persoonsgegevens' (2002) No. 6/7 *Arbeidsrecht*, 3–10.

58. L. Bijlsma and T.C.B. Homan, 'Toepassing Wbp Door Kantonrechter bij Ontslag Werknemer; de Wbp Ontslagen?' (2003) No. 5 *Arbeid Integraal*, 167.

59. P. F. van der Heijden, 'Tussen Paradox en Paranoia: Over Bedreiging van de Privacy op de Werkplek' in *Privacy op de Werkplek*, P.F. van de Heijden (ed.) (Sinzheimer Cahiers 4, SDU Den Haag, 1992).

60. J. Roeloff, *Employability en Assessment Tijdens de Arbeidsovereenkomst, Arbeidsrecht* (1998/1), pp. 3–7; R. Caspers, *Informatiebehoefte van Werkgevers en Privacy van Werknemers, Sociaal Recht* (1992–9), pp. 240–247, in particular pp. 240–241.

61. See S.F.H. Jellinghaus and M. Korpershoek, 'OR en de Wet Bescherming Persoonsgegevens' (2000) No. 3a, special privacy edition, *Sociaal Beleid*.

62. Wet op de Ondernemingsraden (WOR) of 28 January 1971, *Stb.* 54, last revision of 18 March 1999, *Stb.* 184.

63. In theory Art.25 1 under k WOR can also play a role. This article provides the works council with the right of advice when an employer decides to implement a new technological facility. It will depend on the facts and the circumstances whether, and in what way, the definition of Art.25 WOR can be used in situations where employees are monitored. It is not quite clear in what way Art.25-1 under k WOR gives the works council a real form of advice concerning the different technological forms of registration and monitoring. So far no examples concerning Art.25 WOR has made it to court and it seems that in real life Art.27 (under k and l) is of more practical use.

defining the conditions under which processing of personal data is allowed.[64] If there is disagreement between works council and employer, the latter needs to go to court to obtain a substitute consent or approval, which will be provided by the court only if the works council cannot show legitimate reasons to block the employer's decision, or if the employer, alternatively, can show severe reasons to introduce the proposed measures.

The Dutch Data Protection Act is fully applicable in the employment context. This means that personnel filing issues, including medical files, come under the scope of application of the act.

It should be observed that the data protection legislation has to be read in conjunction with other employment and labour legislation. This is specifically the case with, for example, medical employee data in the area which specific labour protection laws apply, or in areas in which discrimination legislation exists.

B.   ELECTRONIC MONITORING

The issue of monitoring and surveillance of employees is, like in many other countries, the subject of much debate in the Netherlands, certainly with the rise of the use of internet and e-mail at work. While other countries have intervened through legislation or other initiatives, the issue remains left to case law and guidance of the Data Protection Commission in the Netherlands (some examples will be given below).

Case law shows a great deal of pragmatism. Many cases involve fraudulent behaviour of employees. What is most clear from the case law is that privacy expectations of fraudulent employees are very low, sometimes non-existent. This may not only be deducted from the case law mentioned above, but also seems to be genuine in the opinion of the Data Protection Commission. In 2004, the Dutch Data Protection Commission approved the use of 'warning lists' of fraudulent personnel in retail business – the Council of Dutch Retail Businesses proposed to introduce a sector-wide warning system, including a list of fraudulent personnel of participating companies, in order to prevent employees who had been dismissed because of fraudulent behaviour being hired by another company in the sector. The Data Protection Commission based its decision on the fact that this warning system was complementary to other pre-employment measures, and on the condition that participating firms would communicate their processing activities to the Commission.[65] Privacy claims are almost never accepted in cases of fraudulent behaviour of employees.[66]

---

64. T.C.B. Homan, 'Medezeggenschap Over Privacy op de Werkplek?' (2002) No. 1 *Privacy & Informatie*, 19–21.

65. Decision of the Data Protection Commission, 17 June 2004, Case 2004–0253.

66. H.H. de Vries, 'Vertrouwelijkheid van E-mail op het Werk' (2000) No. 4 *Privacy & Informatie*, 165.

At the end of 2000, the Dutch Data Protection Authority published a report with an extensive survey of the problems that may occur if an employer monitors the online behaviour of its employees.[67] In this survey the Dutch Data Protection Authority published relevant guidelines that an employer should take into account. With these guidelines it looks like much (but not all) uncertainty among employers has been taken away. A summary of the most important guidelines is as follows:

- Treat problems online the same as offline.
- Use transparent rules with the consent of the works council.
- Make sure that rules or a policy are easy accessible for the employees.
- Make clear in what way private use is allowed.
- Pay extra attention to the position and integrity of the system administrator.
- If a problem occurs, discuss this as soon as possible with the employee in question.
- Give employees the opportunity to check the gathered information from time to time.
- Do not use the gathered information for other purposes.
- Do not keep gathered information longer than necessary.

VII.   SYNTHESIS

The idea of this section is not to give a complete and synthetic summary of all principles to be found in the international and European instruments or the Belgian or Dutch legal regimes as they have been displayed above. A rather pragmatic approach is taken, in order to indicate some relevant discussion points and how they are dealt with under the respective rules and principles.

A.   MONITORING OF PROFESSIONAL COMMUNICATION BY THE EMPLOYER IS GENERALLY NOT DISPUTED, BUT IT IS CONDITIONAL

1.   Openness and Transparency through ICT Policies

One of the most basic general rules of electronic monitoring is transparency. This implies that workers are aware and informed of the fact that they are (able to be) monitored.

Most legal instruments refer to this principle of transparent, fair or open monitoring. The ILO code of practice makes clear reference to it. And the Halford decision of the European Court on Human Rights also made it clear that a lack of

---

67. Dutch Data Protection Authority, 'Goed Werken in Netwerken, Regels voor Controle op E-mail en Internetgebruik van Werknemers' (2000). Available online at <www.cbpweb.nl> (accessed 15 December 2006).

prior warning to the worker could be an element in assessing a violation of the right to privacy.

The Data Protection Working Party's Working Document requires transparency through an obligation to inform the employee about various aspects of monitoring:[68]

1. Providing an e-mail/internet policy within the company, describing the extent to which communication facilities owned by the company may be used for personal/private communications by employees (e.g. limitation on time and duration of use).
2. Reasons and purposes for which surveillance, if any, is being carried out. Where the employer has allowed the use of the company's communication facilities for express private purposes, such private communications may under very limited circumstances be subject to surveillance, e.g. to ensure the security of the information system (virus checking).
3. The details of surveillance measures taken, i.e. who? what? how? when?
4. Details of any enforcement procedures, outlining how and when workers will be notified of breaches of internal policies and be given the opportunity to respond to any such claims against them.

In practice, employers are mostly advised to draft so-called ICT policies, in which they formulate conditions and limitations of an employee's use of the company's equipment and in which the conditions of monitoring are provided. The Belgian CBA No. 81 concerning internet and e-mail at work even suggests the use of these kinds of policies, although other forms of information may be used (like in the individual contract of employment or through work rules).

2. Proportionality

Another principle to be respected in case of electronic monitoring is proportionality. According to the Working Document of the Data Protection Working Party, the proportionality principle rules out blanket monitoring of individual e-mails and internet use of all staff other than where necessary for the purpose of ensuring the security of the system. Where the objective identified can be achieved in a less intrusive way the employer should consider this option (for example, he/she should avoid systems that monitor automatically and continuously).[69]

The monitoring of e-mails should, if possible, be limited to traffic data on the participants and time of a communication rather than the contents of communications, if this would suffice to allay the employer's concerns. If access to the e-mail's content is absolutely necessary, account should be taken of the privacy of those outside the organization receiving them, as well as those inside. The employer, for instance, cannot obtain the consent of those outside the organization

---

68. Data Protection Working Party, *Working Document on the Surveillance of Electronic Communications in the Workplace*, 29 May 2002, 5401/01/EN/final, p. 15.
69. Data Protection Working Party, n. 68 above, p. 17.

sending e-mails to his workers. The employer should make reasonable efforts to inform those outside the organization of the existence of monitoring activities to the extent that people outside the organization could be affected by them. A practical example could be the insertion of warning notices regarding the existence of the monitoring systems, which may be added to all outbound messages from the organization.[70]

In respect of monitoring e-mail and internet use, attention should be paid to an Opinion of the Belgian Privacy Commission regarding internet and e-mail monitoring, of 3 April 2000.[71] In light of the proportionality principle, the Belgian Privacy Commission is of the opinion that systematic registration of all telecommunication details, *a priori*, cannot be allowed. As far as the monitoring of e-mail is concerned, the Belgian Privacy Commission is of the opinion that gaining access to the content of e-mail messages is excessive and thus not in compliance with the law on data protection. According to the Commission, there are several solutions to solve abuse by employees in this respect, such as installing computer software indicating chain messages, or identifying messages which take up too much space on the network, such as music or video attachments. Therefore, e-mail must be monitored on the basis of a list of e-mail traffic and not on the basis of the content of e-mails.

As far as the monitoring of websites is concerned (surfing), the Belgian Privacy Commission is of the opinion that the monitoring must be based on limited objective information, and not on an *a priori* systematic control of the content of all data flow regarding every employee. In this respect, the Commission also indicates that an employer could make up a list of visited websites without identifying every single employee. On the basis of such a list, an assessment of possible problems could be made. Should an acute problem occur, the Commission continues, the employer could at that time undertake individualized action.

Since CBA No. 81, mentioned above, the issue of proportionality has been linked to a certain extent to the referred opinion of the Belgian Privacy Commission.

Under Dutch law, only guidance from case law has to be found, where proportionality is implicitly used, rather than being made explicit.

3. Adequate Monitoring

The Data Protection Directive also provides for a 'fair' data processing principle. Taking this into account, it should also be mentioned that the Data Protection Directive contains the principle of relevancy and adequacy. These principles require that data processing is only lawful if the data are relevant and adequate.

One may, therefore, on this basis, question a business practice whereby the teleworker's working time is monitored purely on the basis of his logging in or out of the company's computer system.

---

70. *Ibid.*
71. Opinion No. 10/2000 of 3 April 2000.

7. E-Monitoring the Teleworker

An interesting application of this principle can be found in a recent decision by the Austrian Data Protection Commission (DPC). In this case, the Ministry of Finance had introduced a new electronic control system for working hours of employees. The beginning and end of working hours could only be entered into the electronic system if the employee opened his workstation in the office. The time of opening the workstation was used for plausibility controls concerning the beginning and end of working hours entered into the electronic system.

The Austrian DPC ruled on the inadmissibility of this system on the grounds of disproportionality, because there are many possibilities why an employee cannot start his working day at the office (like attending a meeting outside the office, travelling for business reasons, etc.). Therefore, this system could not be called appropriate for faithfully recording working time.[72]

4. The Role of Employee Representatives

The role of worker representatives is often mentioned in international instruments on data protection. The ILO code of practice dedicates a paragraph to it.

In the case of Belgium, existing provisions of collective labour law could be applied to electronic monitoring. They can be interpreted as implying that the employer is obliged to inform and consult (consultation means an exchange of view) the works council with regard to (electronic) monitoring practices. The law could also imply that the work regulations have to be amended in case of electronic monitoring (involving the consent of the works council if there is one), if it results in the application of disciplinary sanctions. Nevertheless, the existing collective labour law provisions are to a certain extent outdated, since CBA No. 68 (video surveillance) and CBA No. 81 (internet and e-mail monitoring) expressly provide for involvement of employee representatives.

According to Article 27 of the Dutch Law on Works Councils, the employer needs the consent of the works council when he envisages implementing, modifying or withdrawing rules concerning the processing of personal data. This provision gives the works council a firm position. In general, any form of registration or monitoring will come under the scope of the aforementioned obligation.

5. The Role of the Employee's Individual Consent

It is sometimes argued that relying on individual consent of the employee for electronic monitoring (and therefore limiting his right to privacy) may be problematic. In the European Directive 95/46, explicit consent of the data subject is laid down in Article 8, paragraph 2, a) of the directive. According to Article 2, h) of the directive, the data subject's consent shall mean any freely given specific and

---

72. Working Party on Data Protection, *Eighth Annual Report*, p. 18.

informed indication of his/her wishes by which the data subject signifies his/her agreement to personal data relating to him/her being processed.[73]

It is sometimes doubted that individual consent can be a basis, for example, to monitor the phone calls of employees. The ILO code of practice does not seem to exclude individual consent of the worker for data processing, although certain guarantees have to be respected.[74]

The Data Protection Working Party seems to be more nuanced. The Working Party has already taken the view that:

> Where as a necessary and unavoidable consequence of the employment rela-
> tionship an employer has to process personal data it is misleading if it seeks to
> legitimise this processing through consent. Reliance on consent should be
> confined to cases where the worker has a genuine free choice and is subse-
> quently able to withdraw the consent without detriment.[75]

In the Dutch *Call Centre* case decided by the Dutch Data Protection Commission on 5 July 2005, the Commissioner found that quality monitoring of phone calls can only be based on other justification grounds than the employee's consent. The Commissioner is of the view that unambiguous consent, required by law, will normally not be present in an employment relationship, since the freedom of the employee's will is not guaranteed in case of a subordinate relationship.[76]

B. Monitoring of 'Private' Communication is Generally Reserved for Exceptional Cases

There are many ways to approach the issue of monitoring an employee's private communication. It is much related to the question of whether an employee is entitled at all to private facilities on corporate equipment. One may argue that such private facilities on the employer's equipment cannot be enforced by the employee, so that no privacy rights can be claimed in case of monitoring work tools.

The judgment in the Nikon case made by the French Cour de Cassation on 2 October 2001 is well known.[77] In this case, an employee was dismissed for using data-processing tools at his disposal for personal use. When the employer

---

73. Another important exception for the employment context is laid down in Art.8, para.2, b) of Directive 95/46, providing that the prohibition of sensitive data processing shall not apply where the processing is necessary for the purposes of carrying out the *obligations and specific rights of the controller in the field of employment law* in so far as it is authorized by national law providing for adequate safeguards.
74. 'The issue of consent is of fundamental importance. Informed and explicit consent is referred to in several provisions. The basic reason is to ensure that, when a worker is asked to consent to the gathering or release of certain data, he or she has sufficient information on which to make a decision. Explicit consent would normally mean written consent'. (ILO Code, pp. 11–12)
75. Data Protection Working Party, n. 68 above, p. 21.
76. Dutch Privacy Commission, *Call Centre* case, 5 July 2005.
77. Cass. Fr., 2 October 2002, J.T.T., 37.

searched the hard disk of the computer of the employee, evidence raised against the employee consisted of two e-mails marked 'personal'. The Supreme Court stated the principle that an employer has to respect his/her employee's right to his/her private life, even during working hours. This implies secrecy of correspondence. Employers cannot, according to this court, without violating this fundamental freedom, access and read personal e-mails transmitted or received at work, even when the employer prohibits the use of the computer for private purposes.

1. The position of the law is very unclear as far as the issue of private facilities is concerned. Indeed, the question arises whether individual employees may claim private access facilities with regard to the employer's equipment, like the telephone or the internet, and whether the use of such equipment for private purposes is protected by the law.

There are several principles which defend the employer's right to limit access to its internet and e-mail facilities. The employer has the right to manage the workplace and to exercise authority over the workers. The employer therefore has the right to impose restrictions on the use of computers, internet and ICT at the workplace, these instruments being introduced to reach the company's goals and purposes. Furthermore, the employer is considered to be the 'owner' of the available ICT in the company. At least, the company bears the costs of their use. The fact that these instruments 'belong' to the employer would also imply that the employer has the right to prohibit any use or abuse of equipment or any use for other than the defined purposes.

However, this principle remains open for interpretation, and it is still possible for workers to claim certain rights for the use of company facilities for private purposes.

In the first place, it is possible that the employer allows the use of facilities for non work-related purposes. It happens, for example, that internet policies stipulate that private use of the company's internet is only allowed in limited circumstances, e.g. during (lunch or other) breaks. Under many national laws, this may create an entitlement of the employee to the private use of the internet under the said circumstances, based upon the construction of the 'unilateral obligation' of the employer. Entitlements under a unilateral obligation may not be withdrawn or abolished unilaterally by the employer.

In the second place, there may be an implicit policy of toleration, whereby the employer – often without any express policy on the matter – tolerates the use of the internet for private purposes, as long as this does not lead to excesses. Although mere toleration might hardly lead to an employee entitlement to use facilities for private purposes, some national laws may qualify this as 'corporate custom'. Corporate custom is, for example, a recognized source of rights under Belgian labour law.[78]

---

78. Conditions for 'custom' are: generality, permanence, consistency. Still, rights arising from custom may be excluded in an individual employment contract.

More difficult is the issue of private facilities arising of the employee's right to communication. This concept is quite new, but it may be argued that the employee, like every individual, has a right to communicate with other people, protected under the right to privacy. On this basis, it may be argued that the employee could, for example, claim a right to make a non-disturbing private phone call. However, this line of reasoning is completely underdeveloped in most legal systems.

2. The European Data Protection Working Party seems to follow the view that the employer has the right to determine the extent to which private facilities are granted to employees,[79] although it suggests that companies organize, for practical purposes, a private e-mail account (with limited monitoring rights) separated from the professional mail account (with extended monitoring rights).

According to the Working Party on Data Protection, the principle should be that, where a worker is given an e-mail account for purely personal use or is allowed access to webmail account, opening of e-mails in this account by his/her employer (apart from scanning viruses) can only be justified in very limited circumstances and cannot under normal circumstances be justified on the basis of Article 7 (f) of Directive 95/46, because it is not in the legitimate interests of the employer to have access to such data. Instead, the fundamental right to secrecy of correspondence prevails. Under 'limited circumstances', the Working Party understands actions that would include criminal activity on the part of the worker, in so far as it is necessary for the employer to defend his/her own interests, for example where he/she is liable for the actions of the worker, or where he/she is the victim of the criminal activity.

3. Under Belgian labour law, CBA No. 81 is in full respect of the right of the employer to determine what kind of use will be made of corporate equipment, such as ICT. Still, the CBA does not exclude private use, as it provides for a specific procedure of monitoring communication which cannot be deemed as professional. However, it would seem in recent case law that if an employee abuses the internet system for private purposes, a dismissal may be justified even if procedures are not completely followed.

4. It is interesting that, in the Netherlands, the problem of the private use of e-mail and internet was already on the agenda of the largest Dutch trade union, the FNV Bondgenoten, in 1999. FNV published in that year a model-protocol entitled 'privacy in the use of internet and e-mail'.[80] It provides, for example, that employees are authorized to use the e-mail system for non-commercial transactions in order to send and receive personal e-mail messages, both internally and externally, provided that this does not interfere with their day-to-day work commitments. According to the FNV guidelines, employees are also authorized to use the internet system for non-commercial transactions, provided that this does not interfere with

---

79. Data Protection Working Party, n. 68 above, p. 35 (p.15).
80. See <www.fnv.nl> (accessed 15 December, 2006). The complete text of the protocol can be found in addendum A.

their day-to-day work commitments. However, employees shall not be permitted to deliberately consult websites that contain pornographic or racist matters.

In its Opinion in the year 2000, the Dutch Data Protection Authority published a report with an extensive survey of the problems that may occur if an employer monitors the online behaviour of its employees.[81] It provides as a rule of thumb that the employer should make clear 'in what way private use is allowed'. This seems to reserve the right of the employer to determine private use on the basis of his/her managerial prerogatives.

On the other hand, it should be mentioned that, from Dutch case law, it can be derived that in most cases dismissals for abuse of internet and e-mail have been approved by the courts, although no clear general guidelines are given. Furthermore, to a certain extent, courts accept a limited 'privatization' of the workplace, within which no complete prohibition of personal use of internet or e-mail should be maintained.[82]

An example may illustrate this. It appears, indeed, that the District Court of Amsterdam took the side of the employee.[83] In this case, an employee was sending pornographic e-mails to a colleague. He also had an affair with this woman. The employer, who was using a policy prohibiting the private use of e-mail, dismissed the employee concerned. The court stated, however, that even if an employer has a policy in which he or she strictly forbids any private use of the company network, and specifically prohibits the sending of private e-mails, employees should nevertheless have the right to send some private e-mails. Furthermore, the court stated that sending a pornographic e-mail is no worse than the possession of a pornographic magazine in one's desk. In the end, the court stated that the dismissal was not justified.

5. Conclusively, one may state that the employer has the right to determine the extent of private facilities in the workplace. Nevertheless, most jurisdictions in Europe seem to allow limited private use by the employee, under strict conditions (no influence on performance or during breaks, no illegal material . . .), certainly if it is played off against the employer's interests in a dismissal case. Furthermore, a prohibition by the employer of all private use of the employee of the available ICT equipment would not prevent that a right to privacy could be claimed on information that is explicitly characterized as personal by the employee.

It seems that in the case of telework, this principle needs to be nuanced. In case of home work, the employee has probably enough alternative facilities, i.e. other than those of the employer, to exercise his 'right to communication'. It could be argued that this may reduce his/her claim to private facilities on the company's

81. Dutch Data Protection Authority, 'Goed Werken in Netwerken, Regels voor Controle op E-mail en Internetgebruik van Werknemers' (2000). Available online at <www.cbpweb.nl> (accessed 15 December 2006).
82. J. Terstegge, 'Goed Werken in Netwerken, Achtergrondstudies en Verkenningen' 21, College Bescherming Persoonsgegevens, Tweede druk, 29. Available online at <www.cbpweb.nl> (accessed 15 December 2006).
83. Kantongerecht Amsterdam, 26 April 2001, JAR, 101. See also *Rechtspraak voor Medezeggenschap*, 2001, Nos 8–9, C196, with annotation T.C.B. Homan.

equipment. On the other hand, one may argue that the 'privatization' of the workplace has gone so far in the case of telework that the division between private and professional space has become useless, or at least inadequate.

It is probably in this latter context that the following Dutch case has to be considered. The Dutch Data Protection Commission gave an opinion in a case in which a computer firm stated in its policy that the employer can demand access to the e-mail and voice mail messages of the employees 'for any purpose', and that employees have 'no reasonable expectation of privacy' when they use e-mail and voice mail services in the company. In answering a question of the works council of the firm, the Data Protection Commission is of the opinion that files in which e-mail messages have been stored have to be considered as personal data as understood in the Dutch data protection legislation, as those messages normally contain details regarding name, address of sender or receiver, and an indication of the subject of the message. The Dutch Data Protection Commission also continues by saying that the employer's access 'for any purpose' to e-mail messages cannot be allowed under the data protection legislation. The employer needs to indicate at least the purposes for which such processing is used. Also, the fact that employees have 'no reasonable expectation of privacy' cannot, according to the Data Protection Commission, be upheld.[84]

C.   THE ISSUE OF PERMANENT MONITORING

Many instruments refer to the issue of permanent monitoring. One may think about continuous video surveillance during working hours, but obviously it may concern internet or e-mail monitoring as well.

The Data Protection Working Party puts this issue in the proportionality framework and provides that 'where the objective identified can be achieved in a less intrusive way the employer should consider this option (for example, he/she should avoid systems that monitor automatically and continuously)'.[85]

A case reported by the Working Party originated in Portugal. There, the DPA dealt with a specific case regarding the use of video surveillance in kindergartens, in almost every room, allowing the parents to follow on the internet the daily life of all the children through an access password. The DPA forbade this data processing for being disproportionate, for compromising the children's rights to privacy, and for being abusive to the workers, who would be constantly observed.[86]

In many cases, the idea of permanent monitoring has to be assessed case by case. The ILO too, takes a nuanced approach. It provides that:

> Technical and organizational measures which ensure both the security and proper operation of information systems are necessary for their use (. . .). Such measures, however, imply continuous monitoring, especially of all

---

84. Data Protection Commission, 24 June 1999, 99.V.0141.
85. Data Protection Working Party, n. 68 above, p. 17.
86. Working Party on Data Protection, *Eighth Annual Report*, p. 81.

those working in computer centres. Because there are rules asking for such measures in the interest of efficient data protection in all international and national regulations restricting the use of personal data, the introduction of these measures is probably one of the few cases in which a continuous surveillance of workers is generally acknowledged as indispensable.[87]

---

87. ILO code of practice, p. 13.

Chapter 8

France

Jean-Emmanuel Ray and Jacques Rojot

I.   INTRODUCTION

When looking back on the 1980s forecasts for the forthcoming numbers of teleworkers, one may wonder if there are not now more specialists studying telework
than actual teleworkers! A report from the Directorate for Studies and Research of
the Ministry of Labour for the Forum on Rights on the Internet[1] in June 2004
considered that 48 per cent of French employees in the private sector *could* practice
telework, including 23 per cent part-time. However, only 2 per cent actually teleworked from home,[2] while it is estimated that a further 5 per cent held 'nomad'
positions (travelling salesmen, consultants, on-site advisers), and 10 per cent of the
managerial and technical staff were teleworking either on a rotating, mobile or full
basis, or held 'nomadic' jobs.

However, *informal* telework has developed since 2000, with the development
of more reliable high speed connections and computer equipment, particularly in

---

1. Available on the Forum website at <www.foruminternet.org> (accessed 15 December 2006).
   See also J. Gonié, 'Le Travail en France' (March 2005) *Droit Social*, 273; and A. Probst, 'Le Droit
   du Travail à L'épreuve du Télétravail' (March 2005) Doctoral Dissertation, University of Paris I.
2. DARES, Premières synthèses, No. 51-3, December 2004. Conversely, 1.2 million self employed
   worked at home. 57 per cent highly qualified males, mostly in the sectors of finance and services to
   business. 53 per cent considered mastering their working time, whilst 73 per cent worked at
   weekends and 39 per cent at night (after 10 p.m.).

Blanpain et al., European Framework, Agreements and Telework, pp. 157–170.
©2007, Kluwer Law International BV, The Netherlands.

the so-called quaternary sector.[3] For individual employees it is a case of bringing home a laptop and a high speed connection paid by the employer, with an understanding of showing up at work on an irregular basis, as discreetly as possible, to avoid the curiosity of the labour inspector, as well as the jealousy of other employees. When home or nomad telework has de facto generalized, it requires the information and consultation of an employee representative, but in practice it has seldom been followed by a modification of an individual contract of employment. This has given rise to disputes about which the High Court (Cour de Cassation) began to issue decisions in 2005. However, statutory law[4] has changed deeply since 2005,[5] and many unions now demand that the employer starts negotiations about it at enterprise level, particularly since the national interoccupational collective agreement of 19 July 2005, enacting the European agreement of 16 July 2002, extended by ministerial decree of 30 May 2006, and thus bound all employers in the sectors covered by the employers' organizations.[6]

For enterprises beginning to practise telework, this legislative and contractual framework is useful in order to solve the multiple problems, legal and practical, raised by this new form of work, which upsets acquired habits. However, for the enterprises which have been practising it informally for several years, new problems may appear, as well as for teleworking employees. This is in addition to the need to homogenize within the new legal framework various customs and practices that will have informally arisen in enterprises.

Telework also falls perfectly in step with the newly fashionable Social Responsibility of Enterprises and the new line established by two recent statutory acts: on the one hand, an Act of 23 March 2006 introduces into the Labour Code 'the structuring of occupational and personal and family life'. Fourteen new provisions aim to incite the employer to take into account the family and personal constraints of his/her employees, including the unavoidable additions to the already existing yearly report to the works council on the comparative situation of men and women within the undertaking. Telework obviously has a part to play

---

3. Knowledge workers selling only intellectual performance. With about 10,000 employees, IBM employs 9,000 managerial and technical staff, out of which 90 per cent have their working time, by collective agreement, regulated under the late 1990s legal provisions in terms of a yearly amount of working days (a so-called 'days package') instead of a weekly amount of hours. Top executives under the same legal provisions totally escape working time regulations and the lower tier fall under the 35 hour week regulation for regular employees.

4. And not only in labour law. For instance, the Act of 1 August 2003 on economic initiative with the goal to fight unemployment and to stimulate small business creation contains useful and important provisions for a potential teleworker. For instance, the business can be created at home without the need for a commercial lease (s.6); the home of the teleworker cannot be seized by creditors in case of bankruptcy (s.8); covenant of non competition does not apply for one year (s.15), and the would be teleworker can require from his/her employer either an (unpaid) leave of absence or part-time status. In social security law, deductions for occupational expenses for teleworkers are specially treated.

5. And will change even more if the proposal for a Statutory Act No. 2314, proposed in Parliament on 11 May 2005, integrating more fully telework into the Labour Code, is adopted.

6. Even though telework is not yet one of the, ever expanding, mandatory yearly bargaining topics, but several sections of the agreement refer to collective agreements for its application.

here.[7] On the other hand, telework also fits the Act of 18 July 2005, making compulsory the negotiation of the provisional management of employment and competencies, particularly in view of the occupational and geographical mobility of employees in enterprises of over 300 employees.

In the perspective of the evaluation in 2007 by the social partners of the European Agreement of 2002, seven main issues are raised by telework in French labour law.

II. MAIN ISSUES RAISED BY TELEWORK IN FRENCH LABOUR LAW

A. TELEWORK WITHIN THE MEANING OF THE FRENCH NATIONAL INTEROCCUPATIONAL COLLECTIVE AGREEMENT AND RELATED SITUATIONS

Section 1 of the Agreement defines telework as:

> A form of organization and/or performance of work using information technologies within the framework of a contract of employment and within which work that might also have been performed on the premises of the employer is carried out outside of them on a regular basis.

This definition includes 'nomad' employees, but working outside of the premises of the enterprise cannot alone qualify an employee as a teleworker.

The regular basis demanded by the definition does not require that the work be performed in totality outside of the enterprise, and does not exclude forms of work alternating periods of work outside the enterprise and inside the enterprise.

Therefore, all work 'outside the premises of the enterprise' does not fall within the definition. Besides, it requires in any case the use of information technologies, and on a regular basis. An employee working at home obviously falls within the scope of the French agreement, which expressly also includes the 'nomad'[8] employees and requires an enterprise level negotiation to define the employees covered.

The French agreement legitimately did not create a specific status for the teleworker. He/she is and remains a wage-earning employee. Section 2 mandates that moving to telework, as such, modifies only the way work is performed, and does not affect status as an employee.

Of course, this does not forbid recourse by the employer to independent teleworkers or to French or foreign subcontractors linked or not by high speed internet connections.

Some remarks are necessary:

---

7. Even if in practice it seems to favour men over women (Revue de la Commission, Agenda Social, July 2002, p. 15).
8. The Littré dictionary defines 'nomad' as somebody with no fixed abode, etymologically: shepherd.

1. The teleworker, whether working a lot or a little at home, is not equivalent to the old 'home worker', protected by the Labour Code since long ago (section L. 721-1 and ff.). The condition of subordination of the latter being arguable, he/she is directly assimilated by the law to an employee and benefits from the same provisions, legal or otherwise, than all other employees of the undertaking, in addition to all contractual provisions binding the principal, except if otherwise specified.[9]

The two categories are not superimposed. Telework, etymologically and in the meaning of the agreement of 2005, concerns work 'which could have been performed on the premises of the employer, and using information technologies'. That definition excludes manual work performed at home in the old pattern of home work (assembling garments and the like). However, using information technologies does not concern only the high tech, full-time employee on the computer and internet. In parallel, the only fact to warn his/her employer that his/her work is over by a home working tailor does not qualify him/her as a teleworker. The border remains blurred in many cases, for instance, for translators. It seems, however, that the intent of the parties signatory to both the European and the French agreements is to qualify as telework work which actual making requires the use of the new technologies, and not only the electronic transmission of the final product to the employer.

2. The efficient teleworker must be quite self sufficient and not afraid to remain alone. Then the link of subordination which characterizes the status of wage earner employee in French law is not obviously apparent, either *ab initio* or after a few years. Many teleworkers, questioning the status of subordinate, may come to elect either to work for multiple employers or to set up as independent contractors. This transition might be encouraged by employers preferring to deal with more flexible contract work rather than with a fixed wage bill, given the very high level of wage-based social security contributions. Section 11 of the agreement, by providing that 'teleworkers are identified as such on the single registry of employees', allows unions and/or the works council to check that moving employees to telework is not the first step of externalization of work and/or hidden cutback in the work force, which would legally require the constraining procedure and social plan foreseen for collective dismissals.

3. Telework's growth follows the developments in information and communication technologies, particularly on the internet, with increases in speed, reliability and quality of connections, and decreases in the prices of more and more powerful equipment. Therefore, the legal obligations on the employer for redeployment (for instance for employees becoming unfit for work) or for adaptation of jobs (for instance, for the handicapped, the employment of a percentage of whom is legally compulsory) must now take these factors into account. This is particularly the case for the legally compulsory provisional management of employment and competencies by the employer and the social plan in case of dismissals for economic reasons, when employees may change their place of work. The employer might not want to see his most productive employees shift to telework, and the union will demand to see telework as part of the social

---

9. S.L. 721–6; Cass. Soc. 2 May 2006, No. 04-46.418, Société ABI.

plan to safeguard employment. The classic example is of a call centre moving from Paris to the provinces.[10]

The situation is of course different in the case of internal redeployment (maintaining the contract of employment) and external redeployment (severing the contract of employment and therefore dealing with an independent contractor). In the latter case, the now freelance independent contractor cannot contribute under exactly the same conditions as a wage earner unless his/her freelance status is re-categorized by the judge as a contract of employment (under indefinite duration). For instance, the Court of Appeals of Paris (17° Chambers) on 17 November 2005 held that:

> having a work electronic mail address, Mr N. R. kept working in Paris on the premises put at his disposal since he was hired, with computers belonging to the enterprise, reporting to the manager, who kept giving him work instructions (3D version of the magnetica software, daily e-mails exchanges, report on the work performed). Therefore, the relations between the parties after the dismissal for economic reasons were the ones of wage earning employee to employer.

4. The French national interoccupational collective agreement has a wider scope than the European Agreement since it expressly includes 'nomad' employees. That category includes many more employees than teleworkers, strictly speaking, but with fuzzy borders it will have to be defined by sectoral or enterprise level collective agreements.

B. ARTICULATION OF BARGAINING LEVELS

Since the new rules set up by the Act of 4 May 2004, the lower bargaining level can now depart from, and go against, provisions set up at a higher level, both *in melius* (improving benefits, as it was the case before) and *in pejus* (depriving employees of some benefits granted at higher level, contrary now to the tradition of French public policy in labour law), unless the higher level agreement contains a provision to the contrary. The national interoccupational collective agreement of 19 July 2005 for the first time made use of this new legal mode of articulation of the levels of bargaining in section 12:

> Application: The definition of telework in section 1 paragraph 1 of the present agreement cannot be departed from. It cannot be departed, for its application, from the provisions of section 2 (voluntary character), 4 (similar conditions of

---

10. Paris Court of Appeals, 14 November 2002 (Société Mona Lisa) on the point of a tele-operator in a call centre with a provision accepting geographical mobility in her contract of employment, dismissed for serious offence when rejecting her transfer: 'the enterprise had no legitimate stake in transferring a tele-operator from Paris to Aix-en-Provence whereas the position of Ms. M. might have been kept in Paris, alone, given that it was the work of a tele-operator that might have been performed at home'.

work and employment), 6 (respect of privacy), 8 (health and security), 9 (organization of work), 10 (vocational training), 11 (collective rights) above.

It cannot also be departed from the principle of reversibility and integration (section 3) or from section 7, paragraph 1 (when telework is performed at home, under condition of conformity of electrical equipment and workplace, the employer provides, installs and maintains the equipment necessary for telework). However, the modalities of application may be adapted by collective agreement to the specific characteristics of the sector or enterprise.

It is section 5, regarding data protection, which is not covered. It is up to the employer to take, within the framework of the instructions of the National Commission for Computer Science and Freedom (CNIL), the provisions needed to protect the data used and processed by the teleworker for professional use. The employer informs the teleworker of the legal provisions and enterprise rules regarding the protection and confidentiality of this data. He informs him/her equally of all restrictions in the use of communications and data processing tools, for instance the internet, and in particular of the prohibition of gathering or spreading unlawful material via the internet, and of the penalties incurred for the breach of the rules and prohibitions. It is up to the teleworker to comply with them. However, since it exactly follows the provisions of the acts on computer science and freedom, it is hard to see how an agreement could depart from them.

Therefore, sectoral and enterprise agreements can depart only from the other paragraphs of section 7, regulating very basic but costly issues: costs of telecommunication, technical support, loss or destruction of equipment. Many other issues in that area are not covered by the agreement, such as the cost of maintaining an office and its environment at home, surface of the home taken up by the office, inks, printers, paper and the like. Some enterprises apply a simple rule. If it is the employee who asks to telework, all operating costs are incurred by him/her, except for the equipment and the high speed connection. The reason for the latter is generally not accounted for by altruism, but rather by control and security of data processing.

C. ACCESS TO TELEWORK AND RETURN TO THE ENTERPRISE'S PREMISES

Section 2 of the agreement provides for the voluntary character of telework for both the employee and the employer concerned. Telework can be part of the conditions for hiring, or set up later on a voluntary basis. In that case it is the object of an addition to the contract of employment. If an employee expresses the will to opt for telework, the employer may accept or not.

This necessary double, if not triple[11] voluntary character is a question of common sense and productivity. Telework at home, even part time, may end up

---

11. Besides the employer and the teleworker, efficient telework may require specially trained telemanagers, able to deal with employees under loose (by necessity) subordination.

as detrimental to work and/or family members. To avoid prolonged failure, entry as well as opting out must be the object of consensus.

This is why section 3 provides for reversibility and integration. The national interoccupational collective agreement provides for two cases: first, if telework was not initially part of the conditions of employment, but agreed upon later, both the employer and the employee can take the initiative and reach an agreement to end it and organize the return of the employee within the premises of the enterprise. The modalities of this reversibility are decided by individual or collective agreement.

In the same light, the last paragraph of section 2 provides for an adaptation period during which each of the parties can bring telework to an end, given a term of notice defined beforehand. The employee then gets back to a job on the enterprise's premises, within his skill's grade. This adaptation or probatory period of course cannot constitute another trial period[12] (during which the employee may be dismissed freely). It must last for a minimum of several weeks in order that both parties, but also management and family, can adapt.

The reversibility is double sided: the employer may find the teleworker more costly, or less productive or reliable than the former regular employee. The employee may see his personal or family situation change. However, reversibility cannot occur at will. There must be objective elements, and from the part of the employer it cannot constitute a disciplinary provision, which could not be applied for not included in the formal shop rules. The return of the teleworker may cause multiple problems which should be dealt with in the individual or collective agreement on the modalities of reversibility provided for by section 3. It would be wise to include here a term of notice long enough, and also the consequences of a disagreement of the parties on ending telework,[13] for instance about the fate of the computer equipment put at the disposal of the employee for his work, but also privately used during periods of rest. In light of these problems, some enterprise agreements[14] provide only for experimental short periods of telework, possibly renewable. However, the return of the teleworker, even in that case, still raises practical problems, unless both parties miraculously agree on a given job at the same time.

If telework is part of the conditions of hiring, the employee may apply for any vacant job on the enterprise premises within his skills. He/she benefits from a priority to fill the position.

---

12. The social chamber of the High Court has held that 'in the face of two successive contracts of employment between the same parties, the trial period mentioned into the second contract passed at the occasion of a change of job of the employee can only be a probatory period, whose breach has the only effect to bring the employee back in his former job' (30 March 2005).
13. Under no circumstances can a teleworker who refuses to come back to work on the premises be considered as resigning.
14. Orange agreement of 22 May 2002. Telework is not a right. It is limited to alternate periods to avoid the isolation of the employee. It is at the initiative of the employer for it has a cost for the enterprise. It is limited to a period of six months, possibly renewable if both parties are satisfied.

However, the national interoccupational collective agreement does not provide for an integration of the teleworker in the collective of employees in the enterprise, on the premises, before filling his/her telework position.

D. TELEWORK AND RESPECT OF PRIVATE LIFE

Section 7 of the European Charter of Individual Rights provides for the respect of private and family life, the home and the communications of an individual. Section 6 of the national interoccupational collective agreement provides that the employer must respect the private life of the teleworker.[15] To that effect, he/she establishes, in consultation with the employee, the time slots during which he/she may contact him.

Telework does not constitute a different employee status. The national interoccupational collective agreement, following the European agreement of 2002, sets up a general provision in section 4: equality of treatment of employees on site, nomads or teleworkers at home. But this legitimate principle of equivalence aiming to avoid discrimination against the 'officeless' raises questions. It might seem that the place of work is now irrelevant, that for both sides working at home or in the enterprise is the same thing. Subordination would then be limitless in time and space. Obviously the High Court feels otherwise and has adopted a policy highly protective of the private life and right to rest of the teleworker.

A decision of 2 October 2001 (Abram/Zurich Assurances) established that an employee could not be held to accept to work at home or to install there his files and working equipment. In a case where working at home was agreed upon according to a schedule freely established by the employee, the High Court decided that by demanding that she came back on the premises of the enterprise on a mandatory fixed schedule, the employer had modified the contract of employment. The refusal to comply by the employee did not constitute a cause for dismissal or an offence liable to disciplinary sanctions. On 13 April 2005, the same applied to a sales manager who was authorized first to work at home two days a week and was then required to drive 220 km every day of the week to the enterprise's premises. In both cases, the contractual aspect of telework was doubtful. It seemed to be more tolerated for a limited period by the employer than anything else.

These two examples demonstrate the specificity of working at home in terms of the right to modify the contract of employment. Maybe it constitutes simply a mode of organization of work, but it is so close to private life that it cannot be modified without the express agreement of the employee.

---

15. The second paragraph of this section establishes that if a monitoring device is set up, it must be relevant and proportional to the objective aimed at, and the teleworker must be informed. The employee representatives must also be informed and consulted beforehand. This is to conform to the general rule regarding surveillance of employees by the employer. Webcams may pose specific problems since they are set up in the home of the worker. Before they start operating, after being set up, it is clear that the teleworker must agree to it, maybe by double clicking on an icon.

This specificity was strengthened when an employment contract contained an explicit provision for geographical mobility. A pregnant communications manager was granted by her Paris employer the right to work at home (in the Pyrenees) two days a week with her transportation expenses taken charge of by the employer. At the end of the maternity leave, the employer required her to come back full time on the enterprise premises. When she refused she was dismissed for serious offence (desertion of her post). The social chambers of the High Court on 31 May 2006 decided that when parties contract that part or the whole of work will be performed at home by the employee, the employer cannot modify this contractual organization of work without the agreement of the employee. The requirement by the employer to come back full time at the headquarters, notwithstanding a provision for mobility of the employee, constitutes a modification of the contract of employment that the employee is justified to refuse.

Definitely, home is not a place of work like any other, even in the same geographical sector that the enterprise, even if the presence of a valid provision for mobility invoked in good faith by the employer.

The problem, of course, would be totally different, if, applying the French agreement as well as the European one, a provision for reversibility (in the direction home to office) had been inserted into the contract of employment at the opportunity of an agreement between employer and employee to begin teleworking. It would be, nevertheless, necessary for it to be fully operative to specify in detail the exact conditions and consequences.

E.   TELEWORK, WORKING TIME AND REST PERIODS

Section 9 of the national interoccupational collective agreement provides that the teleworker manages the organization of his working time within the framework of the law, the collective agreements and the enterprise rules applicable.

The workload, production norms and criteria for results required from the teleworker must be exactly equivalent to those required from employees in a similar situation working on the enterprise premises. Notably, workload and performance deadlines must allow the teleworker to observe the law on working time and especially the maximum duration of work and rest periods.

1.   Teleworker and Working Time

The decree of 30 May 2005 extending the national interoccupational collective agreement contains only one reservation concerning the huge and complex issue of the regulation of working time in French law, but it is of importance for the teleworker. It quotes the contents of section L. 212-1-1 concerning the proof of the hours of work performed, including the use of a 'recording automatic system reliable and impossible to forge', and recalls that 'the employer must see to it that the law and regulations on working time are enforced, notably by making sure of the reliability of the system accounting for overtime, even if the employee manages himself the organization of his working time'.

For teleworkers and nomads belonging to managerial and technical staff a simple solution exists since the Act of 19 January 2000: days' packages of work and rest, on a yearly basis, accounting for working time no longer in hours but in days, and applying to managerial and technical staff with sufficient autonomy in the performance of their tasks (section L. 212-15-3 of the Labour Code). It requires a collective agreement implementing these provisions and an amendment to the contract of employment, or a provision to that end in an initial contract. However, in all cases this package accounted for in days must allow for the mandatory daily rest of 11 hours, limiting the working day to 13 hours.[16]

In the case of a regular employee not belonging to autonomous managerial and technical staff, since the Act of 2 August 2005 on small and medium businesses the same system might apply, given that a collective agreement authorizes it and that the employees concerned additionally have individually given their agreement in writing, if they enjoy also a real degree of autonomy in the performance of their work and if the duration of their work cannot be precisely established in advance and predetermined. Nomads, teleworkers and itinerant employees *a priori* fall within this category.

Finally, work on call is prohibited. The Court of Appeal of Paris on 10 February 2006 (18° Ch., No. 04/37674) applied to telework the decision of the High Court recategorizing into contracts of employment for an indefinite duration part-time contracts where an employee was to remain permanently at the disposal of the employer, but was paid only for the time when he/she was asked to work.

2. Telework and Rest Periods

As briefly noted above, even for employees under the packages of days working time system the daily (11 hours) and weekly (24+11=35) rest periods must apply. It was recalled by the Constitutional Council quoted above and by the Court of Justice of the European Communities in its Jaeger decision.[17] Thus, a collective agreement providing otherwise would be void.

F. Telework and the Right to Interrupt the Connection

Going further than the European Agreement, the French interoccupational collective agreement provides that the employer establishes, in consultation with the employee, the time slots during which he may contact him/her. If the employer wants to avoid being sued on that point, he/she must notify not only the

---

16. And a weekly rest period of 35 hours as well. Besides, the yearly number of days' work cannot exceed 218 as the Constitutional Council recalled on 29 July 2005, the legal guarantees regarding the right to health and the right to rest being constitutionally protected.
17. CJCE, 9 September 2003, C-151/02.

managers of the teleworkers, but also any colleagues who might try to contact him/her informally, maybe on his/her own telephone line if the computer is disconnected.

Indeed, on 17 February 2004 the social chambers of the High Court legitimized the 'right to disconnect'. An ambulance driver refused to answer three calls from his employer on his own personal cellular phone during his lunch break (12.30 p.m. to 1.00 p.m.). His dismissal had been approved up to the Court of Appeal of Aix-en-Provence. However, the High Court decided that not being able to be got hold of outside working time through one's own personal cellular telephone did not constitute an offence and therefore did not justify dismissal. It is not a matter of the seriousness of an offence that justifies or not a dismissal, but the very existence of an offence, denied here. This decision institutes a fundamental right to disconnect for every employee, including nomad workers and extended to global positioning systems (GPS) or GSM[18] and, *a fortiori*, a teleworker at home.

G.   COLLECTIVE RIGHTS OF THE TELEWORKER

Without even mentioning the right to strike, mentioning collective rights for employees who seldom, if ever, are physically present among the collective of the employees on site is something of an act of faith. However, these lonely road or home warriors may need representatives near to their employer who really represent their interests. This raises the question if, at some point, as for managerial and technical staff, they should have special representatives elected from their own ranks.

Section 11 of the national interoccupational collective agreement provides that teleworkers have the same collective rights as employees working on the enterprise's premises, particularly as they concern their relationship with employee representatives and access to union information, including the union's intranet, in the same conditions as other employees.

1. This formal equality of treatment may be a source of inequality for the teleworker who cannot be reached physically as easily as if he was on site 9 to 5. Union intranets and electronic mail exist only subject to a collective agreement under the Act of May 4 2004. The office less workers, who can be reached only by cellular telephone or e-mail, are unlikely to receive a visit from a shop steward on union matters, or from a works council member offering the (attractive) social benefits negotiated for employees, such as low cost vacations, cut rate shows and the like. It would therefore be advisable that the collective agreement establishing

---

18. According to the National Commission for Computer Science and Freedom's decision No. 2006-066 of 16 March 2006, employees operating vehicles belonging to an enterprise, private or public, must be warned individually before the instalment of an operating global positioning system for a vehicle: its goal, the nature of the localization data processed and kept, the duration for which they are kept, and the persons having access to them, as well as of their right of access and opposition of this data.

telework in the enterprise also provided for access to teleworkers of employee representatives.

2. Section L. 412-8 of the Labour Code, enacted by the Act of 4 May 2004, provides that an enterprise collective agreement may authorize union literature to be put at the disposal of employees, either on a union site set up on the enterprise intranet or by broadcasting messages on the electronic mail system of the enterprise. In the latter case, the broadcasting must be compatible with the needs of the smooth running of the computer network of the enterprise and must not hamper work performance. The enterprise collective agreement defines the modalities notably by clarifying the conditions of access by unions and the technical rules aiming to safeguard the freedom of choice of the employees to accept or refuse a message.

The equality of treatment set up by section 11 of the national interoccupational collective agreement put teleworkers and nomads under the same rules as their colleagues on the enterprise premises. In the absence of a collective agreement, no employee representative, whether union shop steward, employee delegate or works council member, has access to the enterprise's information systems, unless of course the union has set up its own external site. An employee working on the premises can easily drop into the union or the works council office, but it is another matter for a teleworker who is geographically remote.

Of course, on his/her own computer, at his/her personal address, the teleworker can send and receive all the information that he/she wishes, including the union's. The issue is different on the enterprise's computer at a work address, since the social chambers of the High Court on 25 January 2005 has forbidden a union to send e-mails to employees, from outside of the enterprise, at their professional e-mail address. It would be possible only if provided for within a collective agreement or with the agreement of the employer (unlikely to occur failing a collective agreement).[19]

3. Confidentiality of Communications

The High Court decided on 6 April 2004 that, in the performance of their legal duties and the safeguard of the confidentiality implied, elected employee representatives or union representatives in the enterprise must have at their disposal equipment or a technical process forbidding the interception of their communications and the identification of the callers or persons called. The contents of the union e-mail or the connection by an employee on the works council site must remain impenetrable to the employer under the (criminal) penalties foreseen for hindrance to the performance of the functions of the works council or union delegate, whether on the intranet (if there is an enterprise collective agreement) or the internet (if there is no such agreement). Unless a dedicated server is installed, it could be a nightmare for a network administrator.

---

19. Against the opinion of Pr Ray. An employer can thus by the use of control software block the reception of all union literature, even if sent outside the premises of the enterprise. This further raises to new heights the difficult issue of the difference between personal and professional mail.

The same of course applies to nomad employee representatives. As discussed above for other employees, the GPS of their vehicle must be able to be switched off, and they may switch it off as soon as they act within the performance of their duties as employee representative.[20]

4. Contact with Teleworkers and Time Off for the Performance of Duties by Employee Representatives

The social chambers of the High Court on 10 May 2006 decided that the enterprise collective agreements containing the requirement for an employee representative to complete a voucher for time spent on his/her duties before he/she performs them does not apply to time spent on the telephone by employee representatives and teleworkers. The voucher in that case (meant for warning the employer of the absence at work of the employee representative, only for information) may be completed afterwards. This is the case even if the works council has agreed, because the practice of completing vouchers ahead of time cannot be extended to cases for which it was not established.

---

20. CNIL Decision No. 2006-066 of 16 March 2009.

Chapter 9

Germany

Manfred Weiss

I. INTRODUCTION

In 1983 the German metalworkers' trade union was claiming that telework should be forbidden by law.[1] Social isolation, technological possibilities to monitor the teleworkers' performance and behaviour, monotony of work content, bad career perspectives, destruction of the traditional separation of the spheres of work and family, overburdening of women with family obligations, and dangers of self exploitation and low job security were considered to be factors characterizing telework and thereby endangering all the achievements of the labour movement. This fundamental opposition was soon given up. Telework nowadays is accepted in principle, but has remained a relatively marginal phenomenon, even if it has grown significantly in the last ten years. Estimates range from 875,000 to 1.5 million teleworkers in Germany.[2] There are still quite a few barriers to the further growth of telework. Employers in particular are afraid that the cost/benefit calculation is a negative one for them, that teleworkers cannot be controlled adequately, and that

---

1. See N. Heenen in *Muenchener Handbuch zum Arbeitsrecht*, R. Richarsi and O. Wlotzke (eds), (Vol.2, 2nd edn, 2000), p. 2590.
2. See for the lower figure N. Heenen, n. 1 above, and for the higher one Bundesvereinigung Deutscher Arbeitgeber (ed.), *Konferenz Telearbeit – Praktische Anwendung Europäischer Rahmenvereinbarungen*, (2003), p. 6.

Blanpain et al., European Framework, Agreements and Telework, pp. 171–180.
©2007, Kluwer Law International BV, The Netherlands.

the problems of data protection cannot be resolved properly.[3] The driving force in promoting telework is nowadays the employees rather than the employers. Increase of work autonomy and better compatibility of work and family obligations are the most important incentives.

The predominant pattern of telework in Germany is **rotating telework**. This means that work is performed partly in the company and partly at the telework-place. The latter location may be either in private homes or satellite offices of the company. This type of telework has the advantage that the integration into the workforce of the establishment is maintained to a certain extent. The second pattern is **mobile telework**, a subcategory of rotating telework where work is partly performed in different locations outside the enterprise. The third pattern is **pure telework** where work is fully externalized (be it in the private home or elsewhere). There is no longer real integration into the workforce of the company.

According to a study in the late 1990s, about 95 per cent of teleworkers belonged to the rotating model, more than half of them to the subcategory of mobile telework.[4] Only 2.5 per cent worked exclusively at home. This shows clearly that the big majority are still somehow integrated into the workforce of the company. There is no indication that this has changed in the meantime.

You may be interested to know that almost all teleworkers, be they in the rotating scheme or fully externalized, do have an employment contract. Thereby they enjoy the full protection of labour law. According to the above mentioned study, more than 75 per cent of them were not hired as teleworkers but had already worked as employees in the company. They voluntarily changed to telework by mutual agreement. Different from the pattern elsewhere in Europe, self-employed teleworkers only play a very marginal role.

The study also reveals the high level of education of the big majority of teleworkers in Germany. Only exceptionally is telework a low skilled job.

Since the late 1980s there has been a discussion about whether special legislation for telework is needed. Several drafts were elaborated. In the meantime it looks as if this idea has been given up. The German legislation only rarely refers to telework. The amendment to the Works Council Act specifies that teleworkers are employees in the sense of this act, thereby entitled to vote for the works council and/or to be elected. This, however, is nothing new: it is merely a clarification. Two acts regulating equal opportunities in employment relationships in the public sector, an Act for the Federal Administration and the Federal Courts of 2001,[5] and an Act for the Public Service of the State of Baden-Wuerttemberg of 2005,[6] contain norms according to which telework is to be offered to employees with family obligations if this is possible in the respective context. The provisions also give preference to employees with family obligations if employees for telework are to

---

3. L. Kamp, *Betriebs- und Dienstvereinbarungen Telearbeit – Analyse und Handlungsempfehlungen* (Edition der Hans-Boeckler-Stiftung, No. 31, 2000), p. 7.
4. For all these figures *see* Freudenreich/Klein/Wedde, *Entwicklungen der Telearbeit – Arbeitsrech-liche Rahmenbedingungen, Forschungsbericht im Auftrag des BMA* (1997).
5. Bundesgesetzblatt (BGBl) I 2001, p. 3234.
6. Gesetzblatt Baden-Wuerttemberg (GBl.) 2005, 650.

be chosen. And they expressly state that teleworkers must have the same career opportunities (promotion, training, etc.) as other employees. Finally, telework cannot be taken as an instrument to give teleworkers work of lower value. It, however, is doubtful whether these provisions have a great impact on actual practice.

Not only protection by labour law includes teleworkers. The elaborated legislation on data protection also covers telework.[7] If, exceptionally, teleworkers are not employees but self-employed they may be covered by the Act on Home Work which was established long ago for traditional home work. Of course the rules of this Act are not shaped for modern telework. Nevertheless, they provide significant protection for teleworkers.

As a follow up to the European framework agreement on telework of 2002, the German Confederation of Employers' Associations (BDA) initiated a comparative project and a conference in June 2003 with employers' associations from Austria, Denmark and France and the German Confederation of Trade Unions (DGB).[8] However, this exchange of ideas seems to be the only impact of the European framework agreement. To my knowledge there are no further steps of implementation.

Telework is not considered to be a burning problem in Germany. This is mainly due to the fact that – as will be shown – works councils, in co-operation with management, do have a possibility to conclude tailor-made work agreements for telework in their respective companies. Only to a marginal extent in very few companies (the most prominent being Telekom) has telework become a subject matter regulated by collective agreements concluded between a company and a trade union. Telework, at least so far, is not a topic for sectoral collective bargaining, the still dominating pattern of collective bargaining in Germany. The key player in this context is the works council. Therefore the focus of this short report will be on its role.[9]

II.   THE WORKS COUNCIL'S ROLE IN MONITORING TELEWORK

When the Works Constitution Act was amended in 2001,[10] telework was mentioned in the statute for the first time. Now it is clear that the workplace of a teleworker belongs to the respective establishment for which the teleworker works, no matter whether this is the teleworker's home or a satellite office or whether it is a mobile form of telework (section 5, para.1). The inclusion of

---

7. See, for example, ss. 9, 11 and 38 of the Bundesdatenschutzgesetz.
8. See the report in n. 2 above.
9. For an overview on the works council's role in reference to telework, see T. Schmechel, 'Die Rolle des Betriebsrats bei der Einfuehrung und Durchfuehrung von Telearbeit' [2004] *Neue Zeitschrift fuer Arbeitsrecht*, 237.
10. For this amendment see M. Weiss, 'Modernizing the German Works Council System: A Recent Amendment' [2002] *The International Journal of Comparative Labour Law and Industrial Relations*, 251.

teleworkers in the workforce of the establishment for purposes of the Works Constitution Act is not an innovation: it merely clarifies the status which was agreed upon long before the term found entry into the statute. From the point of view of the Works Constitution Act, the teleworkers are treated the same way as all other employees of the establishment. For inclusion into the works council system it is irrelevant whether from the perspective of employment contract law the teleworkers are employees in a strict sense or self employed. They only have to be linked to the establishment. In this respect they are treated like home workers in a traditional sense.

Teleworkers are entitled to participate in the election of the works council, which takes place every four years. The works council represents the workforce as a whole – unionized as well as non-unionized workers. If teleworkers have been working for an establishment for at least six months, they are also entitled to stand for election into the works council.

Teleworkers are also entitled to participate in the works meetings where four times a year the workforce gathers to discuss issues of joint interest with the works council. At least once a year the employer gives a report to the works meeting on staff questions and social affairs in the establishment, as well as on the financial position of – and trends in – the establishment (sections 42, 43). Thereby the teleworkers have an opportunity to present their views to the works council and the other employees.

The teleworkers are also entitled during working hours to consult the works council (section 39). If teleworkers feel that they are unfairly treated they not only have the right to make a complaint to the employer or his representatives in the establishment, but they are entitled to be supported by a member of the works council (section 84).

The employer has to provide the works council with the technological equipment to be able to continuously communicate with teleworkers. This is implied by the fact that the employer has to provide anything the works council needs to do its job (section 40). The works council is also entitled to visit the teleworkers at their respective workplaces. Otherwise the works council's task to monitor the application of labour standards in the broadest sense (section 80) could not be performed. This is particularly relevant in reference to health and safety standards.

The works council as an actor in the planning stage has numerous rights relating to teleworkers before telework is even introduced. First, an employer has to inform the works council in due time of any plans concerning the technical structure of workplaces and has to consult the works council in good time on the action envisaged and its effects on the employees, taking particular account of its impact on the nature of their work and the implied demands on the employees, so that suggestions and objections on the part of the works council can be taken into account in the plans. In their consultations, the employer and the works council shall bear in mind the established findings of ergonomics relating to the tailoring of jobs to meet human requirements (section 90).

9. Germany

The works council has to be informed and consulted by the employer comprehensively and in good time of all matters referring to manpower planning, including in particular present and future manpower needs and the resulting staff movements and vocational training measures (section 92). This information and consultation of course also refers to the planning of telework.

According to section 92a which was introduced into the Works Constitution Act by the amendment of 2001, the works council is entitled to make proposals to secure and promote employment. This can also refer to the question of whether there should be telework and what modality of telework should be envisaged. If the works council starts such an initiative the employer is obliged to consult on the topic with the works council. If the employer does not want to follow the works council's proposal, he has to justify this rejection by giving reasons. In establishments of more than a hundred employees this justification has to be in written.

If a teleworkplace is actually introduced the position of the works council is very strong: it has a right of co-determination in many respects. Co-determination means that the employer's and the works council's position in decision making are identical. If they do not reach agreement, each of them has access to the so-called arbitration committee which is supposed to resolve the conflict. If the employer acts without the works council's agreement, his/her decision is null and void. The works council by way of court order could stop the employer performing such measures.[11]

There are several rights of co-determination, all contained in section 87, para.1, referring to telework. The most important case for co-determination in this context is 'the introduction and use of technical devices designed to monitor the behaviour and performance of employees' (No. 6). This co-determination right refers to all aspects: whether such a technology is to be introduced and how the modalities are in using it. Transposed to telework this means that the questions of whether there should be teleworkplaces and how the technological devices are to be used by the teleworkers (what kind of measures for data protection are to be taken, what kind of measures to allow or restrict the monitoring of the teleworkers' performance and behaviour, etc.) are to be dealt with and agreed upon. Another important case for codetermination is 'arrangements for the prevention of employment accidents and occupational diseases and for the protection of health on the basis of health and safety regulations' (No. 7). This means that the works council is involved in reference to all health and safety regulations which are not totally predetermined by health and safety regulations but which leave leeway for taking measures. Evidently this plays a big role in the area of telework. Another co-determination right is also important: 'the commencement and termination of the daily working hours including breaks and the distribution of working hours among the days of the week' (No. 2). This implies, for example, arrangements for the availability of the teleworker, etc. Of utmost importance are two other cases of co-determination: 'questions related to remuneration arrangements in the

---

11. For this mechanism, see M. Weiss and M. Schmidt, *Labour Relations and Industrial Relations in Germany*, (3rd ed., 2000), p. 198.

establishment, including in particular the establishment of principles of remuneration and the introduction and application of new remuneration methods or modification of existing methods' (No. 10), and 'the fixing of job and bonus rates and comparable performance related remuneration including cash coefficients' (No. 11). Remuneration arrangements under No. 10 mainly focus on the methods of remuneration, not on the amount, whereas No. 11 also refers to the amount and thereby gives the works council an even stronger position. These are only the most important examples of co-determination rights in the context of telework. There are quite a few more which may become relevant for telework. Co-determination regularly leads to the conclusion of so-called work agreements. These are agreements between works council and employer establishing rights and duties for the employment relationship.[12] They are to be monitored by the works council. In case of violation, the works council as well as individual workers are entitled to enforce them in court.

If a teleworkplace does not correspond with the requirements of ergonomics and thereby a special burden is put on the teleworker, the works council has again a right of co-determination. The works council may request appropriate action to relieve the additional stress or to at least compensate for it (section 91).

If the status of an employee is to be changed into becoming a teleworker, this again is a matter for the works council. Whether the employee agrees to such a change is irrelevant for the works council's right. Under the perspective of the Works Constitution Act this is considered to be a transfer (section 95, para.3). Under certain conditions enumerated in section 99, para.2, the works council may veto such a transfer.

The works council's involvement is particularly important in the area of vocational training. If the employer plans or performs measures which lead to the effect that the work of the affected workers change (by being transferred to telework), and the workers' skills are no longer sufficient for the fulfilment of their tasks, the works council has a right to co-determine the introduction of vocational training in the establishment (section 97, para.2). As far as the performance of vocational training in the establishment is concerned, the works council again has a far-reaching co-determination right. In particular the works council can make sure that such training activities may not be performed by persons who do not have the necessary technical and pedagogic skills. And most important, employer and works council have to agree on who is selected to participate in such courses, be they performed within or outside the establishment (section 98).

The above list of examples may give an impression of the importance of the works council as a key player in the context of telework in Germany. However, it should at least be mentioned that in many small and even medium-sized establishments, works councils – in spite of the law which requires a works council in every establishment of at least five employees – do not exist. For manifold reasons, employees in these small and medium-sized establishments abstain from electing a works council. Of course the protection provided by individual employment law

---

12. See M. Weiss and M. Schmidt, n. 11 above, p. 205.

remains, but there is no collective protection in these establishments. This segmentation is one of the most difficult problems of labour law in Germany. On the other hand it may well be that telework, at least so far, is mainly a phenomenon arising in bigger establishments. Therefore, up to now the lack of a works council in small and medium-sized companies may not yet be dramatic in reference to this very topic.

Instead of giving further examples of works councils' rights in the context of telework, it seems more appropriate to provide some information on the content of work agreements between works council and employer.

III.   THE CONTENT OF WORK AGREEMENTS ON TELEWORK

Work agreements are not easily accessible. Therefore, it is not possible to give a comprehensive up-to-date assessment.[13] In the Hans-Boeckler Foundation these work agreements are collected and analysed. The last publication of this group on telework dates from 2000.[14] There are, however, no indications that things have changed significantly since then.

The author of the study analysed 68 work agreements on telework concluded between works council and employer. Fifty three of them were concluded in 1997 or later which means that they are relatively new. Twenty six of the agreements belong to the public sector. The agreements belonging to the private sector are equally divided between manufacturing and services.

In most of the agreements telework is defined as rotating telework. Telework exclusively performed at home is only very exceptionally allowed. In all 68 agreements telework is defined as something which takes place within an already existing and further continuing employment relationship. This implies that by these agreements the teleworker is guaranteed a right to return to his/her former job or at least to a comparable job in the establishment.

Criteria for telework are defined. These criteria have to be met before telework can be introduced. Astonishingly frequent in this context is the request that the tasks have to be clearly defined and limited and that the results can be measured. This can only be explained by the fact that the companies are interested in being able to monitor the performance efficiently. Other frequently used examples are:

- The work must be such that it can be externalized;
- Work performance is not dependent on a certain time and/or location;
- Permanent presence in the establishment is not necessary;
- There is no need for direct or spontaneous communication; or
- The task can be performed autonomously and distributed autonomously.

---

13. The first work agreement on telework in Germany was concluded at IBM in 1991; *see* M. Koerner, 'Telearbeit – Neue Form der Erwerbsarbeit, alte Regeln?' *Neue Zeitschrift fuer Arbeitsrecht* [1999], 1190.
14. See the publication by L. Kamp, n. 3 above.

In quite a few agreements specific skills for teleworkers are required to be admitted to telework. The emphasis here is on the following items: high degree of autonomy, ability to act on one's own responsibility, psychological ability to work in isolation, high degree of self discipline, high degree of reliability, sufficient technical qualifications to cope with technological disturbances, a family situation which allows for undisturbed work, etc. Only a minority of five agreements provide for a special training period to prepare the teleworkers for their task.

About half of the agreements determine requirements for the teleworkplace. Among these requirements the most frequent ones are as follows: the location has to be appropriate (sufficient space, sufficient light, high rooms, no cellar rooms, etc.), the workplace has to correspond with ergonomic requirements, professional and private sphere have to be strictly separated, protection of data and safety of data are to be guaranteed, the proper working of the technological equipment needs to be guaranteed, etc.

In many agreements it is provided that the teleworkplace is to be inspected by a representative of the company together with the works council before telework can be started. An important role is played by clauses which oblige the employer to inform the teleworker on all relevant health and safety rules.

All agreements define telework as being voluntary. Some expressly state that the employer as well as employees can refuse to accept telework without giving any reasons. In others it is stated that there is no entitlement to telework. In most agreements telework is considered to be only for a fixed term period. This reflects the fact that telework by employers as well as by works councils is apparently still considered to be an experiment which should not be made definite too early. In addition probation periods are regularly required.

The organizational details of telework are left to the work process. However, there are framework rules in the agreements – in particular realistic goals to be achieved by the teleworker should be agreed upon in order to eliminate all dangers of self exploitation. In some agreements it is determined which information is to be given by the teleworker to whom and the other way around.

Working time is an important issue in the big majority of agreements. Examples of these clauses are: distribution of working time between home and establishment or the distribution of working time is to be determined by the teleworker, or the distribution is to be determined by the teleworker within a certain pre-determined range, or distribution of working time is to be agreed upon between management and teleworker with or without a certain pre-determined range. The latter alternative is the most frequent one. In some agreements the time when the teleworker has to be available at the teleworkplace at home is fixed. As far as the working time as a whole is concerned, most agreements refer to the working time which was relevant for the teleworker before. As far as the control of working time at the teleworkplace at home is concerned, most agreements leave it to the teleworker to write it down. Thereby, a sort of diary for working time is established by the teleworker. This registration is also relevant for compensating overtime work.

Clauses on remuneration are rarely included in agreements. In some agreements lump sums for extra availability are provided for.

Most agreements contain rules for establishing continuous communication between the teleworker and the company, in particular with the works council. They also guarantee the teleworker's right to participate in work meetings as described above. In short, there are clauses intending the integration of the teleworker into the establishment of the workforce of the establishment.

An important question contained in the agreements refers to the costs of the teleworkplace. According to all the agreements the employer has to bear all the costs for the establishment and the maintenance of the teleworkplace. The agreements also provide for lump sums to be paid for the rent of specific rooms, for cleaning, electricity, etc. If the building where the teleworker lives has to be adapted to the teleworkplace, the employer regularly bears all the costs. The same happens if after the telework period the building has to be re-adapted. If the teleworker uses private equipment the employer again pays a lump sum. For private furniture used in the teleworkplace again lump sums are provided. Finally there are regulations on how telephone costs are to be reimbursed.

There are clauses which allow and limit the private use of the technological teleworkplace equipment.

A very important item in the agreements refers to the protection of internal data of the establishment and in particular to the protection of personal privacy data. Therefore the agreements regulate in great detail the manifold duties of the teleworker to do everything to protect such data (passwords, codes, virus protection, etc.). The clauses on these duties of protection are related to liability regulations. Here distinctions are made – in line with the rules of employee liability law – between intention, grave negligence, medium negligence and light negligence. In other words, the degree of culpability defines the possibility of being made responsible to pay damages.

There are also clauses protecting the teleworker's privacy in accordance with the rules on data protection in Germany.

In most agreements rules are contained which regulate in detail under what conditions the employer or his representatives are entitled to inspect the teleworkplace. Some agreements require prior notice and define notice periods, whereas others determine that the teleworker always has to allow access to the teleworkplace. Some – fortunately very few – agreements even determine that the teleworker has to leave keys for the teleworkplace with the employer to allow him/her or his/her representatives to enter the teleworkplace at their discretion. As already indicated above, the works council members are entitled to inspect the teleworkplace. However, prior notice and observance of notice periods is also provided for them in some agreements.

Last but not least, the manifold clauses are to be mentioned which guarantee the teleworkers' access to appropriate vocational training.

These examples are not exhaustive by far. And of course the sample of 68 agreements is certainly not representative either. However, the agreements analysed in the study of the Hans-Boeckler Foundation show the wide range of questions dealt with in reference to telework.

IV. CONCLUSION

The sketchy overview on the content of work agreements may be the key to understanding why the European framework agreement on telework in Germany, at least so far, has remained to be without any significant follow up. The shape of telework is considered to be essentially, and first of all, a task for the regulation by work agreement concluded between employer and works council. Since the works council does have a powerful position in this context, there is no danger that telework could be abused to deprive teleworkers of protection. The rules on telework are to be developed and adapted according to the needs of individual companies. These needs, as well as the respective potential of the respective companies, are well known by the works councils. They, therefore, are the ideal actor to co-operate in this respect with the employer.

Trade unions in Germany do have a macro perspective, focusing on the branch of activity as a whole rather than on specific conditions of individual enterprises. This explains why regulations on telework by collective agreement are still a rarity.

The highly decentralized regulation pattern in Germany in reference to telework is considered to be best equipped to deal with the problems arising in this context. Neither the legislator nor the parties to collective agreements are eager to change this situation. This might change if telework were to become a mass phenomenon which – as indicated above – is so far not the case.

The work agreements sketched above show clearly that the requirements of the European framework agreement at least are met where works councils are elected. This means of course that there might be a gap in reference to those establishments without works councils. Collective agreements could not fill this gap since in Germany collective agreements are only binding for unionized employees who are employed by employers who concluded a collective agreement or who are a member of the employers' association which concluded the collective agreement. The non-unionized are not covered. Therefore, the extremely complicated and rarely used mechanism of extension – the declaration of general binding – would have to be applied. This is unrealistic. Given these limitations, only the legislator could fill the gap. However, there is no indication that this will happen in the near future. The legislator only acts if burning needs of regulation have to be met. This cannot be said in the case of telework.

The voluntary European framework agreements are to be implemented 'in accordance with the procedures and practices specific to management and labour and the Member States'. It seems that in Germany, at least up to now, works agreements are the appropriate channel.

Chapter 10

Italy

Michele Colucci

I.   INTRODUCTION

Teleworking is revolutionizing the way we legally frame and perceive work. Tuned to the modern means of communication, it represents an innovative way of working, irrespective of time and place, and adjusted to the worker's own lifestyle and rhythm.[1]

Because of its peculiarities telework has proved successful in a great number of work activities such as, data entry, translation, and in general all the activities where results and quality criteria are measurable.

Of course, not everybody can be a 'teleworker' – only those who have a minimum of computer knowledge, a sense of initiative, and the ability to achieve objectives without the need for strict supervision.

---

1. S. Burns, G. Delle Donne, G. Pinzuti, *Telework in Italy, From Knowledge to Practice*, (Consorzio Tecfor), available at <www.esf-agentschap.be/esf2/europeteleworks/images/pdf/[29814] ESF_Italy.pdf>.

Blanpain et al., European Framework, Agreements and Telework, pp. 181–190.
©2007, Kluwer Law International BV, The Netherlands.

Given its peculiarities and the wide range of activities it covers, we can identify several forms of telework, namely the 'tele home work',[2] the 'telework on location and on the road',[3] and 'telework in satellite offices'.[4]

All these forms of telework mean transforming the traditional organization, i.e. re-structuring productive cycles, information flows, assets and the company's organization chart.

The advantages associated with teleworking can be classified according to the reference object.[5] For employers it means an increase in work flexibility, an improvement in work quality, an increase in the motivation of human resources, a reduction of costs, and of course a reduction of absenteeism.

For employees it means an increase of flexibility, a reduction of home/office transfers, the possibility to choose where to live, and to get more employment opportunities.

On the other side, teleworking could present some drawbacks, such as isolation and reduction of external social relationships, lesser instructions and support in work (self control), reduced identification of employees with their company and employer and company reorganization.[6]

Many factors favour teleworking's expansion: the increase in the use of internet contributing to the creation of a 'net mentality', the necessity to react quickly to market changes, thus increasing productivity and reducing costs.

Before proceeding with the analysis of the relevant legislation on telework, it is important to remind ourselves that telework does not bring about a simple, but a complex form of flexible work, which relies on a wide range of organizational means.

---

2. This is the main form of decentralized work with a contract as employee or co-worker enabling the teleworker to carry out his main activity at home. Some only use telematic connections to communicate with employers or with clients, while others combine working at home with 'conventional' activities inside the company.
3. This type of telework is prevalent mainly among sales people and technical assistants, who communicate with the head office by means of telematic devices and avoid having to return to the office to download data and information contained in the central computer. In that case there is no fixed workplace. Instead, each office disposes of a number of places where it is possible to carry out these specific activities.
4. The 'telework in satellite offices' refers to particular structures in both the private and public sector, where offices, owned by one or more companies, are at the disposal of employees who carry out their work in different locations situated outside the main site of the company.
5. *See* in that regard D. Hobbs and J. Armstrong, 'An Experimental Study of Social and Psychological Aspects of Teleworking' (August 1998) Vol.98, Issue 5, pp. 214–218.
6. R. Donnelly, 'How 'free' is the Free Worker?: An Investigation into the Working Arrangements Available to Knowledge Workers' (2006) *Personnel Review*, Vol.35, Issue 1, 78–97.

II. THE EU FRAMEWORK AGREEMENT

The EU framework agreement on telework[7] is the first to be implemented by the voluntary means expressed in Article 139 EC. It could, therefore, be considered the first real collective agreement on a European level.

The subject matter was particularly suited to such a step forward: in all European Member States the regulation of telework is rarely, or minimally, the result of legislative work.

For evidence of the latter, one must simply look at the inventory of conventions or regulations enforced in each Member State that was enclosed in the Commission's press release on collective agreements.

This is one of the rare occasions where Italy's case stands out. Only in Italy do we find a legislative agreement on telework, the 1998 law on telework in the public sector, and its agreement on telework signed by the CONFAPI, the CGIL-CISL and the UIL is the fifth example of such a collective agreement.

The EU agreement states that the signatory parties view teleworking as a way for employers (both in the private and public sectors) to modernize work organization, to improve their worker's work/life balance and to achieve a greater autonomy in the workplace.

The agreement defines telework as:

A form of organising and/or performing work, using information technology, in the context of an employment contract/relationship, where work, which could also be performed at the employer's premises, is carried out away from those premises on a regular basis.

The condition of 'regularity' in telework, present in the European agreement, seems to exclude all forms of flexible telework, and therefore work taking place both inside and outside of a company premises within the same week.[8]

Teleworkers are awarded the general protection granted to workers based on the employer's premises and the agreement highlights seven key areas where the specificities of telework need to be taken into account.

The agreement aimed to establish a general EU-level framework to be implemented by the members of the signatory parties 'in accordance with the national procedures and practices specific to management and labour'.

The parties make it clear that implementation of the agreement does not constitute valid grounds to reduce the general level of social protection already awarded to workers in this area.

---

7. The signatories were the European Trade Union Confederation (ETUC), the Council of European Professional and Managerial Staff (EUROCADRES)/European Confederation of Executives and Managerial Staff (CEC) liaison committee, the Union of Industrial and Employers' Confederations of Europe (BUSINESSEUROPE)/the European Association of Craft, Small and Medium-Sized Enterprises (UEAPME), and the European Centre of Enterprises with Public Participation and of Enterprises of General Economic Interest (CEEP).
8. D. Gottardi, *L'Accord-Cadre Européen sur le Télétravail Comparé à la Réglementation Italienne*, paper available at <www.telework-mirti.org/comm-gottardi.doc> (accessed 17 December 2006).

It also does not limit the right of social partners to conclude, 'at the appropriate level, including European level', other agreements adapting and/or complementing this agreement in order to take note of the specific needs of the social partners concerned, thus giving a certain amount of flexibility to adapt provisions to specific situations. The text also states that care should be taken to avoid unnecessary burdens on small and medium-sized enterprises (SMEs) when implementing this agreement.

III. THE ITALIAN LEGISLATIVE FRAMEWORK

Although in Italy telework is mainly regulated by collective agreements, a number of bills on telework were presented in Parliament in 1997 and 1998.

All bills used a rather broad definition of telework, namely as 'work performed with the assistance of telematic instruments outside of company premises', and addressed two main issues, namely the rights of teleworkers, and their entitlement to obtain information about the firm for which they work (for example, size, balance sheet, organization chart, branches, statutes, service circulars); they also recognized the right to send and receive messages not related to work (for example, with the users of the company's information system, with the RSU (Rappresentanza sindacale unitaria – Unitary Workers' Representation), with the health and safety workers representatives, as well as the privacy of communications.

The common feature that emanates from the various bills is their overall stance: they all seek to introduce stricter rules and closer external control.

The standards regarding telework must be read in accordance with laws affecting related topics, such as Law 53/2000 which supports maternity and paternity leave, the right to give care and to be trained.[9]

This law pays attention to individual needs, to personalized management and work engagements throughout life, to the ways in which time is spent (both everyday time and life time), and to the need for cures and solidarity towards weaker individuals (within the family, in relationships of a 'good neighbourhood', and in the various forms of 'social solidarity').

The law wants to reconcile care time and work time by offering the possibility to reduce work time, by resorting to forms of telework that offer flexibility with regard to the employee's engagements and family responsibilities (birth, adoption/ entrustment, sick relatives, etc.), and, by regarding care as 'social time'.

Within the context of the modernization operation and the simplification and transparency of public administration – well known as the 'Bassanini reform' – the legislator was obliged to create regulatory standards for 'work at a distance'.

The formal creation of regulatory frameworks helped telework projects to start. Above all, the approval of the Decree on Telework in the Public Administration[10] legitimized the resort as an organizational instrument that favours the

---

9. In OJ No. 60, 13 March 2000.
10. Presidential Decree No. 70 of 8 March 1999 in OJ No. 70, 25 March 1999.

renewal of the structures and practices of service distribution in public administrations.

IV. TELEWORK IN THE PUBLIC ADMINISTRATION

The introduction of telework in the public administration was foreseen by Law. No. 191 of 1998, first in experimental form to increase the efficiency of work organization.

On the basis of this law's provisions, the government approved regulations implementing telework in the public administration in March 1998.[11] These regulations define telework as 'work undertaken by a public employee in a place outside his or her normal work site'.

Compared to the definition offered by the EU collective agreement, the one provided by the national regulations enumerates the tools and the connections necessary to link the teleworker to his administration, but does not specify the quantity of work needed, and does not include the criteria of regularity.

The regulations cover general aspects like pay levels, the teleworker's rights, and working conditions. The definition of more specific rules based on the provisions of the law took place through collective bargaining.

Accordingly, on 21 July 1999 the Aran public sector bargaining agency, the CGIL, CISL, UIL trade union confederations and a number of independent unions signed a framework which regulates telework in the public sector.

Following the agreement the choice of whether or not to take up telework is left to the employee. Priority is given to workers with disabilities, those with family responsibilities, and those who live at a distance from their place of work.

Teleworkers enjoy the same rights as in-office workers. These rights concern such matters as career advancement, pay and training. In order to ensure participation in organizational life and trade union activities, an online noticeboard is created, and each teleworker has an e-mail address. Working hours are the same as for in-office workers, although they may be scheduled differently.

The agreement also focuses on costs and controls for teleworking: the cost of installing computers and other equipment (modem, printer, etc.) and their maintenance will be met by the authority employing the teleworker. The equipment can be used only for the purpose of work. Also foreseen are lump-sum reimbursements for telephone and electricity charges.

According to the provisions of Italy's Workers' Statute legislation, checks by the employer are not allowed, and this also applies in the case of teleworkers.[12]

The framework agreement lays down only the basic principles for the introduction of telework in the public administration. By means of bargaining in the

---

11. M. Trentini, *Agreement Signed on Telework in the Public Administration* (Eironline), available at <www.eiro.eurofound.eu.int/1999/08/feature/it9908344f.html> (accessed 17 December 2006).
12. See also M. Colucci, 'The Impact of the Internet and the New Technologies in the Workplace' (2003) *Bulletin of Comparative Industrial Relations*, No. 43, Kluwer Law International.

individual sectors of the administration it is possible to introduce rules which suit the requirements of individuals.

The agreement signed in the public administration laid the basis for the increase of this new form of work.

V.   THE ITALIAN NATIONAL AGREEMENT ON TELEWORK

On 9 June 2004, 21 employers' associations representing all sectors, and the three main trade union confederations[13] signed an interconfederal agreement implementing the EU framework agreement on telework.[14]

The interconfederal agreement defines the general regulatory framework for telework, leaving ample space for collective and individual bargaining, though the latter must respect the minimum conditions for protection established by the text.

It does not affect collective agreements already concluded on the matter: as we will see there are a number of national, industry-wide collective agreements in Italy which regulate telework, for example in the retail, service sectors, telecommunications, small and medium-sized enterprises and the public sector.

The signatories to the agreement recognize that telework is 'a means to modernise the organisation of work and that it may furnish a better work–life balance by giving the workers concerned greater autonomy'.

Moreover, they consider that telework should be encouraged by making the best use of new technologies, so that flexibility can be combined with job security, the quality of work improved, and greater opportunities for people with disabilities to enter into the workforce.

The interconfederal agreement recognizes the voluntary and reversible nature of telework.

Unless explicitly stated by the contract, the worker is entitled to accept or refuse telework, and refusal does not constitute grounds for the termination of the employment relationship.

The teleworker enjoys the same rights as those established by the law and collective agreements for a 'comparable' worker on the employer's premises.

The employer is normally responsible for furnishing, installing and maintaining the equipment necessary for the telework. The employer also reimburses or pays costs deriving directly from the work, in particular communication costs.

---

13. The General Confederation of Italian Workers (Confederazione Generale Italiana del Lavoro, Cgil), the Italian Confederation of Workers' Unions (Confederazione Italiana Sindacati Lavoratori, Cisl), and the Union of Italian Workers (Unione Italiana del Lavoro, Uil).
14. The text of the agreement is available at <www.uil.it/pol_contrattuali/accordo_telelavoro 2004.pdf> (accessed 17 December 2006).

The teleworker's privacy is guaranteed. Following the Italian Workers' Statute, if the employer decides to install control devices, these must be proportionate to their purpose.[15]

The employer is responsible for protecting the health and safety of the teleworker and must provide all information on company health and safety policies, especially as regards the use of visual display units.

In order to ensure compliance with health and safety regulations, the employer, the workers' representatives and the competent authorities have right of access to the premises where telework is undertaken. This access is subject to the consent of teleworkers if they work in their own home.

Likewise, in order to ensure that the health and safety regulations have been correctly applied, teleworkers have the right to ask for the inspection of the premises in which they work.

Within the limits established by the law, collective agreements and company regulations, teleworkers are responsible for the organization of their working time.

Particular attention is paid to preventing the isolation of teleworkers by ensuring access to company information and regular meetings with work colleagues.

Teleworkers are guaranteed the same training and career development opportunities as those working on the employer's premises, and are subject to the same assessment criteria. Moreover, they are entitled to receive specific technical and organizational training.

Teleworkers have the same collective rights as their colleagues working on the employer's premises and can vote or stand as a candidate in elections for workers' representatives. Finally, their communications with workers' representatives must not be obstructed. The introduction of telework is subject to information and consultation of the workers' representatives.

VI. SECTORAL AGREEMENT: TELEWORK IN THE COMMERCE SECTOR

The two industry-wide agreements covering telework are as follows: the one signed by the telecommunications companies affiliated to Intersind (the association of state-owned enterprises which, as a result of privatization, is now part of Confindustria), signed in September 1996; and the agreement reached in the commerce sector in June 1997.

The national contract for the commerce sector offers the most complete definition of teleworking by identifying four types of telework: 'home working', when the work is performed in the worker's own home; 'out working', when the work is performed at a distance from the company's premises in a variety of locations (examples being maintenance services or on-site assistance to clients); 'remote

---

15. Art.4 of the Italian Workers' Statute, Law No. 300 of May 20 1970, containing 'rules on the protection of the freedom and dignity of workers and of trade union freedom and union activity in the workplace, and rules on the public employment service'.

working', when the work is performed at a collective work station at a distance from the company but still belonging to it; and 'hoteling', when work stations are made available in the company for workers who usually operate off site.[16]

The commerce agreement guarantees that for those engaged in teleworking, both at home as well as in special centres outside the companies, the contractual rules in terms of salary, career opportunities, trade union and training rights set by the industry-wide agreement for all workers in the distribution sector are valid.[17]

Teleworking can concern new employees or workers who already work for a company. It cannot be imposed on the worker, but can only be proposed by the enterprise to the worker, who is free to accept or refuse it voluntarily. The possibility of a teleworker returning to work in the company after a set time is also foreseen.

The company can exercise control from a distance, but it has to follow criteria of absolute transparency. The teleworker has to work with diligence and discretion, and cannot carry out work for his or her own sake or for a third party or in competition with the company which employs him or her.

Finally, the agreement extends the contractual and legislative rules on health and safety and includes insurance against injury for the places in which telework occurs, and for the people that have access to them.

VII. COMPANY AGREEMENTS

On the basis of the existing agreements signed at company level, it appears that telework in Italy is used mainly by companies operating in the telecommunications and information technology sector.[18]

Collective bargaining has covered all the issues related to telework.

A company agreement on telework typically includes the definition of telework, the status of teleworkers, the circumstances in which telework may be started and those in which it can be discontinued, responsibility in terms of health and safety rules, wage scales, overtime regulation, expense coverage by the employer and the teleworkers, the provision and maintenance of the equipment required for telework, the guarantee of access to training and career opportunities, and rules on regular meetings in the company and on access to company and union information.

---

16. The text of the Agreement is available at <www.cgil.it/documenti/accordotelelavoro.htm> (accessed 17 December 2006).
17. D. Paparella, *Commerce Sector Agreement Seeks to Regulate Telework* (Eironline), available at www.eiro.eurofound.eu.int/about/1997/07/inbrief/it9707118n.html (accessed 17 December 2006).
18. R. Pedersini, *Company Agreements Focus Attention on Teleworking* (Eironline), available at <www.eiro.eurofound.eu.int/about/1997/12/feature/it9712218f.html> (accessed 17 December 2006).

Significant company agreements on telework have been reached in companies like Telecom Italia, Seat, Saritel, Italtel, and Digital Equipment.

Under the terms of the Tim Agreement, telework aims to achieve a significant improvement in the quality of the service.

In the case of maintenance services, the innovation has reduced the amount of time spent on the company premises, given that a number of operations (including clocking in and out) can be performed using a computer provided by the company. There is no change in the working hours of maintenance staff or in the places where they perform their job tasks, which remain the same as those of their colleagues, with work organized along 'traditional' lines. However, controls on their work activity have changed.

The sales personnel will be given apparatus (computer, printer, mobile phone with a modem) which will enable them to 'hook up' to the company's information system and thus work in constant contact with headquarters. The aim of the initiative is to increase the sales personnel's response capacity when dealing with clients by enabling constant online consultation with the company.

If, on completion of the experimental period, the system is extended to all the maintenance and sales staff, around 35 per cent of the company's personnel might be involved in telework.

The Electrolux Zanussi agreement aims to enhance the work experience, professional development and career advancement of pregnant women and women with young children.

Assignment to telework is voluntary. The system has the following features: a work area separate from those normally devoted to everyday family life must be made available in the teleworker's home; this work area must comply with health and safety regulations; working hours are distributed throughout the day at the worker's discretion, according to the tasks to be performed.

However, the worker must be present at certain times of the day to receive communications from the company – since working hours can be organized as the worker wishes, extra payments for overtime, night work and weekend work are not envisaged. The equipment necessary for telework is installed by the company, and at the company's expense.

The worker may use this equipment only for company purposes. Moreover, the worker must guarantee access to the equipment for maintenance; the worker receives a lump-sum payment to cover the costs arising from the telework, like the occupation of space, electricity, telephone charges.

VIII.   CONCLUSION

Telework regulation is the ideal test to prove that flexibility can be combined with security.

Italy has been a pioneer in developing collective agreements on telework in the public sector where government and unions have played a leading role on this subject.

In contrast, Italy has limited experience in telework in the private sector where all company agreements have concentrated mostly on home working and out working. They all cover only the pilot phase of telework experiments.

Moreover, telework diffusion should be based on a clear regulatory framework for the protection of employees and to avoid telework being exploited as an unofficial or illegal activity.

This does not mean that closer external control and stricter rules than those already foreseen by the Italian legislation are needed, but rather that employers should be put in a condition to adopt telework in all its forms for the good of their company and its employees.

IX.   REFERENCES AND FURTHER INFORMATION

A.   LEGISLATION

Preparatory Works

Bill No. 2305 (03/04/1997) Standards for the Promotion of Telework
Bill No. 3123 (10/03/1998) Standards for the Regulation, the Protection and the Development of Telework
Bill No. 3489 (30/07/1998) Standards for the Development of Telework

B.   LAWS

Law No. 191 of 16 June 1998 in OJ No. 142 of 20 June 1998.
Law 53/2000 of 8 March 2000 in OJ No. 60 of 13 March 2000.
Presidential Decree No. 70 of 8 March 1999 in OJ No. 70 of 25 March 1999.

C.   COLLECTIVE BARGAINING AGREEMENTS

Interconfederation Agreement on Telework of 9 June 2004

D.   WEBSITES

(accessed 17 December 2006)
(accessed 17 December 2006)
<www.eurofound.org> (accessed 17 December 2006)
<http://telelavoro.formez.it/> (accessed 17 December 2006)
(accessed 17 December 2006)
<www.ires.it> (accessed 17 December 2006)
<www.homeworkers.org> (accessed 17 December 2006)

Chapter 11

The Netherlands

A.T.J.M. Jacobs

I. INTRODUCTION

Telework is only slowly gaining ground in the Netherlands. In 1997 the number of teleworkers was estimated at less than one per cent of the working population. In 1999 it was estimated at 2.6 per cent (200,000 people).[1] Another survey of 1999, however, indicated that 8.3 per cent of the working population of the Netherlands performed telework as a primary way of working and another 6.3 per cent as a secondary way of working.[2] A survey in 2000 mentioned a percentage of 7.[3] So the size of telework in the Netherlands is not exactly known. It seems that much depends on the definition of telework. If any size of telework is taken into account, then already more than 40 per cent of the working population of the Netherlands may be performing telework!

A survey of 2002 indicated that approximately 43 per cent of the workers were keen to perform at least part of their work by way of telework.[4]

In 2003 a sharp increase in telework was predicted by TNO Labour thanks to technological developments, notably the introduction of cell phones with access to

---

1. De Volkskrant, 6 February 1999.
2. See *STAR-Recommendation on Telework* (The Hague, 2003), p. 6.
3. European Foundation for the Improvement of Living and Working Conditions, *Third European Survey on the Working Conditions* (Dublin, 2000), p. 19, fig. 3.
4. *STAR-Recommendation*, n. 2 above, p. 6.

Blanpain et al., European Framework, Agreements and Telework, pp. 191–204.
©2007, Kluwer Law International BV, The Netherlands.

internet.[5] In 2004 the research institute Ernst &Young predicted a sharp increase in telework in the information, communication and technology (ICT) sector. There the ratio of telework had already jumped from 10 per cent in 2002 to over 35 per cent in 2003.[6]

Research reveals further that in The Netherlands the main motives for telework are: undisturbed working, more efficient working and reduction of travel time.

Telework is indeed often seen as a way to reduce transport congestion and related problems, but again, it is uncertain to what extent this is effectuated. Privately conducted research in 2003 concluded that telework may lead to a better distribution of traffic over the hours of the day, but not to less use of cars and less miles driven.[7]

Another motive for telework is a better compatibility of work and family life obligations – many teleworkers are looking after their children while working at home.

In the Netherlands telework is also often seen as a useful way to help disabled workers obtain or maintain employment. The Dutch legislation (formally Wet REA, now Wet WIA) offers employers various subsidies to establish and adapt workplaces in order to encourage partly disabled workers to stay in/resume employment. These subsidies can also be used to create telework places for partly disabled employees. However, it is unknown to what extent this has been effectuated.

As well as the advantages, the disadvantages of teleworking are also often mentioned. Work site dispersion complicates team work and may contribute to social isolation of employees. Telework can intrude upon personal and family privacy. Employers often think that it may be difficult to direct or to monitor the employee's performance if he or she is not based on the employer's premises.

Quite remarkably, one of the pioneer employers to use large scale telework in The Netherlands (Otto Nederland, daughter of the German Otto group, a mail order business) stopped teleworking in 2003 because the returns did not counterbalance the costs. The reason given was changes in the employment legislation and the collective agreement that apparently had made telework more costly than work at a central office.[8]

However, the dominant opinion is that family friendly, flexible and fair work arrangements, including telecommuting, can benefit individual employees and their families, employers, and society as a whole.

Although in The Netherlands there are no statutes especially promoting telecommuting, the Dutch Government supports telework and telecommuting, but it is not very consequent in this respect. Initially, the acquisition of personnel

---

5. De Volkskrant, 7 January 2003.
6. Ernst & Young ICT Barometer, 'Thuiswerken Breekt in 2004 Definitief Door' <www.ey.nl> (accessed 18 December 2006).
7. Metro, 25 November 2003.
8. Brabants Dagblad, 19 February 2003.

computers and the installation of a teleworkplace have been encouraged by tax facilities,[9] but some of them have been cancelled now. Most zoning laws are interpreted favourably by the courts for telework,[10] but housing regulations still do not require newly built houses to contain the necessary ICT facilities for telework.

II.   THE LEGAL POSITION OF TELEWORKERS IN THE NETHERLANDS

The Netherlands does not have specific legislation as regards home-based work in general or telework in particular. There is only a special regulation for state civil servants, the Framework Decree on Telework (Besluit Raamregeling Telewerken) of 12 March 2001. However, a good deal of labour law and social security law in general may be applicable to telework.

The European framework agreement on telework contains a number of rights and obligations. Some of them are already clearly laid down in statutory employment law in The Netherlands. Other rights and obligations can be easily derived from general rules and court cases. Is there a case for saying that the European framework agreement on telework is already implemented by existing Dutch employment law, as it is laid down in statutes and case law?

A.   THE VOLUNTARY CHARACTER

Dutch labour lawyers[11] are convinced that under the general principles of the law of the employment contract, the employee cannot be obliged against his/her will to perform his/her duties by way of telework. It is uncertain, however, whether under Dutch law the employer can be required, against his/her will, to allow the employee to perform part or all of his/her duties by way of telework. In extreme cases the test will be 'reasonableness' (Article 7:611 Dutch Civil Code) as there are no specific statutory provisions in this respect. There is no case law in this area.

In theory indirect pressures to accept or to offer telework are contained in the Dutch legislation on unemployment insurance benefits (WW), disablement benefits (Wet WIA) and social assistance (WWB). For instance: whether an unemployment insurance benefit claim will be granted may turn on such considerations as whether a worker has adequate justification to decline available telework. Again, there is no case law in this area.

---

9. Art.11 (1), sub p and q; and Art.15 jo. Art.15b Wet op de Loonbelasting.
10. 'The possibility of telework is inherent in the notion of 'residence' and therefore allowed in all zones indicated as residential areas', ruled the Dutch Council of State, 3 April 2002, LJN: AE 0960, 200104569/1.
11. W.C.L. Zegveld a.o., *Handboek Telewerken* (Assen, 1995), pp. 118–119; F.J.L. Pennings, *Telework in the Netherlands, Labour Law, Social Security Law and Occupational Health and Safety Aspects* (Amsterdam, 1996), p. 23.

If telework is agreed between employer and employee this must, according to Article 7:655 Dutch Civil Code (implementing Directive 91/533/EC), be communicated in writing to the employee.

B.   EMPLOYMENT CONDITIONS

According to the general principles of Dutch labour law it seems self evident that teleworkers benefit from the same rights, guaranteed by applicable legislation and collective agreements, as comparable workers at the employer's premises. However, there are no specific statutory provisions in this respect and there is no case law.

C.   DATA PROTECTION

According to Dutch law, employer and employee have indeed a shared responsibility in complying with the rules on data protection, as described in the European framework agreement on telework (point 5). Some of these rules follow from the Act on the Protection of Personal Data (Wet Bescherming Persoonsgegevens) – others can be derived from the general principles of Dutch labour law. There is no case law.

D.   PRIVACY

According to Dutch law the employer must respect the privacy of every worker, therefore also of the teleworker. This principle is derived from Article 10 Dutch Constitution, and Article 8 ECHR (which is directly applicable in The Netherlands).[12] However, according to Dutch lawyers[13] and case law this respect for privacy is not absolute. By entering in an employment contract the worker gives up part of his/her privacy. The employer may have justifiable grounds for limiting the privacy of the worker. In case of conflict the courts must weigh the various interests at stake. There is no specific case law in the area regarding telework.

Of course management may use, by way of quantitative or qualitative checking facilities, the employee's computer equipment to monitor the work rate. However, this is subject to the provisions of the Act on the Protection of Personal Data and to health and safety provisions aiming to prevent stress by an over emphasis on output speed. Moreover, if the company has a works council, any

---

12. Dutch Supreme Court, 9 June 1987, NJ 1987, 928.
13. H.H. de Vries, *Juridische Aspecten van Huistelematica* (Deventer, 1993), pp. 99–102; Pennings, n. 11 above, p. 29; W.C.L Van der Grinten, Arbeidsovereenkomstenrecht (Deventer, 2002), p. 67.

kind of monitoring system may only be put into place after the consent of the works council (Article 27 Works Councils Act).

E. EQUIPMENT

Telework requires the equipment of a proper working place at home (desk, chair, computer with ISDN or ADSL connection, printer, etc.) which may cost at least 2000 Euro or more. It is assumed that employers requiring telework have to pay that. If the telework is solely due to the desire of the employee employers may refuse to compensate these costs, but in reality even in these cases the employer usually does pay.

It is uncertain whether Dutch law requires an employer to absorb fully or partly the costs of establishing, equipping and operating (heating, electricity, water and space usage) a home office. Dutch labour law has only a few general rules on the basis of which can be determined who is responsible for providing, installing and maintaining the equipment for telework and for compensating or covering its costs. Lawyers agree that on the basis of the general rules of labour law (Article 7:611 and 7:661 CC) the employer is in principle responsible for providing, installing and maintaining the equipment for telework and has to bear the costs of it. The worker can only exceptionally be charged with responsibilities and costs in this area (for example if he has wilfully abused or damaged the equipment (Article 7:611 and 7:661 CC).

Here lies one of the main needs for further specification of the European framework agreement on telework by way of collective agreements or individual employment contracts. Such specification is also due because Dutch tax laws offer special tax facilities for telework, taking into account the question of who is financing the teleworkplace.[14]

The only point which is very clear is about the health and safety aspects of the equipment of the workplace. The Health and Safety at Work Act contains some rules laying down the responsibility on the employer of providing protecting equipment, and he also has to bear the costs of it (see Article 44 Arbeidsomstandighedenwet).

F. HEALTH AND SAFETY

The Health and Safety at Work Act (Arbeidsomstandighedenwet 1998) applies to all telework performed by an employee. All employers are responsible for complying with this Act. Exceptions are made for work on the employee's home, for performing domestic household tasks, care and for the work of those who perform a

---

14. *See* Art.11 (1) (r) and 15b (1) (f) Wet op de Loonbelasting – see Court of Appeal Arnhem, 24 October 2002, LJN: AF 2700, 02/01739.

profession or deliver services to third parties.[15] Besides this exception, all employers who make use of telework – whatever the legal status of the teleworker – must comply with the general obligations of the Dutch Health and Safety at Work Act, such as workplace analysis and hazard prevention, information and training. This covers all the obligations contained in Directive 89/391/EEC and its relevant daughter directives. On the other hand, many secondary rules on health and safety laid down in the Health and Safety at Work Decree (Arbobesluit) are not applicable to telework, as the Arbobesluit says that its rules are only applicable to worksites in an employee's home, if that has been determined explicitly (Article 1.43 Arbobesluit). Such explicit determinations have been made notably for the rules on the use of dangerous materials, fire protection, lighting, cooling, heating and ventilation of the workplace, visual display units (in conformity with Directive 90/270/EEC), ergonomics and electric equipment.[16]

Dutch law does not contain any specific obligation on the employer to prevent the worker becoming isolated from the rest of the labour community in the enterprise.

A problem here is that the employer under Dutch law is not entitled to enter the home of the teleworker for inspection against the will of the employer.

In principle the Dutch Labour Inspectorate has the power to inspect the working place of the teleworker (Article 24 (3) Arbeidsomstandighedenwet). However, in reality the Dutch Labour Inspectorate respects the privacy of the home and has never systematically conducted inspections of teleworkplaces.

G. CIVIL RESPONSIBILITY FOR WORK ACCIDENTS AND OCCUPATIONAL ILLNESSES

The civil responsibility of the employer for work accidents and occupational illnesses of his/her employees (Article 7:658 Dutch Civil Code) may be weak in the case of telework as the Dutch Supreme Court has refused to extend this liability to damages deriving from accidents outside the employer's premises. However, the courts in these cases have pointed to the possibility that the employer may be liable for accidents outside the employer's premises, but linked to the fulfilment of the contractual obligation of the employee, not on the basis of Article 7:658 CC but on the basis of Article 7:611 CC (bona fides).[17] It seems evident to me that employers are responsible in home worksites for hazards caused by materials, equipment or work processes which the employer provides or requires to be used in an employee's home, but there is as yet no case law in this field.

---

15. *See* Art.1, lid 2, Arbowet 1998, jo. Art.1, lid 2; H. de Vries, *Thuiswerkers Onder de Arbowet* (Den Haag, 1998).
16. Art.1.44 to 1.46, 4.110 to 4.115, 5.14 and 5.15, 6.30, 7.40 to 7.42 and Art.8.15, Arbobesluit.
17. E.H. de Joode, 'De Virtuele Werkplek' (Arbeidsrecht 2001/6-7), p. 17.

H.   ORGANIZATION OF WORK

The Dutch Working Time Act (Arbeidstijdenwet) is applicable to teleworkers with a genuine employment contract (or civil servants' nomination). The reality, however, is different. A teleworker organizes the work him/herself without taking into account the working time schedules in the law and in the enterprise. It is hard to see how this can be disciplined by an employer. In this context it is also difficult to keep track of possible overtime work. Again, there is no case law in this area.
     Dutch law does not contain any rules on workload and performance standards.

I.   TRAINING

There are no specific provisions in Dutch law about training. All Dutch lawyers will agree that according to general principles of labour law, teleworkers are entitled to the same rights to training as comparable workers at the employer's premises. However, there is no case law in this area.

J.   COLLECTIVE RIGHTS

There are only a few dispositions in Dutch law protecting the rights of employees to organize for the purpose of collective representation. Most violations of such rights may be challenged in court on the basis of provisions in international labour law.[18] Dutch lawyers will agree that this protection is equally available for teleworkers. Of course the efforts to organize employees or to effectuate collective labour rights are complicated by the lack of or reduced opportunities for face-to-face contact at or near the employment establishment. There is no case law in this area.
     Some Dutch lawyers doubt whether full-time teleworkers are entitled to fully participate in the Dutch system of works councils. There is, however, no case law supporting these doubts and to my view they are not justified.
     For the inclusion into the works council system it is, however, relevant whether from the perspective of an employment contract the teleworker is an employee in a strict sense or self employed.[19]
     Teleworkers, as far as they are working on a formal contract of employment, *must* be involved in the functioning of the works councils system. Teleworkers not working on a formal contract of employment *may* be involved (Article 6(4) Works Councils Act).
     The last lines bring us to the very important question of the legal nature of telework.

---

18. See on this Antoine T.J.M. Jacobs, *Labour Law in The Netherlands* (Deventer, 2004), pp. 131–132.
19. Pennings, n. 11 above, p. 94; De Vries, n. 13 above, p. 5.

III.   THE LEGAL NATURE OF TELEWORK

All the aforementioned rights can be invoked when the teleworker is working on a genuine contract of employment. However, telework may also be performed by self-employed persons.

The European framework agreement on telework deals with telework 'in the context of an employment contract/relationship (point 2)'. The word 'relationship' notably refers to civil servants (who therefore are also covered by the European Agreement). However, it seems evident that the European Agreement does not cover telework in self-employment.[20]

The problem here, of course, is that it may be unclear whether the teleworker is working on an employment contract or as a self-employed person, or that there is a situation of quasi-self-employment. Like in all countries employers sometimes attempt to evade employee protective statutes by asserting that the teleworker's enhanced independence transforms the relationship from employment to independent contractor, a relationship with less statutory protection.

How is this problem dealt with under Dutch law?

There is as yet no judgment of the Dutch Supreme Court on the legal nature of telework. However, judgments of the Dutch Supreme Court in other types of home-based work[21] indicate that home-based work may or may not be performed as a formal contract of employment. Whether it is a formal contract of employment should be judged for each contract taken apart. Notably the criterion of 'subordination'/'authority' is crucial.[22]

Thus, the reality is that under Dutch law much telework is performed in the nature of a genuine contract of employment, but at the same time much telework is also performed outside the nature of a contract of employment.

This reality makes the legal position of teleworkers in the Netherlands very uncertain, as many parts of labour law and social security law are only applicable to teleworkers when there is a genuine contract of employment.

So, for example, the provisions of the Civil Code on holidays with pay (Article 7:634, etc.), on the transfer of enterprises (Article 7:661, etc.), and on dismissal (Article 7:667, etc.) are only applicable on contracts of employment in the formal sense.

This uncertainty is partially remedied by a number of legal tools.

Firstly, since 1999 there is a provision in the Dutch Civil Code which provides that any person who for the benefit of another person performs work for remuneration by such other person for three consecutive months weekly or for not less than 20 hours per month is presumed to perform such work pursuant to a contract of employment (Article 7:610a CC).

---

20. See S. Clauwaert & O. Deinert, *A New Milestone in the EU Social Dialogue, the Telework Agreement – Its Interpretation and Implementation* (European Union Yearbook 2002, ETUI 2003), p. 42.
21. Dutch Supreme Court, 17 November 1978, NJ 1979, 140; Dutch Supreme Court, 16 October 1981, NJ 1982, 123; Dutch Supreme Court, 5 November 1982, NJ 1983, 231.
22. *See* Jacobs, n. 18 above, pp. 45–47/50–51.

Secondly, since 2001 self-employed workers without personnel can obtain from the social security authorities a declaration that they are not subject to social security schemes for workers.

Finally, it should be recalled that not all labour laws and social security laws are narrowly confined to persons working on a genuine contract of employment. A number of labour and social security laws have a somewhat wider scope and may cover a peripheral group of workers not working on a genuine contract of employment, but considered as equally in need of protection.

It should also be noted that the scope of a number of Dutch labour laws has been extended beyond the narrow definition of a genuine contract of employment. Such statutes therefore are not only covering telework performed on the basis of a contract of employment, but also telework performed on some other legal basis.

- Various provisions prohibiting discrimination and unequal treatment in labour conditions are covering all discrimination in offices, occupation and trade and therefore protect the teleworkers, irrespective of their legal status, be it either employer or self employed.
- The civil responsibility for work accidents and occupational illnesses (Article 7:655 Dutch Civil Code) is not limited to employees working on a genuine employment contract, but is extended to all persons who are performing work for a business.
- The Compatibility of Labour and Care Act (Wet Arbeid en Zorg) which entitles leave and payments in cases of maternity, parenthood, adoption, etc. is also applicable to a number of self-employed teleworkers, which are put on a par with teleworkers working on a genuine contract of employment.
- Article 7:655 Dutch Civil Code (containing the obligation to provide the employee with a written statement about his employment conditions) also applies to contracts under which one party, being a natural person, undertakes to perform work for the other party for remuneration, unless this contract is entered into in the conduct of a profession or business.
- The Dutch Extra Ordinary Decree on Labour Relations (requiring that an employer needs a permit for every dismissal and for every reduction in working hours with corresponding wage reduction) is also applicable for a teleworker who is not working on a formal contract of employment, if he/she is working for two principals at most, is assisted by two persons at most, performs the work personally, has engaged him/herself to perform the work for at least 30 days, while the telework is for him/her more that just a sideline, unless this contract is entered into in the conduct of a profession or business.
- The Dutch legislation on minimum wages and minimum holiday allowances is also applicable to a teleworker who is not working on a formal contract of employment, if he/she works for two principals at most, is assisted by no others than family members, performs the work personally, has engaged him/herself to perform the work for at least three months, the period between two charges being less than 31 days and telework being performed during at least five hours, unless this contract is entered into in the conduct of a profession or business.

- All teleworkers, irrespective of their legal status, are covered by the statutory social security schemes embracing the entire population: the Old Age Pension's Act (AOW), Survivors benefits Act (ANW) and Child benefits Act (AKW).[23]

The statutory social security schemes for employees are also applicable to a teleworker not working on a formal contract of employment, if he/she works for two principals at most, is assisted by two family members at most, performs the work personally, earns with the telework at least 40 per cent of the statutory minimum wage, and has engaged him/herself to perform the work for at least 30 days, unless this contract is entered into in the conduct of a profession or business.

Authors and editorial staff are excluded,[24] as are teleworkers who work for their own limited company.[25]

The effectuation of these rules is sometimes problematic and may give cause to fraud. Cases have been discovered by the social fraud inspectorate in which the employers had registered some persons as independent home workers and thus had not paid taxes and social security contributions, while in reality such workers were performing work on the premises of the company.[26]

IV. THE IMPLEMENTATION OF THE FRAMEWORK AGREEMENT IN THE NETHERLANDS

The European framework agreement on telework has been translated into the Dutch language by the Stichting van de Arbeid (STAR, the Foundation of Labour, a bipartite forum embracing the representatives of all the major confederations of trade unions and employers' associations in The Netherlands).

Subsequently these representatives have, within the framework of the STAR, negotiated on the implementation of the European framework agreement in The Netherlands. This negotiation resulted on 11 September 2003 in a formal recommendation of the STAR on telework. The STAR published this recommendation on its website.[27]

The contents of the STAR recommendation are rather poor.

After having called attention to the creation of the European framework agreement on telework and its 'voluntary' character (which means that the Agreement must be implemented by the affiliated members of the signatory parties), the STAR recommendation says:

> Against this background the STAR brings the European Framework Agreement on Telework to the notice of the enterprises and sectors of industry and adds to it some suggestions for implementation.

---

23. The only problem here may result form telework performed outside the Netherlands.
24. Beschikking van 23 December 1986, Stcrt. 1986, 251.
25. *See* Art.6 (1) (d) ZW/WAO/WW.
26. NRC, 2 December 2003.
27. *See* <www.stichtingvandearbeid.nl> (accessed 19 December 2006).

11. The Netherlands

The STAR aims with this Recommendation to stimulate teleworking in such a way that it strengthens the knowledge economy, modernises the organisation of labour, increases the quality of work and enlarges the chances on the labour market.

Finally, the STAR recalls that the members of the parties which have signed the European framework agreement have bound themselves to implement the agreement before 16 July 2005. 'The framework-agreement will be elaborated at different levels: in collective agreements, in arrangements with the works council and or in individual telework arrangements'.

The STAR says in its recommendation that arrangements in collective agreements or in co-operation with the works council may embrace the following aspects:

- The definition of telework;
- The voluntary character of telework;
- The equality of the working conditions with comparable employees;
- The use and the compensation for equipment;
- Training and career perspectives.

However, in reading the European framework agreement critically one discovers other aspects, such as privacy, health and safety, data protection and the organization of work. Does it mean that for these aspects, as well as other aspects like working hours, attainability, information and instruction, contact possibilities, assessment and coaching, STAR recommends putting detailed arrangements in the individual employment contracts?

Then the STAR in Annex 1 gives a number of examples of existing provisions in collective agreements dealing with telework. If one considers these provisions it becomes clear that they are only rather summary provisions. They do not cover all the various aspects mentioned in the European framework agreement.

In Annex 2 of the STAR recommendation reference is made to some existing statutes in relation to telework, notably the Health and Safety at Work Act (Arbeidsomstandighedenwet), the Act on the reintegration of disabled workers, and the Act on Data Protection. Moreover, the various facilities for telework in Dutch tax law are mentioned.

The drafting of the STAR recommendation was not an easy affair. A working party of the STAR, set up to implement the European framework agreement on telework, could not reach an agreement, because its trade union members wanted to adapt the European framework agreement to the situation in The Netherlands, which did not please the employers' members of the working party. They were only prepared to communicate the framework agreement to the bargaining parties at enterprise and sectoral level in the most neutral and meagre way.

Which indeed had been the outcome of one year of deliberations in the STAR.

The STAR recommendation in fact does hardly anything more than communicating the text of the European framework agreement under addition of some 'suggestions for implementation'. These last words indicate that the STAR holds the opinion that it has not itself implemented the European framework agreement on telework.

The main Dutch trade unions' confederation, FNV, has also itself communicated the STAR recommendation to its affiliated members. It also included a paragraph on telework in its Collective Bargaining Manual 2006, destined to its affiliated members. The minority trade union, De Unie, (strong under white collar workers) has communicated the European Agreement and the STAR recommendations to all its negotiators in an 'advisory letter'.

One will be curious to know to what extent and in what way the European framework agreement on telework and the STAR recommendation have been implemented by collective agreements and arrangements with the works councils.

Regrettably there are no representative research results in this field.

The FNV has not effectuated an evaluation of the way and the degree in which the STAR recommendation has been effectuated in practice. Nor has the official Dutch Labour Inspectorate effectuated such an evaluation.

From a quick scan on digitalized collective agreements, the author of this contribution has learned that there are meanwhile more collective agreements with provisions on telework than a few years ago. New texts can be found in the company collective agreements with KPN, Fortis, CWI and Arbo Unie and in the sectoral collective agreements for higher education and universities, research institutes, educational services, energy and water suppliers, distribution and cable services, youth care and medical insurances.

In theory collective agreements can play a good role as regards telework, because the Dutch law on collective agreements does not limit the binding force of collective agreements to formal contracts of employment. They may also deal with the carrying out of particular jobs and agreements for the performance of services (Article 1(2) Act of Collective Agreements).

In practice, however, not many collective agreements do play such a role.

A number of companies and institutions have personnel agreement manuals which contain regulations for telework: standing orders as well as a model for an individual telework contract of employment.

The introduction of telework can be seen as an important change in the organization of work and is therefore subject to information and consultation of the works council (Article 25 Dutch Works Councils Act). The works council has the power to appeal such managerial decisions by the court of Amsterdam (Article 26 Works Councils Act). Any policy regulations of the employer on the organization of telework must have the consent of the works council if they were not already laid down in collective agreements with the unions. In case of no consent there is mediation foreseen and a decision by the courts (Article 27 Works Council Act).[28]

So, in theory, in the Netherlands like in Germany, the works council may be a key player in the context of telework.

---

28. For this mechanism see Antoine T.J.M. Jacobs, *Labour Law in The Netherlands* (Deventer, 2004, pp. 180–185).

There is, however, no research available to confirm to what extent works councils in The Netherlands in practice are performing this function. Like in Germany it should be recalled that most small and medium sized enterprises do not have a (well-functioning) works council.

In the Netherlands the binding force of STAR recommendations is dubious.[29] There will be no sanctions on the parties to collective bargaining on inferior level if they do not follow a STAR recommendation.

It should be recalled that the Dutch Government, in the context of the ratification of ILO-Convention 177 on home work, has declared that its intention is to follow closely the developments on home work, e.g. to watch the development of telework, and to launch further research or policy initiatives.[30]

However, there is at the moment no public or political debate on the fact that the European framework agreement on telework has been carried out so poorly. So it is not to be expected that the Dutch legislator will intervene to implement the European framework agreement.

The question remains whether the European framework agreement on telework and the STAR recommendation can have a direct effect on individual employment contracts.

In this respect the situation in The Netherlands may be more promising than in other countries. Dutch courts are generally prepared to give a wide interpretation to the notion of bona fides contained in the Dutch Civil Code. It provides that the employer has to behave as a 'good employer' (Article 7:611 Dutch Civil Code). This article can be used to give effect to the protections offered in the European framework agreement on telework.[31] Also, other articles in the Dutch Civil Code which offer a certain margin of interpretations for the courts, such as the provisions on dismissals (Articles 7:681 and 7:685 Dutch Civil Code), make it possible that the European framework agreement on telework and the STAR recommendation can have a direct effect on the contract of employment when it comes to court decisions.

However, up until now there is no case law confirming this.

V.   CONCLUSIONS

The Dutch legislator has done nothing to customize employment standards and benefits to the unique characteristics of telework. Courts and administrative agencies have up until now only been seldom faced with specific issues of

---

29. *See* M.A.C. de Wit, *Het Goed Werkgeverschap als Intermediair van Normen in het Arbeidsrecht* (Deventer, 1999), pp. 95–113; A.H. van Heertum-Lemmen and A.C.J.M. Wilthagen, *De Doorwerking van Aanbevelingen van de Stichting van de Arbeid* (Sinzheimer Cahiers, No. 12, Den Haag, 1996), p. 33.
30. Parliamentary Papers 2001–2002, 28 436, Nos.390 and 1, pp. 7–8.
31. M.A.C. de Wit, n. 29 above, pp. 99 and 100.

telework. The legal aspects of telework have scarcely been researched in The Netherlands.[32]

As the European framework agreement on telework contains many norms which sound very plausible, but which have not been laid down in Dutch law equivocally, this Agreement can be considered as a welcome addition to Dutch labour law.

Therefore it is regrettable that in The Netherlands the European framework agreement on telework has been implemented so poorly. It is submitted that the best way to implement the European framework agreement on telework would have been the conclusion of an all-industry collective agreement, adapting the norms of the European Agreement to the domestic situation, as has happened in Belgium with the Collective Agreement No. 85, concluded in the National Labour Council on 9 November 2005 (see Chapter 6).

Having failed to do that the text of the European framework agreement on telework has only obtained a weak knowledge in The Netherlands, even if it is probable that in court cases the European Agreement may produce direct effect. However, because of the weak knowledge of the European Agreement, not many people will be aware of that.

Finally, the question should be raised whether a correct implementation of the European framework agreement on telework could be counterproductive for Dutch teleworkers. Is it not to be feared that in that case employers would be enticed to refrain from using telework in subordination and to only demand telework done by self-employed persons, for which it is much more doubtful whether they are covered by the norms of the European Agreement? And is it not to be feared that employers could be enticed to only demand telework from workers outside the EC and therefore not covered by the European framework agreement.[33] In The Netherlands these possibilities have never been researched.

---

32. H.H. de Vries, n. 13 above; Penning, n. 11 above; H. de Vries and T. Weijers, *Zicht op Tele-werken* (Den Haag, 1998); J.W. Broekema and J. Karreman, *Telwerkwijzer: Het Wat en Hoe van Telewerken* (Deventer, 2001); W. Eveleens & C. Stephan, *Telewerken* (2003).

33. The status under international private law of the various norms in telework contracts with an international aspect have never been tested in Dutch case law.

Chapter 12

Poland

Andrzej Swiatkowski

I. INTRODUCTION

As part of the European employment strategy, the European Council invited the
social partners to negotiate normative agreements modernizing the processes
related to human resources management and enabling greater flexibility of
working arrangements. On 16 July 2002 the European social partners[1] concluded
a voluntary agreement setting forth basic employment conditions with regard
to telework. It is estimated by the European Commission that there are currently
10 million teleworkers in the EU Member States. Approximately 4.5 million of
them are employed under employment contracts. According to the European social
partners – signatories of the voluntary agreement of 22 June 2002 – telework, as a
new form of employment, helps to reduce costs of employment, increase
efficiency, and successfully combine two key components of a contractual employment: flexibility of working arrangements and social security. The European social
partners perceive telework as an opportunity for professionally active people to
reconcile their career commitments with family obligations.

---

1. European Trade Union Confederation (ETUC); the Council of European Professional and Managerial Staff (EUROCADRES)/European Confederation of Executives and Managerial Staff (CEC);
   Union of Industrial and Employers' Confederations of Europe (BUSINESSEUROPE)/European
   Association of Craft, Small and Medium-Sized Enterprises (UEAPME); European Centre of Enterprises with Public Participation and of Enterprises of General Economic Interest (CEEP).

Blanpain et al., European Framework, Agreements and Telework, pp. 205–216.
©2007, Kluwer Law International BV, The Netherlands.

II.   TELEWORK AND THE POLISH LABOUR CODE

The Polish Labour Code does not provide any legal definition of telework. In publications dealing with labour law, telework is treated as one of the atypical forms of employment.[2] The discrimination between typical and atypical forms of employment, based on a dichotomic criterion, is quite distinctive. The baseline for this discrimination is one type of employment contract – a full-time employment contract for an unspecified period. Such discrimination between types of employment contracts does not admit precise distinguishing of employment contracts categorized as atypical. This is so because this group comprises all limited time employment contracts and part-time unspecified time employment contracts. The mere fact that telework has been categorized as an atypical form of employment does not allow for highlighting the unique features of this form of employment.[3] One of the basic features of telework is the impossibility of direct supervision and control over employees by the employer. A person performing telework communicates with the employer via electronic means of communication. This, however, is not unique to telework. Employees working in the employer's premises also, on a regular basis, communicate with the use of high technology solutions (e-mail, the internet, mobile phones). The definitions of telework, which focus on the form of organization and/or performing work with the use of high technology for communication purposes, do not get to the heart of the matter. Equally unsuccessful in capturing the essence of telework have been attempts to demonstrate that one of the characteristics distinguishing telework from other forms of employment is the right of a teleworker to choose their place of work. Authors engaging in the discussion on telework point out that telework may be performed at home or in other places.[4] Hence, a characteristic feature of telework is the consent of the employer to perform work outside the employer's premises. Telework may be performed at home (home-based teleworking), in a centre equipped with high-tech means of communication (telecottages), or in any other place chosen by a teleworker. Telework does not have to be performed in one place – it may involve movement from one place to another (nomadic teleworking). As I see it, the most characteristic feature of telework is the combination of the means of communication used by a teleworker with the right to choose the place of work. Telework is performed in the most convenient place. The choice of such a place is made jointly by a teleworker and by the employer.

---

2. L. Mitrus, 'Telepraca Jako Nowa Forma Zatrudnienia' ('Telework as New Form of Employment') (2001) Vol.3 *Transformacje Prawa Prywatnego* (*Transformation of Private Law*), 10 *et seq.*
3. D. Ksiazek, 'Telepraca' ('Telework') (2004) No. 7 *Praca i Zabezpieczenie Społeczne* (*Labour and Social Security*), 8 *et seq.*
4. R. Blanpain, 'Legal and Contractual Situation of Teleworkers in the Member States of European Union. Labor law Aspects including Self-employment' in *The Jagiellonian University Yearbook of Labour Law and Social Policy*, A. Świątkowski (ed.) (Vol.10, Cracow, 1998/1999, p. 46); R. Depta, 'Teleworking Jako Alternatywna Forma Pracy w Przyszłości' ('Telework as Alternative Employment in the Future') (1998) No. 4 *Praca i Zabezpieczenie Społeczne* (*Labour and Social Security*), 9; L. Mitrus, n. 2 above, pp. 11–12.

12. Poland

Article 22, section 1 and 2 of the Labour Code, states that the situation where an employee undertakes to perform personally specific work for the employer and under the employer's supervision, in the place and time specified by the employer, in return for remuneration, is an instance of contractual employment, regardless of the name of the contract concluded.[5] The same type of work may be performed under an employment contract or any type of civil law contract. Due to the specific nature of telework, the entity for which telework is performed is unable to use traditional means of supervision in order to check whether the work is performed personally by the employee concerned. The personal risk of the employer, who is liable for actions and negligence of the employees, does not admit the employee engaging any third parties to perform the work. In the case of teleworking, an employee obliged to perform the work personally, technically speaking, has virtually unlimited possibility to subcontract the performance of the work to another party who is not bound by any contractual employment to the employer for whom the teleworker should perform the work personally. In the event of loss suffered by a third party, the teleworker's employer is liable towards the injured party for having employed an unsuitable employee – a person responsible for the damage caused during the performance of the work (Article 120, section 1 of the Labour Code). The employer is not liable for any damage caused by another party engaged by the teleworker to perform the work. The actual possibility of engaging a third party by a teleworker to perform the work that the teleworker should perform personally is blurring the borderline between an employee and a person conducting a business activity or providing services on their own (self employed) in telework, which is very different from a traditional form of employment. A teleworker engaging third parties to perform the duties specified in their employment contract ceases to be an employee in the meaning of Article 2 of the Labour Code and becomes an employer employing another employee.

Decisive for the purpose of distinguishing employment under an employment contract from the employment under any other civil law contract are the requirements set forth in Article 22, section 1 of the Labour Code. The provision does not, however, lay out the employment conditions. It only governs legal consequences of establishing a legal relationship under which:

> An employee undertakes to perform a specific work for the employer, under the employer's supervision, and in place and time specified by the employer, whereas the employer undertakes to employ the employee in return for remuneration.

The legal relationship established under such a contract, regardless of its name, if any, is considered by the Polish legislator a contractual employment (Article 22, section 2 of the Labour Code). The problem is that section 1 of Article 22 of the Labour Code refers to the employment conditions, whilst in section 2 of Article 22 of the Labour Code the legislator uses the term 'employment

---

5. A. M. Świątkowski, *Polskie Prawo Pracy* (*Polish Labour Law*) (Warsaw, Wydawnictwo Praw-nicze, LexisNexis, 2003), p. 25 *et seq.*

upon conditions specified in section 1'. In the Polish language, the statutory term 'employment' has two meanings. It refers either to the process of work or to the place of work.[6] Both meanings are crucial in the analysis of the legal status of telework. As a result of granting a teleworker engaged under an employment contract the right to employ a third party, the said contract named 'employment contract' loses the characteristic qualities of an employment contract and becomes a civil law contract under civil law. A contract for performing telework may not contain any provisions obliging a teleworker to perform the work personally. In this case, consequent upon discovery by the employer that a teleworker engages a third party to perform the work, there is a different assessment of the legal status of the contract. Although the parties to such a contract have originally agreed that a teleworker employed under the employment contract falling within the scope of labour law regulations enjoys the status of an employee in the meaning of Article 2 of the Labour Code, as a result of the fact that the teleworker has engaged a third party to perform the work under the said contract, the employment is not compliant with the requirements laid down in Article 22, section 1 of the Labour Code and, thus, cannot be considered a contractual employment, although the legal basis for such employment is a contract referred to by the parties as the employment contract. The above conclusion is drawn from an *'a contrario'* interpretation of Article 22, section 1 and 2 of the Labour Code.

Quite different is the situation of a teleworker engaged under an employment contract which contains the provisions obliging the teleworker to perform the work personally. The breach of this obligation entitles the employer to terminate the employment contract without notice, pursuant to Article 52, section 1, Part 1 of the Labour Code. Yet it does not deprive the contract of the qualities characteristic for employment contracts.

The place where the work is performed is treated by the Polish legislator as *essentialia negotii* of an employment contract (Article 29, section 1, Part 2 of the Labour Code). The parties are obliged to determine the place of work. A failure to fulfil this obligation results in the presupposition that the work is performed on the employer's premises. The parties enjoy full freedom of selection of the place of work. It may be one permanent place of work, or it may change. The changeability of the place of work may be consequent upon its nature (specificity).[7] Telework is the perfect illustration of an argument concerning the freedom of choice of the place of work enjoyed by the parties to an employment contract. Because of information, communication and technology (ICT) development, there are no global constraints for setting zones defined in terms of administrative units (countries, continents) in determining the place of work. In the case of telework, the place of work is chosen taking into account the specificity of work and the preferences of the parties. There are no reasons to introduce any restrictions with

---

6. S. Skorupka, H. Auderska, Z. Lempicka (eds), *Maly Slownik Języka Polskiego* (*Polish Language Dictionary*) (PWN, Warsaw, 1968), p. 987.
7. A. M. Swiatkowski, *Kodeks Pracy* (*Labour Code*), Vol.I: *Commentary to Article 1–189*, C. H. Beck (Warsaw, 2004), p. 184.

respect to the choice of the place of work, but technical (concerning the possibility of communication) and logistic (concerning time differences around the world) ones. The already quoted provision of Article 22, section 1 of the Labour Code states that the work should be performed in a place specified by the employer. The employer concluding an employment contract with a teleworker is in no way bound by any restrictions as to the place of work. In extreme cases the employer may agree with a teleworker that the place of work will be the globe. The method for specifying the place of work depends on the type of work to be performed under the relevant employment contract. The work which does not require the employee's presence in a specific time and place or the employee's co-operation with other employees does not have to be performed within the employer's premises. The labour law had been originally designed as factory law providing a legal framework for the performance of team work (co-operative work) by employees working in one place (employer's premises) and in one time (time of work) under the management of the employer (work under supervision).[8] New technologies and means of telecommunication admit performing work without direct contact with supervisors and other employees. The employer may, thus, permit teleworkers to perform the work in the place most convenient for them.

Article 22, section 1 of the Labour Code says that the place of work is chosen by the employer. In the case of telework, the employer supervises the choice of workplace because the employer has an exclusive right to choose the place of work for a teleworker. The scope of supervision exercised by the employer as regards the workplace of a teleworker depends on how this place of work has been specified in the employment contract. If the parties to the employment contract agree that a teleworker will perform the work in a particular room within their own house, apartment or telecommunication centre, the moving of a computer to another room in the same building would require the consent of the employer to the change of workplace. On the other hand, if the parties define the place of work as a geographical area (town, municipality, district, region, country, continent, or even the globe); a teleworker is free to move within the specified area without the need to negotiate with the employer the consent to the change of workplace. In Poland, work outside the employer's premises has been performed by persons working under a home work contract. In such instances, the work is usually done at home. There is no legal definition of outwork provided in the Labour Code. It only authorizes the Council of Ministers to specify the scope of application of the labour law provisions with respect to outwork (Article 302 of the Labour Code). An outwork services contract is not a contract governed by labour law provisions. Similarly, neither a person providing outwork services nor a person or an institution financing such outwork are the parties to a contractual employment. A person providing outwork services is not obliged to perform the work personally, nor is he/she subordinated to the entity or person commissioning the work. Such people work at their own risk. Their remuneration depends on the effects of work. They are

---

8. A. M. Świątkowski, 'Indywidualne Prawo Pracy' ('Individual Labour Law') [2001] *Infotrade*, Gdańsk-Kraków, s. 18 i nast.

free to choose the place of work. The government ordinance of 31 December 1975 on facilitating the conditions of work for persons providing outwork services[9] requires the parties to the contract to define the minimum monthly work volume to be done by the commissioned party. From the legal perspective, a commissioned party cannot be considered an employee and the commissioning party cannot be considered an employer.[10] A commissioned party enjoys social and employee rights inasmuch as they are granted in the above mentioned government ordinance. The resemblance between the actual situation of a teleworker and an outworker stems exclusively from the fact that in both cases the work is done outside the employer's premises or outside the place of work indicated by the employer, and is true only in the event that a teleworker works at home. Hence, the legal situation of a teleworker and an outworker cannot be compared.

The employer is entitled to specify – within the statutory daily and weekly working time limits – the working hours of an employee (Article 22, section 1 of the Labour Code). The time and place of work are key elements of any employment contract (Article 29, section 1, Clause 4 of the Labour Code). Employees may be engaged under full-time (eight hours a day, on average 40 hours a week in an average five-day working week – Article 129 of the Labour Code) or part-time employment (fewer working hours than basic daily and weekly limits set forth in Article 129, section of the Labour Code). The schedule is to be determined by the employer. In the case of telework, the employer indicates the working hours which have to be in compliance with the requirements set forth in Part VI of the Labour Code. The employer is obliged to pay a teleworker for overtime and for working at night, as well as to grant a teleworker additional days off for working on Sundays and holidays. Telework justifies the implementation of a task-based working time system. Article 140 of the Labour Code allows for the implementation of a task-based working time system upon agreement with the employer. In the case of telework, due to the character and the place of work, the task-based working time system is justified because the employer is unable to supervise the employer and the work. While implementing a task-based working time system the employer has to assign a teleworker tasks which can be reasonably performed if working, with average efficiency, the statutory eight hours a day and 40 hours a week.[11] If the daily and weekly working time limits are exceeded by a teleworker engaged under a task-based working time system, the teleworker is entitled to claim extra pay for overtime (Article 151, section 1 of the Labour Code). The employer engaging teleworkers is obliged to keep individual working time records for each teleworker – subject to the same requirements as in the case of other employees, working in the employer's premises – where all details concerning working time are entered (the number of hours worked each day, including working Sundays and

---

9. OJ No. 3, 1976, Item 19 as amended.
10. A. M. Świątkowski, *Kodeks Pracy* (*Labour Code*), Vol.II: *Commentary to Articles 190–305*, C. H. Beck (Warsaw, 2004), p. 813.
11. D. Bielecka, 'System Zadaniowego Czasu Pracy' ('Organisation of Work Based on Results') [2005] No. 6 *Monitor Prawa Pracy* (*Labour Law Monitor*), 149 *et seq.*

holidays, overtime and at night, as well as days off resulting from the working time schedule in an average five-day working week).[12] In principle, keeping working time records consists of an employee completing individual working time sheets, an average of eight working hours a day. Teleworkers working overtime, on statutory holidays, on their days off resulting from their working time schedules, or at night, are obliged to keep their own working time records. A precondition for receiving extra pay for overtime is the supervision exercised by the employer over the employee's working hours. In the case of telework, the fulfilment of this obligation is difficult or even impossible. In the event that employees work outside the employer's premises on a regular basis and, thus, cannot be supervised by the employer, Article 151, section 5 of the Labour Code allows the parties to conclude an agreement under which extra pay for overtime will be replaced with a regular fixed allowance. Such a fixed allowance for working overtime cannot considerably differ from extra pay for overtime calculated subject to the statutory provisions: 100 per cent of normal pay for working overtime at night, on Sundays and holidays which are not working days subject to the relevant working time schedule of a given employee as well as for working on the days off granted in return for working on Sundays and holidays; 50 per cent of normal pay for working overtime on other days (Article 151, section 1 of the Labour Code). When a fixed allowance for working overtime is agreed upon, the employer is exempt from the obligation to keep working time records, if accurate control of overtime hours worked is particularly difficult.

For working at least three hours a day between 21.00 and 7.00, i.e. at night, an employee is entitled to extra pay (20 per cent of hourly rate calculated on the basis of the statutory minimum pay – Article 151, section 1 of the Labour Code). If an employee working at night performs particularly dangerous jobs, or jobs requiring exceptional physical or mental effort, the working time at night cannot exceed eight hours per day (Article 151, section 3 of the Labour Code). Whether a job is done at night or not is decided on the basis of local time. In the event that the indicated place of work is located on another continent, the working hours specified for a teleworker employed under a contractual employment in the time zone applicable to the employer's premises should be such that the teleworker is not forced to work at night, according to the time zone applicable to the teleworker's place of work.

The employer supervises the employee and has the right – within the scope of work specified in the relevant employment contract – to give the employee orders concerning the manner in which the work is to be performed. The employer may also occasionally order the employee to perform some work outside the place of work specified in the employment contract. An employee who is ordered by the employer to work in a town/city/village other than the one specified in the employment contract is entitled to a daily business trip allowance (Article 77, section 1 of

---

12. Sec. 8, para.1 of the ordinance of the Minister of Labour and Social Policy on the scope of records kept by employers concerning matters related to contractual employment and on the method for keeping employees' personal records of 28 May 1996: OJ No. 62, Item 286 as amended.

the Labour Code).[13] The type and amount of allowance paid to employees engaged in undertakings categorized as state-owned entities or budgetary units managed by local authorities are governed by two Ordinances of the Minister of Labour and Social Policy of 19 December 2002. One of them specifies the amount and requirements for calculation of domestic allowances,[14] the other of foreign business trip allowances.[15] The entitlement to these allowances depends on how the teleworker's workplace is defined. If a particular city/town/village is indicated as the teleworker's workplace, the employer is obliged to pay the business trip allowance every time the teleworker has to travel to a place other than the place of work specified in the employment contract. Thus, the scope of entitlement of a teleworker to business trip allowances and of the obligation of the employer to pay them is defined in terms of administrative borders.

Modern means of telecommunication do not limit the employer's ability to give orders to teleworkers. It is rather unlikely that telework which does not admit everyday direct contact of the employer with an employee in any way reduces the supervisory powers of the manager. An opinion quite common in the literature dealing with labour law that supervisory powers can only be exercised via direct shaping of the working process by means orders[16] is rather outdated. In the case of telework the employer is able to interfere in a teleworker's working process. I disagree with the authors claiming that in the case of telework, the scope of supervisory powers over an employee is limited to assigning tasks and assessing the results.[17] Neither the nature of telework, nor the contract concluded with a teleworker, justifies the conclusion that the difference between the employment under a contract for telework services and the employment under any other typical employment contract is that a teleworker undertakes to achieve the objectives set forth by the employer and not – as is the case with the employment under other employment contracts – to act with due diligence in performing the work.

In the examples discussed so far, falling under the provisions of individual labour law, there are practically no differences in the legal situation of employees and teleworkers. Teleworkers enjoy the same social and employee rights as any other employees. The employer has to respect a teleworker's personal dignity. Hence, the employer is not allowed to use electronic devices deployed by the teleworker to monitor the teleworker during his/her time off. Furthermore, the employer has to inform a teleworker that he/she might be monitored during working hours.[18]

---

13. A. Sobczyk, 'Podróż Służbowa' ('Service Trip') [2005] No. 8 *Monitor Prawa Pracy* (*Labour Law Monitor*), 207 *et seq*.
14. OJ No. 236, Item 1990 as amended.
15. OJ No. 236, Item 1991 as amended.
16. H. Lewandowski, *Uprawnienia Kierownicze w Umownym Stosunku Pracy* (*Managerial Rights in Employment Relationship*) (Wyd. Prawnicze, Warsaw, 1977), p. 21; L. Mitrus, n. 2 above, p. 16.
17. L. Mitrus, n. 2 above, p. 17.
18. D. Dörre-Nowak, 'Monitoring w Miejscu Pracy a Prawo do Prywatnosci' ('Monitoring the Place of Work and the Right to Privacy') [2004] No. 9 *Praca i Zabezpieczenie Spoleczne* (*Labour and Social Security*), 8 *et seq*.

Devices or equipment used in teleworking are, in Polish legislation, treated as tools. They are the property of the employer, given in use to a teleworker who is obliged to care for the employer's property and, after the termination of the contract, to return any such devices or equipment or to account for each and every piece of equipment (tool) given in use by the employer. Parties to the contractual employment under which a teleworker is employed may conclude an agreement on financial responsibility for the property (tools) given in use by the employer to the employee. The basis for financial responsibility of a teleworker for any damage suffered by the employer or a third person during, or in connection with, the performance of the work is regulated in Part V of the Labour Code, 'Financial Responsibility of Employees'.

Quite noticeable during the analysis of the specificity of telework become the problems faced under the individual labour law provisions currently in force in Poland with respect to solving certain issues connected with the limited powers of employers to have direct access to the place of work in order to check whether the working conditions of a teleworker are in compliance with the provisions of Part X of the Labour Code, 'Health and Safety'.[19] The employer is obliged to ensure that all employees work in safe and healthy conditions. Article 207, section 1 of the Labour Code, states that 'the employer is responsible for ensuring health and safety conditions of work in the establishment'. The Polish legislator does not define the term 'establishment'. Under the previous labour law provisions where the entity employing employees was referred to as the 'establishment' and the 'employer', the literature of the subject made the distinction between the 'establishment as an entity' and the 'establishment as an object'.[20] The first term denoted the employer as an entity employing employees. The other term referred to the establishment as a building, including equipment, machinery, tools and materials used by employees while doing their work. As a consequence of the amendment to the Labour Code consisting in the introduction of the term 'employer' to denote a person or an organizational unit employing employees, the former distinction between two meanings of the term 'establishment' are no longer applicable. Therefore, 'an establishment' can now be understood as denoting the place where an employee performs his/her work. Hence, Article 207, section 1 of the Labour Code, imposes on the employer of a teleworker the obligation to ensure safe and healthy working conditions in the workplace of a teleworker. The employer cannot be released from this obligation, or pass this obligation on any third party, e.g. a teleworker. Except for home teleworking, the employer and labour inspectors have the right and duty to control whether the places of work comply with the health and safety regulations. Under the law of 6 March 1981 on the National Labour Inspectorate,[21] the inspectors are vested with the power to carry out, without prior notification,

---

19. See K. Zakrzewska-Szczepańska, 'Bhp Przy Telepracy' ('Safety and Health in Telework') [2005] No. 9 *Praca i Zabezpieczenie Spoleczne* (*Labour and Social Security*) 34 *et seq.*
20. Z. Hajn, *Pojecie Zakladu Pracy Jako Podmiotu Zatrudniąjacego* (*The Notion of Undertaking as an Employer*) (Warsaw, 1988).
21. Unified text: OJ No. 124, 2001, Item 1362 as amended.

inspections concerning compliance with the health and safety regulations in force, at any time of day or night (Article 8, section 2). In the case of telework performed from abroad, the inspectors' ability to execute this power in relation to teleworkers working in places other than Polish establishments, is, *de lege lata,* limited. Under the law of 6 March 1981 on the National Labour Inspectorate currently in force, the inspectors may perform their statutory duties in establishments located within the jurisdiction of a district labour inspectorate. After the adoption of the Freedom of Services Directive, the supervision over obligations imposed on employers exporting services and employing people for the purpose of providing these services will be exercised by the labour inspectors competent for the official seat of the employer.[22] In the wake of freedom of movement of goods, employees and entrepreneurs, the freedom of movement of labour inspectors for the purpose of performing their duties is to be introduced.

In the case of home teleworking, neither the employer nor a labour inspector has the right to carry out an inspection of the workplace with respect to its compliance with health and safety regulations without the consent of the teleworker concerned.

Telework does not pose any difficulties as regards the application of the provisions of collective labour law. Teleworkers are granted the same rights provided for in the collective labour law as other employees.[23] They have the right to organize in trade unions; their representatives have to be informed by the employer on the situation and probable development concerning the employment and the establishment, subject to the applicable legal provisions, particularly to the Law of 23 May 1991 on trade unions.[24] Trade union organizations representing and protecting the rights of teleworkers have the right to negotiate collective and other normative agreements. In the event of a collective dispute, trade union organizations representing teleworkers have the right to organize protests, including strikes. Pursuant to the Law of 23 May 1991 on settling collective disputes,[25] a strike is a collective cessation of work by employees (Article 17, paragraph 1). The statutory requirement that a group of employees employed by a particular employer have to participate in a strike cannot be understood as the requirement that the employees participating in the strike have to be gathered in one place. A legal strike action cannot be considered equivalent to an occupational strike. The specific nature of telework does not deprive teleworkers of the rights granted to other employees. None of the actions mentioned above falling under the collective labour law provisions – exchange of information, consultation, negotiation of collective agreements, organizations of protests and strikes – require direct

---

22. See R. Blanpain (ed.), *Freedom of Services in the European Union. Labour and Social Security Law: The Bolkestein Initiative* (Bulletin of Comparative Labour Relations, Vol.58, Kluwer Law International, 2006).
23. cf. B. Cudowski, 'Podstawowe Problemy Zbiorowych Stosunków Pracy z Udzialem Pracowników Tymczasowych' ('Basic Issues Concerning Collective Labour Relations of Temporary Workers') No. 4 [2005] *Monitor Prawa Pracy (Labour Law Monitor),* 93 *et seq.*
24. Tekst Jednolity: OJ No. 79, 2001, Item 854 as amended.
25. OJ No. 55, Item 206 as amended.

contact between teleworker and employer. All these actions provided for in collective labour law require only communication between the parties to individual and collective employment contracts/agreements. Modern means of telecommunication enable teleworkers to make use of all rights granted to them in the collective labour law provisions.[26] There are no reasons why teleworkers should not be organized in working teams, why they should not form establishments managed by telemanagers. The concept of virtual teams, virtual undertakings or virtual employers is not at variance with the concept of an employee, employer, individual employment contracts and collective employment agreements defined in the Polish Labour Code.

The relevant provisions of Polish labour law to be abided by the parties to the contractual employment (individual and collective) established under one of the procedures set forth in Article 2 of the Labour Code – employment contract, appointment, nomination, or election – are also applicable in the case of telework.

III. CONCLUSION

A framework agreement concluded by the European social partners on 16 July 2002 is not binding upon the EU Member States. The implementation of the agreement consists in making the employers and employees aware of the benefits they can derive from making use of a flexible form of atypical employment such as telework. Telework does not change in any way the legal status of either party to the contractual employment (individual or collective). It only makes it more difficult for employers and labour inspectors to supervise the compliance by some teleworkers of health and safety provisions.

---

26. cf. A. Drozd, 'Wykonywanie Obowiązków Informacyjnych Pracodawcy w Formie Elektronicznej' ('Performing Employers' Duties in Electronic Form') No. 8 [2005] *Monitor Prawa Pracy* (*Labour Law Monitor*), 210 *et seq.*

Chapter 13

Sweden

Birgitta Nyström

I. TELEWORK IN SWEDEN – AN INTRODUCTION

Traditionally home work was different kinds of manual work that (mainly) women performed in their homes, but this kind of home work has practically disappeared in Sweden. Instead, during the 1990s the number of employees working in their own homes or elsewhere outside their normal workplace and the employer's normal premises began to increase. This was due to developments in telecommunications and computer technologies. The number of teleworking male employees increased and also the number of teleworking white-collar workers.[1] Today, the typical Swedish teleworker is a male, middle-aged, well-educated white-collar employee performing work from his home some days a week.

Discussions regarding telework started in Sweden during the oil crisis in the 1970s, as telework could result in less travelling. In the 1980s the discussions shifted towards telework as an opportunity to live and work in remote geographic regions, and in the 1990s the focus shifted once again and was now directed towards large workplaces in the big cities.

A State Committee was appointed by the Swedish Government in 1997, and in 1998 this Committee on Telework (Distansarbetsutredningen) published a

---

1. In this chapter I have tried to use English expressions and definitions which are used by Reinhold Fahlbeck and Tore Sigeman, *The European Employment and Industrial Relations Glossary: Sweden* (Office for Official Publications of the European Communities, Sweet & Maxwell, 2001).

Blanpain et al., European Framework, Agreements and Telework, pp. 217–228.
©2007, Kluwer Law International BV, The Netherlands.

comprehensive report on telework.[2] The aim of the Committee was to identify various obstacles to telework. Telework was considered to be desirable both for individual employees and for society as a whole, and the committee could – if it found it appropriate – suggest legislative changes aimed at promoting teleworking and secure good working conditions for teleworkers. The work of the committee led to a new rule in the Employment Protection Act (see section II.D below).

In Sweden there is a wide meaning given to the notion of 'employee'. Although no definition of the concept exists under Swedish law, its meaning has been clarified in an extensive body of case law. The fact that someone is performing work from another location than the principal ordinary workplace is normally not a relevant factor here. Home workers and teleworkers are normally deemed to be employees under Swedish law and thereby covered by the labour law and general collective agreements. The presumption is that an employee is under the employer's immediate direction and control, but this is not always true when it comes to teleworkers. The teleworker enjoys equal status with comparable workers at the regular principal workplace and all legislation regarding equal treatment and anti-discrimination applies.[3]

A.   FREQUENCY AND DEFINITION

Teleworking is, according to several studies, most prevalent in northern Europe, and telework seems to be rather common in Sweden compared to most other countries. One reason for the Swedish potential for telework is that IT is well developed and most employees have access to computers and the internet in their homes.

There is no overall statistical data available regarding the frequency of telework in Sweden. According to a survey conducted in 1998,[4] nine per cent of all Swedish employees do work in their homes regularly or occasionally, but there was almost nobody working from home full time. In 2000 it was estimated that 15 per cent of employees were teleworking. There is uncertainty, though, about the numbers of employees engaged in telework. Figures between 1 per cent and 30 per cent, between 30,000 employees and one million employees, have been mentioned. This uncertainty is mainly due to the lack of a general definition of 'telework'.

The teleworker's own home is by far the most frequent place for teleworking, and employees working from their homes are considered to be teleworkers. Also, people working elsewhere away from the employer's ordinary premises, in for

---

2. *Distansarbete. Betänkande av Distansarbetsutredningen* (*Telework. Report from the State Committee on Telework*) (SOU 1998:115).

3. A self-employed person is under Swedish law someone who works for remuneration but not in subordination, meaning under command and control of another person. A self-employed person is an independent entrepreneur and responsible for all social costs and tax payments. General contractual law applies, not labour law.

4. (SOU 1998:115), pp. 52–59.

example satellite offices, are considered to be teleworkers. Most teleworkers work from home only to a limited extent and also work in the ordinary workplace regularly. There is no definition deciding if occasional work from home could be telework, or if it has to be on a more regular basis, if it is enough to work one day a week from home to be considered a teleworker, or if it has to be more frequent. Another example is call centres that are increasingly common in Sweden. They are often situated in less densely populated areas far away from the big cities where unemployment is high. Employers contract out their telephone operating and booking service to the call centre. Communication is done by telephone, data operating or the like, and is independent of geographical distance to the employer's normal workplace.[5] Call centres have in some surveys been considered as telework and in others as a form of work of its own.

The Telework Committee 1998 underlined the difficulties in defining telework. In the Government's directives to the Committee, telework was defined as 'work performed using IT, in the employee's home or elsewhere away from a traditional working place'. The Telework Committee nevertheless concluded that the use of IT could not be a determinable factor in the definition. In this chapter I have chosen a wide definition of a teleworker: an employee who performs full time or occasionally in his/her home or any other chosen place (close to home), satellite office or the like, outside the employer's ordinary or standard workplace.

B.   ADVANTAGES AND PROBLEMS – EQUAL OPPORTUNITIES

Employers consider voluntary telework to be good personnel policy and hope that it will lead to increased productivity. On the other hand, many employers are worried that their direction and control over the employee and his/her work will diminish. One of the foremost advantages with telework is that the employee feels more freedom and flexibility. The employee is undisturbed and able to concentrate more. Initially, trade unions paid attention to expected problems such as difficulties in dividing work and leisure time, women returning to their homes, and an even more divided labour market in male and female jobs, deteriorating working conditions, etc. Swedish trade unions became gradually more positive towards telework at the end of the 1980s, realizing that many of their members were interested in the possibility to work from home. But Swedish trade unions are generally negative to full-time work from home and underline the importance of trade union involvement when agreements on telework are concluded.

The Telework Committee established in 1998 that telework was mainly performed by employees with the competence and working conditions to decide when and where they should perform, and also had employers willing to supply

---

5. The Telework Committee named this distance-independent work.

them with technical equipment. Obstacles to telework were considered to be special work tasks and also the needs of colleagues.[6] The Committee anticipated an increase in the total amount of teleworkers.

Recent signs are, on the contrary, that the interest in teleworking may be on the decline in Sweden.[7] One explanation for this might be the rapid changes in today's working life, and that employees are keen to be on the spot to find out what is going on. The teleworkers' colleagues are not always satisfied. They sometimes complain that they have to take over tasks from people working at home, for example receive visitors.[8]

Telework has, according to several studies, not turned out to be the expected trap for women. Nevertheless, it has been mentioned above that the number of teleworking male employees have increased, but when it comes to the teleworkers that spend all their working time in their own home or at a call centre, these groups are dominated by women. Studies have shown that the consequences of teleworking are different for men and women. Men generally draw a sharper line between work and family life, have a separate working room at home, and fixed working hours. Women teleworking from home find it more difficult to demand the rest of the family to do their share of the housework and have to adapt to the rest of the family.[9] Freedom and flexibility in teleworking means different things for men and women. For men it is reduced travelling hours and more freedom in how to perform the work and when to do it. For women, freedom and flexibility stand for an opportunity to combine childcare and work.[10]

II.   LABOUR LEGISLATION AND TELEWORK

Sweden initially adopted ILO Convention No. 177 (1996), but decided in 1998 not to ratify it. The reason for this was that home workers are normally considered to be employees and thereby protected by Swedish labour legislation and general collective agreements, and the employers were opposed to ratification. Today, there does not seem to be any legal obstacles to ratify since the earlier derogations for home work in the Working Time and Annual Holidays Acts were abolished some years ago.

---

6. The Telework Committee has summarized several studies regarding telework (SOU 1998:115), pp. 61–81.
7. Trine P. Larsen/Søren Kaj Andersen, *Frivillige Aftaler – en Ny Europaeisk Reguleringsform. Et Empirisk Studie af Implementeringen af Teleaftalen i Danmark, Sverige, Tyskland og Ungarn* (*Voluntary Agreements – a New European Form of Regulation. An Empirical Study of the Implementation of the Telework Agreement in Denmark, Sweden, Germany and Hungary*) (Faso Forskningsnotat 070, 2006), p. 34.
8. <www.arbetslivsinstitutet.se/distansarbete> (accessed 19 December 2006).
9. Kerstin Hultén, 'Leva och Arbeta i Hemmet. Effekter av Distansarbete för Privatliv och Arbetsliv' ('Living and Working at Home. Effects of Teleworking for Private and Working Life') [11 February 2005] *Arbetsmarknad & Arbetsliv*, 123–136.
10. (SOU 1998:115), p. 64.

13. Sweden

General Swedish labour law provisions are applicable to telework.[11] However, there are a few special provisions regarding telework in the Employment Protection Act and regarding the work environment.[12]

A. WORK ENVIRONMENT

The work environment is one of the crucial questions regarding telework. There are both negative and positive expected work environment consequences. On the one hand, telework is an advantage because travel hours are reduced; the work can be done in an undisturbed environment, etc. On the other hand, the localities, lights, and equipment like desks, chairs, etc. may be inadequate. Studies show that teleworkers often work longer days than they should have done at the office. There is also a risk of isolation, demands of constant accessibility, and an increase in working hours and workload, and also problems in relation to family life.

The 1977 Work Environment Act protects teleworkers to the same extent as other employees. The teleworker should enjoy the same conditions as comparable workers who perform at the standard workplace.

Most often it is the employer that takes the costs and responsibility for computer equipment, etc., but it is rather common that it is the employee that is responsible for other work equipment like desks, chairs, lights, etc. The safety of machinery and other equipment that has been handed over to the employee, to be used in the employee's home or elsewhere, is the employer's responsibility. It is also the employer's responsibility to make sure that safety measures are taken and that satisfactory information is given.[13]

Additionally, employers should take account of the special risks of ill health and accidents that attend working alone. When an employee has to work alone, the work should be organized in such a way that the danger of being physically or psychologically hurt does not increase. The employer's obligations with regard to internal monitoring also cover teleworkers. The Occupational Health and Safety Board[14] have issued a number of non-statutory regulations on working alone.[15] The Board has underlined that the rules regarding work environment are

---

11. *See* also Niklas Bruun/Märeta Johnson, *The Legal and Contractual Situation of Teleworkers. Labour Law Aspects* (Arbetslivsrapport 1995:32, National Institute for Working Life, 1995).
12. There are other legal aspects than labour law regarding telework. For example: responsibility for damages, insurances regarding computers and other equipments and for the teleworker him/herself, personal integrity, secrecy, taxation problems, etc. These questions will not be discussed in this chapter.
13. Prop. 1976/77:149 p. 212 *et seq.*
14. The central government authority responsible for work environment issues. The Agency can supplement legislation with more detailed requirements in the form of legally binding non-statutory regulations. At local level the Agency is also responsible for the supervision of individual places of work.
15. AFS 1982:3 *Ensamarbete* (*Working Alone*) is the most important non-statutory regulation in this area.

applicable, regardless of the employee's workplace. The employer is always responsible for working environment and it is not possible to agree upon anything else.

The Work Environment Act does not, however, provide the possibility to appoint a safety representative where a worker works alone. There has to be a minimum of five employees in the same location for that.

Regarding the work environment for employees working in their own homes there is a special problem: the possibility to control that prevailing rules regarding the work environment are applied in a correct manner is limited. The employee has no general obligation to allow the employer, the safety representative or the Occupational Health and Safety Board access to his/her home if this has not been agreed upon. Inspection by the Board can only take place in a home at the request of the employer or employee, or if there is a particular reason for inspection. Access to the workplace in the teleworker's home is often regulated in agreements (see section III below).

B.   WORKING TIME AND ANNUAL HOLIDAY

Formerly, the 1982 Working Time Act did not entail home workers and forms of remote working, and the 1977 Annual Holidays Act had a corresponding exception. It was considered impossible for the employer to control the actual time such an employee spent working. The Telework Committee suggested in 1998 that the exceptions regarding home work in both Acts should be abolished and this proposal was followed soon after.

The teleworker as a main rule organizes the work him/herself within the framework of the prevailing working time schedule at the standard workplace, but there could be many variations due to the line of work and the individual agreement between the employer and the employee.

C.   COLLECTIVE LABOUR RIGHTS

Teleworkers enjoy the same collective labour rights as other employees in Sweden. They enjoy freedom of association like anybody else, and teleworkers are found in many different trade unions, mostly under the federations TCO, the Swedish Federation of Professional Employees (Tjänstemännens Centralorganisation), and SACO, the Swedish Confederation of Professional Associations (Sveriges Akademikers Centralorganisation). The Swedish labour law system is built upon the notion that it is the labour market parties that have the main responsibility for regulating pay and other working conditions by means of collective agreements. Trade union representatives who perform their duties during paid working hours are key actors in labour market relations at the workplaces.

According to the 1998 Telework Committee there could, however, be a few problems regarding collective labour rights and telework. The first deals with the possibility for trade union representatives to visit teleworking members in their home during the union representative's paid working time. A trade union representative can perform trade union work during paid working hours only in their own working place. But there does not seem to be a serious problem here. The teleworker's home should in this respect be deemed to belong to the ordinary workplace. The second question relates to the teleworker's own ability to be an employee representative. This is also dependent on how the notion 'workplace' is defined. When telework is regulated in a collective agreement it is often clarified that the 'teleworkplace' is considered to be a part of the employer's ordinary workplace. It is true, stated the Telework Committee, that it could be more difficult to give information to, and to keep contact with, teleworking trade union members. The Committee therefore suggested that the possibility of a trade union representative using the employer's intranet, etc. to give the union members information should be dealt with in collective agreements.

The Telework Committee underlined that the rules in the 1976 Co-determination Act regarding an employer's duty to negotiate and to give business information should also be applied with regard to teleworkers. According to the Co-determination Act, an employer has a duty to take the initiative to commence negotiations with the trade union which has concluded a collective agreement with the employer[16] before the employer makes a decision in major questions regarding the running of the business. These negotiations are aimed at giving the employee side information and influence on the employer's decisions in the conduct of business. To introduce or to abolish telework is normally to be considered as a major change and will thereby fall within the employer's duty to take the initiative to negotiate.

D. EMPLOYMENT PROTECTION

The 1982 Employment Protection Act prescribes that employment of an unspecified duration (permanent employment) is the normal case, and that the employer must have a just cause for dismissal. Redundancy is such a just clause. In a redundancy situation the employer must observe a specified order of selection for dismissal. A separate order of selection is normally drawn up for each group of employees who belong to the same area of collective agreement coverage in the establishment. The position of the individual employee in this order of selection for dismissal is normally based on the length of service with the employer.

The concept of an 'establishment' is determined in geographical terms, in principle a part of a business situated within the same building or the same enclosed area. Since 2001 the Employment Protection Act protects the home working employee by stating that the mere fact that an employee's workplace is in his/ her own home does not signify that the workplace constitutes a separate

---

16. In the main only such an established union has the right to take part, but in some situations unions without collective agreement also have a right to take part in negotiations.

establishment. The home working employee should belong to the group of employees in the employer's ordinary establishment where he/she would have been working if he/she had not been teleworking.[17] This new rule solved a problem that was often paid attention to in earlier individual or collective agreements.

III.   THE VOLUNTARY CHARACTER OF TELEWORK: COLLECTIVE AND INDIVIDUAL AGREEMENTS

There is consensus that telework is voluntary and needs agreement from both parties. In fact, the initiative for teleworking is often taken by the employee. Employers' organizations and trade unions have issued a number of joint policies or guidelines on telework. There are also policies from employers and employers' organizations. The trade unions are concerned that teleworkers should enjoy strong protection, and several unions have drawn up model agreements to regulate the relationship between the employer and individual teleworkers.

Specific conditions can be laid down in collective or individual agreements in order to take account of the specific aspects of telework. Individual contracts between the employer and the teleworkers are normal, even in situations where telework is regulated in a collective agreement. Individual agreements are often informal, verbal contracts between the employee and his/her employer, but sometimes they are in writing. In some sectors of the labour market the national general collective agreement contains clauses referring to telework. At individual company level one can find agreements on telework in forms of collective agreements.

In 1998 the Telework Committee studied over 30 collective and individual agreements, joint guidelines, trade unions and employers' organizations or employers' policies, at both nationwide and local level. The committee found that these agreements, guidelines and policies mainly regulated the same questions, like, for example, where the teleworker belongs in the employer's ordinary organization, working place, equipment, insurance, working time, availability, and time of notice if the employer or the employee wants to terminate the agreement on telework. The employer is, as a main rule, responsible for equipment and it is rather common that the teleworker according to the agreement is forbidden to use the equipment for private purposes. It is often stipulated that it is the employer who is responsible for the working place and that the employee is obliged to co-operate regarding security questions and work environment, for example giving the employer and/or the safety representative access to the workplace. It is not uncommon that it is agreed that the employee has to be present at the ordinary workplace at least one day a week. There are examples in individual agreements that the teleworker is not allowed to keep his/her ordinary working room at the employer's ordinary workplace, but can share another room there with others. It was the Commission's impression that regulation at lower levels followed regulation and policies issued at higher levels. The Telework Committee concluded that

---

17. Prop. 1999/2000:86.

the most important questions regarding telework seemed to be regulated in the agreements and guidelines.

Regarding call centres, there is, since the early 2000s, a general nationwide collective agreement between the Union of Salaried Employees (Handelstjänste-mannaförbundet, HTF) and the Swedish Service Employers' Association (Almega). This is only a special supplementary agreement to the general collective agreement for the white-collar service area and regulates questions mainly regarding fixed-term employment, working time and special remunerations. Since the employee does not work from his/her home, but from a satellite office or the like, there is no need to regulate equipment, etc.

After the European Agreement on Guidelines on Telework in 2001, developments in collective agreements at nationwide level began to increase in order to implement the European framework agreement (see section IV below).

IV. IMPLEMENTATION OF THE FRAMEWORK AGREEMENT

Implementation activities have taken place both at national and sectoral levels. In May 2003 the main organizations in the Swedish labour market – the Confederation of Swedish Enterprise (SN Svenskt Näringsliv), the Swedish Agency for Government Employers (Arbetsgivarverket), the Swedish Federation of County Councils (Landstingsförbundet), the Association of Local Authorities (Kommunförbundet), the Swedish Trade Union Confederation (LO Landsorganisationen), the Swedish Confederation of Professional Employees (TCO) and the Swedish Confederation of Professional Associations (SACO) – agreed on guidelines for the implementation of the European Agreement on Guidelines on Telework in Commerce (the framework agreement). The parties agreed that the European Agreement should serve as guidelines when Swedish collective agreements about telework are concluded, with due consideration to different branches, sectors, undertakings, authorities and employers. The Swedish guidelines for implementation do not take the form of a collective agreement, and are not binding for the parties.[18] Nevertheless, it is important that all the main organizations covering in principle the entire Swedish labour market have agreed to try and implement the European Agreement.

Developments in sector agreements after the abovementioned guidelines of implementation in 2003 have been somewhat slow in parts of the private Swedish labour market. It is only in the public sector that all sectoral agreements have

---

18. According to a recently published research report the SN did not want binding Swedish rules implementing an unbinding European agreement and therefore rejected concluding a collective agreement. See Trine P. Larsen/Søren Kaj Andersen, *Frivillige Aftaler – en Ny Europaeisk Reguleringsform. Et Empirisk Studie af Implementeringen af Teleaftalen i Danmark, Sverige, Tyskland og Ungarn* (*Voluntary Agreements – a New European Form of Regulation. An Empirical Study of the Implementation of the Telework Agreement in Denmark, Sweden, Germany and Hungary*) (Faso Forskningsnotat 070, 2006), pp. 31–35.

implemented the European framework agreement, mostly in forms of references to the framework agreement. Explanations for this could be that telework is not – at least not yet – a question that concerns major parts of the Swedish labour market. Agreements on telework are, for example, rare in the blue collar area. Another explanation could be that telework does not seem to be a very controversial issue. The typical teleworker is a well-educated employee with a strong position on the labour market, and most commonly the teleworker is present at the ordinary workplace one or a couple of days a week, thereby eluding several expected negative consequences of working from home.

There are examples of collective agreements stating that the parties have noticed the European framework agreement, but established that telework is not applicable in their sector (for example, regarding seamen).

The framework agreement was implemented for state sector employees during the general collective bargaining rounds in 2005. The new rules are built upon earlier agreements and guidelines for the state sector. A framework agreement, 2004–2007, between the Swedish Agency for Government Employers and the Public Employees' Negotiations Council (OFR Offentliganställdas förhandlings-råd) states that the social partners at the workplace are supposed to support equal opportunities for men and women at the workplace. This includes possibilities to combine work and family life. The organization of work and working time as well as possibilities of teleworking are to be considered in this context. There are similar articles in other collective agreements in the state sector. Additionally, there is a special agreement on telework concluded in late 2005 between the Swedish Agency for Government Employers and its trade union counterparts. This agreement considers the European framework agreement and states that it should serve as guidelines in the state sector. In government agencies where telework is decided there should be guidelines for the specific agency, and local co-operation regarding telework should be regulated locally by the social partners. Furthermore, details regarding telework should be taken care of in written agreements between the employer and the individual employee.

In the municipal sector the 2005 collective agreements entail a reference to the framework agreement. In the private sector the picture is more fragmented (for examples, *see* below). It seems to be rare in the private sector that the framework agreement is implemented by a collective agreement, but on the other hand it seems to be rather common that the social partners give a reference to either the framework agreement or the Swedish Guidelines in their collective agreement. Nevertheless, in 2006 the majority of the sectoral collective agreements in the private sector of the Swedish labour market had not implemented the guidelines on telework.[19]

---

19. Trine P. Larsen/Søren Kaj Andersen, *Frivillige Aftaler – en Ny Europaeisk Reguleringsform. Et Empirisk Studie af Implementeringen af Teleaftalen i Danmark, Sverige, Tyskland og Ungarn* (*Voluntary Agreements – a New European Form of Regulation. An Empirical Study of the Implementation of the Telework Agreement in Denmark, Sweden, Germany and Hungary*) (Faso Forskningsnotat 070, 2006).

13. Sweden

The collective agreement in the banking area between the Employers' Association of the Swedish Banking Institutions (Bankinstitutens Arbetsgivareorganisation) and the Financial Sector Union (Finansförbundet) has a relatively extensive regulation of telework. The agreement defines 'telework' as work that an employee performs regularly and at least one day a week from his/her home or another agreed place outside the employer's ordinary premises, and where there exists an agreement about telework. The following rules are compulsory: Before introducing telework, negotiations between the employer and the trade union according to the Co-Determination Act should be conducted. The teleworker should be considered to belong to the employer's ordinary workplace. The employer has the responsibility for the workplace regarding the work environment, but the teleworker is supposed to co-operate and is obliged to follow security rules. The employer should have admission to the workplace. Working time schedules for teleworkers could be decided either according to the general rules in the collective agreement, or the teleworker could have the working time in his/her own command within the stipulated 38 hours and 30 minutes a week. Further, the collective agreement mentions a wide range of issues that could be regulated between the employer and the teleworker, for example regarding presence at the ordinary workplace, when to be available, travel rules, questions regarding work equipment, insurances, secrecy, etc. A similar collective agreement has been concluded between the Employers' Association of the Swedish Banking Institutions and the trade union for university educated workers in the banking area (within the SACO).

In the collective agreement between the Swedish Newspaper Publishers' Association (Tidningsutgivarna) and the Graphic Workers' Union (Grafiska Fackförbundet Mediafacket), the parties have agreed that they will inform the employers in writing about the European framework agreement in order that it should be observed when individual agreements about telework are concluded. The collective agreement regarding white-collar employees in the graphics industry between the Swedish Graphic Companies Federation (Grafiska Företagens Förbund) on the employers' side and the Swedish Association of Graduate Engineers (CF Civilingenjörsförbundet) and the Swedish Union of Clerical and Technical Employees (SIF) on the employees' side includes a similar regulation.

In the collective agreement between Almega Samhall Employers' Association (Almega Samhallförbundet) and SIF, there is a reminder of the guidelines that the main organizations have agreed upon for the implementation of the European guidelines on telework. The parties also notice that there are agreements regarding telework between employers and unions at company level.

The Swedish Construction Federation (Sveriges Byggindustrier) and their counterpart the Swedish Association of Graduate Engineers agreed, in 2004, to set up a working group to discuss the implementation of the European framework agreement. A similar paragraph can be found in the collective agreement between the Swedish Forest Industries (Föreningen Sveriges Skogsindustrier) and the Paper Workers' Union (Svenska Pappersindsustriarbetareförbundet).

In all sectors there exists supplementary collective agreements at local and company level regulating telework in more detail.

V.   CONCLUDING REMARKS

Telework is supposed to be on the increase and in Sweden teleworking seems to be rather common compared to most other countries. Nevertheless, there are still few employees teleworking on a more extensive and/or regular basis on the Swedish labour market. The circumstances have shifted during the years. From the beginning home work was mainly manual work conducted by women. Nowadays telework is mainly conducted by well educated white-collar men by means of telecommunication. Discussions regarding telework have also shifted. Telework has been considered to save travelling time, including costs and pollution, to be a means to help distant regions to survive, or a way to combine family and working life and to raise productivity. Telework has, on the other hand, been accused of trapping women in their homes, deteriorating working conditions, etc.

Today, telework is not considered to be a major problem in Swedish working life. One reason for this is probably that it is rare that an employee is teleworking full time. Mostly, the employee works from home one or a couple of days a week and keeps his/her workplace intact at the ordinary workplace, thereby also remaining an integrated part of the ordinary daily organization at the workplace and among colleagues. Other reasons are that a teleworker is normally considered to be an employee protected by labour law, and the trade unions paid early attention to problems that might occur and issued guidelines, etc. The most complicated questions relating to telework seem to be work environment issues.

Developments in collective agreements have by Swedish means been rather slow. The European framework agreement has put focus on telework, and since 2003 the number of collective agreements taking telework into consideration has increased. Still, the more detailed agreements regarding telework mainly have the form of individual agreements between the teleworker and his/her employer.

The European framework agreement states that it shall be implemented 'in accordance with the procedures and practices specific to management and labour in the Member States'. Nevertheless, the Swedish implementation strategy reflects an innovation. The main organizations on the Swedish labour market agreed on national non-binding guidelines that do not have the form of a collective agreement for implementing the framework agreement. This is an entirely new way of regulating questions between the Swedish employers' organizations and Swedish trade unions, probably influenced by the specific nature of the European framework agreement.

Chapter 14

The United Kingdom

Alan C. Neal

As an Information Society, the UK has a lot going for it. It has a liberalised telecommunications regime, substantial network investment, very strong telecommunications and broadcasting companies, a healthy publishing industry and established library and information networks. Like the US, it also has a head start in that English is recognised as the common language of the Internet and is increasingly becoming the common language of global communications. Given all these advantages – and more besides – the UK should be a world leader of the Information Society.

House of Lords, *Agenda for Action in the UK* (1996)

I. INTRODUCTION

The advent of the social partnership Framework Agreement on telework in July 2002 has arguably not produced any significant policy shift in United Kingdom (UK) labour market terms. On the other hand, it may have proved, over the past four years, to have provided added impetus to the development of a species of 'soft' social dialogue in the traditional 'home of collective bargaining'. More generally, it may offer a useful focus for evaluation of the development of the 'information society' in that country.

Blanpain et al., European Framework, Agreements and Telework, pp. 229–244.
©2007, Kluwer Law International BV, The Netherlands.

In terms of the development of activities capable of being described as 'teleworking',[1] the UK had long been in the vanguard of technical developments for the provision of the relevant necessary communications infrastructure.[2] Perhaps more importantly, however, the UK had been a focal point for developments in the 'flexible workforce' (including varieties of 'teleworking'), both as part of the radical shake up of the labour market model stimulated by the industrial relations policies introduced under Prime Minister Mrs Margaret Thatcher,[3] and as a direct concomitant of the 'market driven' labour market policies introduced throughout the 1980s and early 1990s.[4]

Indeed, not long after a 'new labour' government had been elected to office in 1997, the EU Commission was describing the UK situation in the following terms:

> UK has the highest penetration of Internet use among the major European economies and substantially the highest take up of teleworking, with estimates of between 1 – 2 million people teleworking on a full or part-time basis and in a variety of modes. It also has had the fastest rate of introduction of 'concentrative teleworking', as banks, insurance companies and other sectors switch from High Street presence to telephone-based sales and support.
>
> Factors promoting the adoption of Information Society methods include the early liberalisation of telecommunications, which has led to price reductions and a proliferation of competition and new services, together with a lightly regulated labour market that presents few barriers to innovation. Telework adoption has been accelerated by Europe's most well-established telework association, which has positively influenced media coverage as well as providing information services to the public.[5]

---

1. L. Haddon & R. Silverstone, *Information and Communication Technologies in the Home: The Case of Teleworking*, Working Paper 17, SPRU CICT (University of Sussex, Falmer, Brighton, BN1 9QN, UK, October 1992); U. Hotopp, 'Teleworking in the UK' (2002) *Labour Market Trends*, 311; Y. Ruiz & A. Walling, 'Home-based Working Using Communication Technologies' (2005) Labour Market Trends, 417; Trades Union Congress, The Future of Work Looking Ahead – the Next Ten Years (London, 2000).
2. Department of Trade and Industry, *Moving into the Information Age 1999* (London, HMSO, May 1999).
3. J. Atkinson, *Manning for Uncertainty: Some Emerging UK Work Patterns* (Brighton, University of Sussex Institute of Manpower Studies, 1984); J. Atkinson, 'Manpower Strategies for Flexible Organisations' [1984] *Personnel Management*, 28; A. Pollert, 'The Flexible Firm – Fixation or Fact?' (1988) 2 *Work, Employment and Society*, 281.
4. M. Cully, S. Woodland, S. O'Reilly & G. Dix, *Britain at Work: As Depicted by the 1998 Workplace Employee Relations Survey* (London, 1999); N. Millward, A. Bryson & J. Forth, *All Change at Work? – British Employment Relations 1980 – 1998, as Portrayed by the Workplace Industrial Relations Survey Series* (London, 2000); B. Kersley, C. Alpin, J. Forth, A. Bryson, H. Bewley, G. Dix & S. Oxenbridge, *Inside the Workplace: Findings from the 2004 Workplace Employment Relations Survey* (London, Routledge, 2006).
5. European Commission, *Telework 1998: Annual Report from the European Commission* (Luxembourg, 1999).

It therefore comes as little surprise that the impact of the 2002 Framework Agreement in the UK has been more focused on addressing the content of the agreement in terms of how it fits an already developing and developing pattern for this sector, and of encouraging various 'soft' forms of supporting supervision and quasi-regulation.

II. DEFINING 'TELEWORKING'

In 1990 the International Labour Organisation (ILO) proposed the following definition of telework:

> 'A form of work in which (a) work is performed in a location remote from central office or production facilities, thus separating the worker from personal contact with co-workers there; and (b) new technology enables this separation by facilitating communication'.[6]

By 2001, a report for the European Foundation for the Improvement of Living and Working Conditions[7] was suggesting that:

> Telework is the work performed by a teleworker (employee, self-employed, home worker . . .). Mainly or for an important part, at (a) location(s) other than the traditional workplace for an employer or a client, involving the use of telecommunications.

In the same year, in further work for the ILO, Di Martino sought to offer indications of the detailed kinds of work encompassed within the notion of 'teleworking'.[8]

For some time, the UK has operated on the basis of a trio of categorisations for 'teleworkers' in the labour market. So far as the national statistical material is concerned, the Labour Force Survey (LFS) defines teleworkers as 'people who do some paid or unpaid work in their own home and who use both a telephone and computer', and includes people who (i) mainly work from home in their main job – so-called 'teleworker home workers'; (ii) work from home in various locations but use their home as a base – described as 'home based teleworkers'; and (iii) do not usually work at home or use home as a base but did so for at least one day in the reference week – labelled as 'occasional teleworkers'. The statistical series tends to present data for 'all teleworkers', which reflects the situation for the combination of all three of these categories.

---

6. V. Di Martino & L. Wirth, 'Telework' (1990) Vol.9 No. 1 (special issue) *Conditions of Work Digest* (Geneva, International Labour Organisation).
7. R. Blanpain, *The Legal and Contractual Situations of Teleworkers in the European Union, Consolidated Report* (Dublin, European Foundation for the Improvement of Living and Working Conditions, 2001).
8. V. Di Martino, *The High Road to Teleworking* (Geneva, International Labour Organisation, 2001).

The Labour Force Survey has also made use of another, narrower, definition, which includes only those workers for whom both a computer and a telephone are essential for them to be able to perform their job – a sub-group of 'all teleworkers' sometimes referred to as 'TC teleworkers'.

This follows out of a rather more colourful denomination of workers undertaking activity of the kind associated with 'telework', as can be seen from the 1995 report of a House of Lords committee, which identified four categories:[9]

Home Telework

The 'traditional' form of telework, where the worker undertakes paid employment from home by means of information and communication technologies (ICTs). Work could be undertaken full or part-time whether as a direct employee or self-employed.

Telecottages

These offices or work centres are equipped with ICT facilities both for on-site work and for teleworking to remote locations. Such facilities may be shared by a number of commercially-oriented organisations, their employees, independent freelance professionals, small businesses etc.

Nomadic workers

Workers who are mobile, using portable equipment and telecommunications facilities to maximise their time 'on the road' or at customer's premises.

Distance (remote) offices

Firms reorganise across space. In some cases, they may centralise functions and use ICTs to site these offices at lower cost locations. In others they may redesign services around the use of ICTs – e.g. in call centres or telecentres.

Even before the social dialogue initiative at European level, some evidence of efforts to define (first) 'homeworking' and (later) 'teleworking' for the purposes of agreements to be entered into by employers and unions in the UK could be seen emerging in a number of sectors.

One of the pathfinding agreements in the field of teleworking, entered into by the communications organisation British Telecom on 20 January 1992 – an 'Agreement between BT operator services and the UCW on the teleworking experiment at Inverness' – is interesting more for the fact that there is no specific definition of 'teleworking' included either in the agreement or in the model statement of variation of terms of employment to be used in relation to staff moving to telework within that organisation.

A similar lack of concern for definition can be seen in the agreement made on 27 March 2000 between Prudential Assurance Company Limited (Home Service Division) and the Manufacturing Science and Finance Union (MSF), relating to what are described as 'outdoor staff' at the company.

---

9. House of Lords, *Working at a Distance – UK Teleworking and its Implications* (London, 1996).

An early example of definition by a major employer (British Gas) in relation to 'homeworking' can be seen in that organisation's 'Service Joint Committee (gas staff and senior officers) home working/home based working agreement' of 13 October 1995, where three categories of home worker are identified:

Category A
Home start or District start – where employees spend most of their time in the field, but use their home as a starting and/or finishing base instead of having to report to a British Gas location on a daily basis.

Category B
Home based working where employees are expected to use their home as an office for frequent short periods, e.g. Central Heating Representatives.

Category C
Home based working where employees are expected to undertake a significant amount of administrative work at home, e.g. Field Managers.

An interesting example of definition for the purpose of an agreement on teleworking between UK collective bargaining parties can be seen in a 2000 draft model agreement drawn up by the MSF for use between itself and compliant employers, where it is provided that:

For the purposes of this agreement a Teleworker shall be understood as an employee who undertakes work that was previously or would be performed on the company premises but is now to be mainly performed from the employee's home with the support of decentralised information-processing or communications devices and equipment. The collectively agreed or regular individual working hours are therefore worked primarily in the employee's home (domestic workplace).

Since the adoption of the 2002 Framework Agreement at European level, the UK has seen the development of guidance, agreed between the social partners under the auspices of the relevant ministry.[10] This takes a non-prescriptive approach to the question of defining telework, by stating that:

There is no definition of teleworking in UK law. Telework is not a job but a method of working. The essential feature is the use of information and communications technologies to enable remote working from the office, either for:

(i) Workers who work at home full-time or part-time;
(ii) Workers who divide their time between home and the office; and
(iii) Primarily mobile workers using their home as an administrative base.

---

10. Department of Trade and Industry, *Telework Guidance, as Agreed by CBI, TUC and CEEP (UK)* (London, HMSO, August 2003).

III.   A LEGAL DEFINITION FOR 'TELEWORKING'?

The various definitional endeavours in the UK may be contrasted with the 'definition' adopted for the purpose of the 2002 Framework Agreement, which, in Article 2, states that:

> TELEWORK is a form of organising and/or performing work, using information technology, in the context of an employment contract/relationship, where work, which could also be performed at the employers' premises, is carried out away from those premises on a regular basis. . . . A teleworker is any person carrying out telework as defined above.

In particular, one can see the attempt, in the Telework Guidance published in 2003, to integrate the 'descriptive' profile contained in the Framework Agreement with the 'trilogy' of situations in respect of which UK official labour market statistics have been compiled in respect of teleworking practices.

What is most significant, however, is the reality that – as openly acknowledged in the Guidance – 'there is no definition of teleworking in UK law'.

This confirms the situation that, for a 'teleworker' (howsoever defined) to enjoy most of the individual employment rights provided by modern UK labour law, it will be necessary for that person to show that he is a 'worker' or (in relation to many of the most important of those rights) an 'employee', as defined by the legislator.

The definition of 'worker' is set out in section 296(1) of the Trade Union and Labour Relations (Consolidation) Act 1992 and in section 230(3) of the Employment Rights Act 1996, in terms that:

> 'worker' (subject to the following provisions of this section) means an individual regarded in whichever (if any) of the following capacities is applicable to him, that is to say, as a person who works or normally works or seeks to work –
>
> (a) under a contract of employment; or
> (b) under any other contract (whether express or implied, and, if express, whether oral or in writing) whereby he undertakes to do or perform personally any work or services for another party to the contract who is not a professional client of his; or
> (c) in employment under or for the purposes of a government department (otherwise than as a member of the naval, military or air forces of the Crown) in so far as any such employment does not fall within paragraph (a) or (b) above.

Meanwhile, the narrower definition of 'employee' – which is required for individual employment rights such as the statutory protection against 'unfair dismissal' – is to be found in section 295(1) of the Trade Union and Labour Relations (Consolidation) Act 1992 and in section 230 of the Employment Rights Act 1996, in terms that:

> 'employee' means an individual who has entered into or works under (or, where the employment has ceased, worked under) a contract of employment.

14. The United Kingdom

Although there is no definition in the UK legislation of 'teleworker', there has been, since 1998, recognition of a 'home worker' as a particular species of worker. Thus, for the purposes of the National Minimum Wage Act 1998, a 'home worker' is defined in section 35(2) as:

> An individual who contracts with a person, for the purposes of that person's business, for the execution of work to be done in a place not under the control or management of that person.

While it is important not to fall into the trap of equating 'homeworkers' with 'teleworkers' in an unnuanced fashion, the existence of a specific provision covering persons who perform work in certain circumstances while at home is clearly of relevance when considering the extent to which UK labour law provisions can be said to be applicable – other than in the normal course of events where the individual concerned satisfies the definition of 'worker' or 'employee' – in the context of telework.

This tension is, of course, not unique to the UK, as has been noted by reference to telework arrangements and regulation in the context of 'flexible work patterns' designed to reconcile work and family life:[11]

> In several countries employers offer the opportunity to work part-time. In addition, most other flexible working-time patterns like teleworking are settled at the level of the firm. Teleworking is less common, though, than part-time employment and national legislation on teleworking is generally absent in European countries. The majority of teleworkers are employed in the public sector, non-profit sector or commercial services. In contrast to part-time work, telework increases with educational level.

The issue of coverage and scope for the Framework Agreement is central to the likelihood that the initiative can deliver meaningful regulations for teleworkers, not only in the UK but across the whole of the EU. Nor is the problem confined to defining 'teleworkers' and 'homeworkers', but embraces issues relating to the protective coverage of labour law provisions to other groups, such as the self employed. As the Trades Union Congress (TUC) lamented during the course of the implementation scrutiny process (following a meeting of the ETUC's Social Dialogue Committee on 16 May 2006):

> ETUC affiliates met in May 2006 to review progress on the agreement. Progress varies across the member countries, according to a preliminary assessment carried out by ETUC. It found there was confusion over whether or how the agreement applied to self-employed workers, whether teleworkers should have the same employment rights as other employees, and on the workability

---

11. European Commission, *Report of an EU Expert Group on Gender, Social Inclusion and Employment* (2005). See <http://bookshop.eu.int/eubookshop/FileCache/PUBPDF/KE6905828ENC/KE6905828ENC_002.pdf> (accessed 20 December 2006).

of the voluntary agreement. There was also the issue of homeworkers, who ETUC found only had limited protection.[12]

Indeed, the ETUC, in preparation for its subsequent meeting on 28 June 2006, felt obliged to address these issues from a cross-national perspective – recognising that the problems involved are not specific to particular Member States, but reflect some of the most fundamental challenges to modern labour law throughout the European Union.[13]

So far as the UK is concerned, there has long been controversy over the way in which modern labour law provides substantial individual employment protections for 'employees', with a narrower group of 'workers' enjoying only a limited selection of those protections, while persons who may be active in the labour market but fail to satisfy the requirements that their activity falls within the definitions of 'employee' or 'worker' are left entirely outside the coverage of the statutory labour law rights.

Although 1998 saw, as has already been indicated, the addition of a category defined as 'home workers' for the purposes of the National Minimum Wage Act, along with a further category defined as 'agency workers' (in relation to both the National Minimum Wage Act 1998 and the Working Time Regulations 1998), little reform has been witnessed to the basic dual qualification status since the development of modern employment protection measures in the mid-1960s and early 1970s. Even a 2002 Government 'Green Paper', purporting to address some of the issues arising in this context, adopted an approach of describing who enjoyed, and who did not enjoy, various statutory employment protections, and sought views about 'possible reform' – rather than putting forward any strategic or analytical framework within which a coherent structure for the enjoyment of employment protections might be developed.[14]

It is, of course, also noteworthy that the preparations leading up to the adoption by the ILO, at its 2006 conference, of a recommendation on the employment relationship,[15] never saw truly positive progress in this direction, given the strength of fundamental objections from the employer side to any regulation, let alone nuanced regulation, of the employment relationship.

It may be suggested that, so far as the UK is concerned, without a radical 're-casting' of the framework within which individual employment protection rights are awarded by the legislator, there is little prospect for a particular structure of statutory rights for teleworkers (or, for that matter, any other specific group within the developing modern labour market) to be established or developed. Furthermore, against a background of sloganistic policy-making in the name of 'globalisation', 'market

---

12. Trades Union Congress 73 *Changing Times News* [31 May 2006].
13. European Commission, *The Evolution of Labour Law 1992 – 2003* [2 volumes] (Luxembourg, 2005).
14. Department of Trade and Industry, *Discussion Document on Employment Status in Relation to Statutory Employment Rights* (London, HMSO, July 2002).
15. International Labour Organisation, *The Employment Relationship*, International Labour Conference, 95th Session, 2006, Report V (1) (Geneva, International Labour Office, 2005).

forces', and the like, no such fundamental 're-casting' of the present paradigm is likely to be undertaken in the foreseeable future.

IV. THE PROBLEM OF 'VOLUNTARY' AGREEMENTS IN THE UNITED KINGDOM

The issue of definitional coverage for employment protection in the UK has to be seen alongside additional, though related, problems which arise out of the way in which the law in that country treats collective agreements and the contractual or non-contractual force of 'agreements' made in various industrial relations and labour market contexts.

This matter can probably be summed up best by recalling the classic 1969 enunciation of the legal status of the collective agreement under the common law:

> Agreements such as these, composed largely of optimistic aspirations, presenting grave problems of enforcement and reached against a background of opinion adverse to enforceability are, in my judgment, not contracts in the legal sense and are not enforceable at law. Without clear and express provision making them amenable to legal action, they remain in the realm of undertakings binding in honour.[16]

This common law judicial approach has to be seen together with the modern statutory provision in section 179 of the Trade Union and Labour Relations (Consolidation) Act 1992, which raises a statutory presumption that the parties to the collective agreement (i.e. the employer and the trade union) do not intend their agreement to create legal relations. This has been held by the courts to mean that the agreement so formed is not a contract at law, since it is said that 'the intention to create legal relations' constitutes an indispensable element in the formation of a contract under English law.

Given this background, the prospects for any 'voluntary agreement', such as the Framework Agreement reached between the European social partners on telework, taking on binding legal force without the intervention of the legislator are so remote as to be almost non-existent. Nor is this confined to the modern examples of 'social dialogue agreements', as exemplified by the telework agreement and the related social dialogue agreement on stress at work.[17] The problem goes to the heart of the regulatory system established by the UK's statutory labour law framework in the context of the common law concerning contracts between private

---

16. *Ford Motor Co. Ltd v. Amalgamated Union of Engineering and Foundry Workers* [1969] 2 QB 303 (330H – 331A).
17. See DTI, *Work-Related Stress: A Guide – Implementing a European Social Partner agreement* (HMSO London 2006), in the context of the social partnership *Framework Agreement on Work-Related Stress* of 8 October 2004. See also *Alan C. Neal*, 'The Collective Agreement as a Public Law Instrument', in F.K. Banakas (ed), *United Kingdom Law in the 1980s* (London 1988) and M. Freedland, *The Personal Employment Contract* (OUP, Oxford 2003).

parties. The difficulties of transposing 'externally agreed norms' into the body of the individual employment contract have been explored in detail over many years,[18] and the obstacles in the way of converting European social dialogue arrangements into binding legal obligations under UK law remain as formidable as ever.

Nor should it be overlooked that scepticism over the potential to convert 'social dialogue agreements' into 'hard' normative provisions as a part of the regulatory systems of individual EU Member States has not been confined to the particularly problematic context of the UK. Thus, in the course of considering a variety of emerging 'new social risks' in the enlarged EU, Trieb and Falkner, having noted that the underlying object for the social partnership negotiations preparatory to the adoption of the Framework Agreement on telework was 'only a document of voluntary character since BUSINESSEUROPE considered telework as a form of working (and not a legal status) and argued that it was inappropriate for a statutory instrument', conclude that:

> This agreement will serve as the crucial test case for the potentials of a purely voluntaristic approach to EU-level industrial relations, and to the 'regulation' of new social risks.[19]

V.   MEASURING THE EXTENT OF TELEWORKING IN THE UNITED KINGDOM

Before embarking on a brief presentation of the available statistical data on tele-workers in the UK, it is as well to sound a word of warning about the reliability of such data, both nationally and across the EU. Interesting examples are available on the European Telework Online website[20] of how outcomes may vary depending upon the methodology and definitions used. Suffice it to say that most observers appear to agree that officially available statistics are likely, for a variety of reasons, to understate the incidence of teleworking.

Turning specifically to the UK, and drawing primarily on the data collected for successive labour force surveys, a steady increase in teleworking can be observed between 1997 and 2005. This increase has built upon an already significant base figure recorded by 1997. Indeed, it is the early development of teleworking in the UK, as part, *inter alia*, of the dramatic restructuring and flexibilisation of the workforce following the return to power of a conservative government under

---

18. F. Schmidt & A. Neal, 'Collective Agreements and Collective Bargaining' [1984] Vol. XV *International Encyclopedia of Comparative Law*, Tübingen, Ch.12; see also Neal, 1986, Neal, 1997 and Freedland, 2004.

19. O. Trieb & G. Falkner, *The EU and New Social Risks: The Need for a Differentiated Evaluation*, Paper prepared for presentation at the 14th Biennial Conference of Europeanists, 'Europe and the World: Integration, Interdependence, Exceptionalism?' Chicago, USA, 11 – 13 March 2004 (Vienna, Institute for Advanced Studies, 2004).

20. *See* <www.eto.org.uk>

Prime Minister Mrs Thatcher in 1979, which marks that country out from the majority of EU Member States.

In the same period, a steady increase can be discerned in the incidence of home working in the UK. All of these figures can be seen in the context of a growing number and percentage of the active working population undertaking employment within the UK labour market throughout the same reference period.

Growth in home working and teleworking: millions and % of UK workforce

	1997	*2001*	*2005*
Home workers	2.3 (9%)	2.6 (10%)	3.1 (11%)
Teleworkers	0.9 (4%)	1.5 (5%)	2.4 (8%)

The early phase of this development (1997 – 1999) suggests the following division by reference to the tripartite reporting definitions used for the labour force surveys:[21]

	1997	*1998*	*1999*
Teleworker home workers (narrow definition)	225,000	256,000	255,000
Teleworkers using home as base	504,000	589,000	693,000
Occasional teleworkers	285,000	301,000	357,000
Total (wide definition)	1,014,000	1,146,000	1,305,000

Looking at the sectors where teleworkers are occupied, data from 2001 suggests the following:[22]

	all	*employee*	*self employed*
Managers and senior officials	424,111	328,988	90,989
Professional occupations	378,666	242,011	135,841
Associated prof. & technical	365,532	169,451	193,531
Administrative and secretarial	132,170	79,512	36,314
Skilled trades	230,379	48,102	181,526

---

21. Presentation by Andrew Miller MP, 'Flexible Work 99' [3 November 1999].
22. *Labour Force Survey* (London – Statistical Series, HMSO, 2001).

	all	employee	self employed
Personal services	31,620	17,382	13,921
Sales and customer services	39,580	24,591	14,139
Process, plant and mechanical ops	27,578	2,033	25,545
Elementary occupations	23,104	5,367	16,106

Furthermore, it is suggested that the body of workers making up the teleworking workforce is significantly better qualified than the average for the UK labour market, such that:

> Compared with the rest of the workforce, UK teleworkers are a highly qualified bunch. . . . They are more than twice as likely to be graduates, with 36.5 per cent having a university degree or equivalent, compared with only 15.1 per cent of the total workforce, and only 4.8 per cent having no formal qualifications (compared with 16.26 per cent of the workforce as a whole).[23]

	workforce	teleworkers
University Degree or equivalent	15.13	36.50
Higher education	8.26	12.71
GCE A Level or equivalent	23.87	24.07
GCSE grades A – C or equivalent	22.16	14.56
Other qualifications	13.64	7.03
No qualification	16.26	4.82

VI.   COMMENTS AND CONCLUSION

To describe the agreed 'guidance' published in the names of the UK 'social partners' as 'implementation' of the European Framework Agreement would be to commit an act of 'economy with the truth' on a scale which only politicians could appreciate.

The 'guidance' is no more than just that – a selection of observations about the understanding of those responsible for its drafting as to the current state of UK law in respect of a variety of issues touched upon by the words of the Framework Agreement. It is hard to discern any 'normative' addition to the legislative *status quo* prior to the conclusion of the agreement at European level. Furthermore, given the state of UK law in relation to agreements referred to as 'collective agreements'

---

23. *Ibid.*

in that country, there is no binding legal effect which follows from the typesetting of the words of the Framework Agreement and their subsequent publication on glossy paper available from Her Majesty's Stationery Office.

In short, the response of the UK to the Framework Agreement illustrates precisely why 'social dialogue' in that Member State is little more than a fig leaf for empty aspirations on the parts of self-appointed interlocutors who purport to fulfil a role spelled out in the European order established by the Treaty of Amsterdam, but who, in reality, lack any of the legitimacy, authority or normative power which would be necessary to undertake such a role.[24]

The notion – propounded by some commentators – that the UK Confederation of British Industry (CBI) and TUC (along with the so-called CEEP (UK) – a *deus ex machina* if ever there were one) – can be considered 'social partners' in the sense in which that term is understood in a variety of European industrial relations systems is nothing more than a cruel myth perpetrated to cover the weakness of the situation in which the parties to employment relations find themselves after a quarter of a century undermining by conservative and 'new labour' governments alike.[25]

Nor is this the occasion on which where that reality has been exposed. With the arguable exception of the preparatory arrangements prior to implementation of Directive 2002/14/EC establishing a general framework for informing and consulting employees in the European Community,[26] the nature of the contacts which have faithfully been reported in successive NAPs drawn up by the UK Government as examples of developing 'social dialogue' in the 'home of collective bargaining' has offered little more than a chance for the remnants of collective labour/management representatives to partake of a listening role in the face of an inevitable introduction of measures already determined and dictated from Whitehall.

Far from being some form of 'soft' law developed by and through modern UK 'social partners',[27] the best that can be said for the current position is that it appears to constitute a species of 'soft social dialogue' – with neither creative input over and above the words agreed in the course of the European level discourse, nor normative consequences at the domestic level, even for those EU-inspired words.

---

24. A. Neal, 'We Love You Social Dialogue – But Who Exactly Are You?' in *La Contrattazione Collettive Europea: Profili Giuridici ed Economici*, Fondazione Giulio Pastore (Milan, FrancoAngeli, 2001), pp. 113 – 127.
25. R. Hyman, 'The Europeanisation – Or the Erosion – of Industrial Relations?' (2001) 32 *Industrial Relations Journal*, 280; *cf.* E. Heery, 'Partnership versus Organising: Alternative Futures for British Trade Unionism' (2002) 33 *Industrial Relations Journal*, 20.
26. A. Neal, 'Information and Consultation for Employees – Still Seeking the Philosopher's Stone?' in *Quality of Work and Employee Involvement in Europe*, M. Biagi (ed.) (Deventer, 2002) 83.
27. K. Sisson & P. Marginson, *'Soft Regulation' – Travesty of the Real Thing or New Dimension?*, Paper produced for the Economic and Social Research Council's research project on 'Emerging Boundaries of European Collective Bargaining at Sector and Enterprise Levels', within the context of the 'One Europe or Several?' programme (Working Paper 32/01, June 2001).

Little surprise, therefore, that fundamental and key issues such as 'employee status', the legal effect of collective agreements in a historically 'voluntarist' system, and the continuing fruitless search for a 'social partnership' continue to dominate the debate over measures such as the Framework Agreement on telework and other creatures of a similar nature.

Until such time as the UK develops – if it ever does – a relational framework for modern 'social partnership' in relation to labour market regulation, the notion of European-level 'social dialogue agreements' being transformed into effective normative regulatory instruments in that country remains a distant dream. More problematically, propositions such as that by the Secretary-General of the TUC, Brendan Barber, do little to disguise the inherent weakness of the TUC and other labour market organisations in the labour market regulation of the 21st Century UK:

> The joint guidance also shows that when social partners work together on issues relating to employment they find much to agree on and can produce guidance for employers and employees which is clear, comprehensive and workable.[28]

Nor does the statement by the Executive Director of CEEP (UK), Charles Nolda, offer anything other than an illustration of the extent of self-delusion which is rife in the modern-day United Kingdom, to the effect that:

> We can rightly be proud of the constructive way in which this guidance has been drafted and indeed to be among the first countries to implement this European accord.[29]

The chilling truth of the matter is to be discerned in the observations of the Director General of the CBI, Digby Jones, who observes that:

> Voluntary, non-binding guidelines such as these represent the way forward in employee relations, enabling business and employees to find the right solutions without unnecessary prescription, and I wholeheartedly welcome them.[30]

What could the UK's main employers' organisation have to fear from such a source? No wonder, either, that the responsible minister at the time – Gerry Sutcliffe MP, Parliamentary Under Secretary of State for Employment Relations, Competition and Consumers – felt able to opine that:

> I am delighted to see that the CBI, TUC and CEEP UK have worked so productively together to produce this document. I welcome and endorse the valuable information this guidance provides and I am sure it will be a useful

---

28. Department of Trade and Industry (2003), n. 9 above, 3.
29. Department of Trade and Industry (2003), n. 9 above, 4.
30. Department of Trade and Industry (2003), n. 9 above, 2.

resource for business when identifying and assessing the key issues when introducing a telework policy.[31]

'Much ado about nothing!' one might cry. But the truly damning indictment must be of the delusions under which the modern successors to the UK labour movement and their employer counterparts are labouring in one of the most deregulated and 'flexible' labour markets so far developed in the global information society.

---

31. Department of Trade and Industry (2003), n. 9 above, 1.

Chapter 15

United States of America

Alvin L. Goldman

I. AMERICAN VIEWS CONCERNING THE VALUE OF TELEWORK

In the United States, 'telecommuting', 'telework', and 'virtual office' are terms used to describe a variety of arrangements that utilize remote communication techniques in order for work to be performed and monitored even though those who manage the work do not have direct physical contact with the workers.

In one sense, the techniques of telework have been around for a very long time. In ancient days, by use of signal flags, smoke, drums, bugles and similar devices, legions and fleets were able to carry out the directives of their generals and admirals. Similarly, runners, carrier pigeons, and other physical modes of long-distance communication enabled generals, admirals and ambassadors to follow the directives of their emperors and kings. At the commercial level, letters of credit enabled buyers and investors to ensure that work at distant locations would be performed according to their dictates prior to payment being made. However, in these examples the desired work efforts could be carried out only at the remote location. Therefore, they involved a different category of work effort than is encompassed by the modern notion of telework. Closer to the modern concept were the ancient cottage industries which allowed capital to conduct manufacturing without providing a common workplace. The required degree of uniformity, quality and productivity were achieved through the use of templates, mock-ups, piece rates,

Blanpain et al., European Framework, Agreements and Telework, pp. 245–272.
©2007, Kluwer Law International BV, The Netherlands.

and circuit riding agents.[1] Eventually, the factory and office systems were adopted to facilitate better co-ordination of work activity; permit more exacting oversight; use larger, more complex machines; and harness superior energy sources.

However, the trend toward greater centralization of work activity has been at least partially reversed by the electronic age's development of new means of rapid, long-distance communication, computation, monitoring, and operational control. More and more frequently, American workers and managers are recognizing that telework can offer a variety of advantages over work performed at a central, common work site. Often at-home telework is seen as a means of reducing the tensions between the competing demands of work and family responsibilities with the result that it can be performed under less stress. Similarly, telework facilitates adjusting the work schedule, pace and environment to each worker's life style preferences and idiosyncrasies. It also permits disabled workers to enjoy needed privacy; avoid hazards unique to their predicament; overcome difficulties or the impossibility of commuting to a traditional work site; and maximize utilization of specialized tools, equipment or aides required to cope with their disabilities. From a broader social perspective, telework additionally can help reduce burdens on energy, transportation, urban space, and other resources, and decrease the accompanying financial, social and environmental costs to workers and employers. Finally, events of recent years reveal that telework can make it possible for many workers to remain productive in the face of mass disasters, or the fear thereof, whether generated by terrorists, pandemics, temporary infrastructure breakdowns, or forces of nature such as hurricanes, tsunamis, earthquakes, and the like.[2]

On the other hand, telework can introduce or exacerbate problems associated with employment relations. Some, for example, contend that the virtual workplace increases gender inequality both in the workplace and at home.[3] Also, techniques of electronic monitoring can intrude upon personal or family privacy, and the separation of workers from one another can reduce organizational opportunities of those who share a community of economic and social interests. At-home telework, additionally, may blur the lines between work and family or personal time

---

1. Until the industrial revolution, most commercial activity was carried on at or about the home of the farmer or artisan, including the work of those employed to assist in those activities. N. Garnett, 'On Castles and Commerce: Zoning Law and the Home-Business Dilemma' (2001) 42 *Wm. and Mary L. Rev.* 1191 at 1191–92.
2. K. Dutrow, 'Note & Comment: Working at Home at Your Own Risk: Employer Liability for Teleworkers under the Occupational Safety and Health Act of 1970' (2002) 18 *Ga. St. U.L. Rev.* 955 at 955–57; J. Natale, 'Exploring Virtual Legal Presence: The Present and The Promise' (2002) 1 *J. High Tech. L.* 157 at 174–75. An assessment of the positive and negative effects of telework is offered by W. Crandall & L. Gao, 'An Update on Telecommuting: Review and Prospects for Emerging Issues' (2005) 70 *S.A.M. Advanced Management J.* 30.
3. M. Travis, 'Equality in the Virtual Workplace' (2003) 24 *Berkeley J. Empl. & Lab. L.* 283, 285; M. Travis, 'Telecommuting: The Escher Stairway of Work/Family Conflict' (2002) 55 *Maine L. Rev.* 262 at 265–66, 270, 275–76.

with the result that telecommuting can intrude on non work activities and leisure.[4] Finally, work site dispersion complicates performance assessment and advancement evaluation,[5] and encumbers enforcement of policies designed to establish worker protections and minimum standards. Thus, in reality the impact of telework has the potential of reducing benefits, protections, and fair treatment of affected workers.

II. EXTENT OF TELEWORK IN THE UNITED STATES

A. GENERALLY

A Bureau of Labour Statistics (BLS) study estimated that as of May 2004, 20.7 million American workers did at least some work at home as part of their primary job. (This was close to a third of the entire US workforce, including government workers.) The survey also reported that about 15 per cent of the non-agricultural workforce worked at home at least once a week.[6] In mid 2005, a privately conducted survey estimated that in the US, 26.1 million people worked from home at least one day a month. This included 22.2 million who did so at least once a week.[7] It is unlikely that telework grew so dramatically in the little more than a year between these two surveys. Rather, the differences more likely reflect a considerable margin of error in gathering such data. However, it should also be noted that to the extent these estimates are reliable they understate the number of teleworkers, since the researchers did not count those working in mobile virtual offices, satellite offices, or telecommuting centres (see below).

A more reliable source of data respecting teleworking, based on the US census studies for the year 2000, reported that 4.2 million, or 3.3 per cent of all workers, stated that they usually worked at home. 'Usually' was defined to mean most days

---

4. See, for example, E. Hill, A. Hawkins, B. Miller, 'Work and Family in the Virtual Office: Perceived Influences of Mobile Telework' (2006) 45 *Family Relations* 293 at 297–98, reporting survey findings that although three quarters of those surveyed thought they benefited personally from telework and a majority thought their family life was improved as a result of telework, almost a fourth said it blurs the distinction between family life and work life and over 15 per cent said it makes them feel like they are always working. Also, in P. Jackson & J. Van Der Wielen, *Teleworking: International Perspectives* (1998), see M. Kimpast & I. Wagner, 'Telework: Managing Spatial, Temporal and Cultural Boundaries', 95 at 115–16; L. Haddon, 'The Experience of Teleworking', 136 at 143; and A. Büssing, 'Teleworking and Quality of Life', 144 at 161–62.
5. For example, a study of lawyers found that many organizations put a high value on being available for face-to-face consultation and meetings, regardless of whether such availability has been proven to increase performance productivity or quality. J. Williams, C. Calvert & H. Cooper, 'Better on Balance? The Corporate Counsel Work/Life Report' (2004) 10 *William & Mary J. Women & L.* 367 at 392–93, 420.
6. BLS, *Work at Home – 2004* (US Department of Labour Document 05-1768, September 22 2005). Workers employed in professional and business services, financial activities, education and health services were the most likely to work at home.
7. Dieringer Research Group, '2004–2005 American Interactive Consumer Survey' reported in summary form by the study sponsor, ITAC News, October 4 2005.

during the week. Thus, those who worked at home part of the week, but worked elsewhere more days than at home, were not counted as at-home workers, thus partly explaining the much lower figure.[8]

B.   FEDERAL GOVERNMENT SECTOR

In October 2000, the US Congress adopted a law which promoted the use of telecommuting by federal government employees by mandating that such opportunities be expanded and by appropriating funds to provide needed equipment and facilities for such efforts.[9] More specifically, the new law called for each executive branch agency to 'establish a policy under which eligible employees of the agency may participate in teleworking to the maximum extent possible without diminished employee performance'.[10] Pursuant to this law, many federal agencies, which sometimes refer to the goal as 'flexiplace arrangements',[11] have adopted telecommuting guidelines and regulations.

Federal agency guidelines identify several alternative means of telecommuting. One method, referred to as a 'mobile virtual office', involves equipping an employee with electronic and mechanical devices that permit work to be performed under supervision by the employee's home office while away from a permanent duty station. Another means of telecommuting is through an agency's 'satellite office'. This is an equipped office arrangement shared by multiple workers in the same geographical area. It allows them to work at a site removed from their usual business office.[12] A variation of an agency satellite office is a 'telecommuting center'. This is a facility established by the federal General Services Administration (GSA)[13] to house employees of more than one agency, and includes work spaces and equipment common to the normal contemporary office environment.[14] Finally, 'work-at-home' is a telework arrangement in

---

8. US Bureau of Census, '2000 PHC-T-35. Working at Home: 2000', Table 1.1.
9. General information about the federal government's programmes can be found at <www.telework.gov/> (accessed 20 December 2006).
10. Public Law No. 106–346 § 359, adopted October 23 2000. An earlier law, 31 US Code § 1348, adopted in 1995, permits agencies to use their appropriated operating funds 'to install telephone lines, any necessary equipment, and to pay monthly charges, in any private residence or private apartment of an employee who has been authorized to work at home'. This language does not appear to allow for government payment for the residential space used as an office.
11. General Services Administration, *OAD P 6010.4* ¶ 11, available at <www.telework.gov/policies/gsapolic.asp> (accessed 20 December 2006).
12. Department of Housing and Urban Development, *Telework Guidelines* § 1.0.4, available at <www.hud.gov/offices/adm/jobs/telework/telwork4.cfm> (accessed 20 December 2006).
13. Among other things, this agency has general responsibility to procure and maintain building sites, other facilities and goods and services used in the operations of the federal government.
14. The employing agencies contribute an hourly or daily fee to the GSA for the amount of use made by their employees. General Services Administration, *OAD P 6010.4* ¶ 11(d), available at <www.telework.gov/policies/gsapolic.asp> (accessed 20 December 2006). As of the end of 2005, 17 such centers had been established, all in the area surrounding Washington DC and its suburbs.

which an employee performs duties in a specified suitable area of his or her home.[15] Depending on the causes that give rise to the telework arrangement, the telecommute arrangement can constitute the employee's regularly scheduled workplace or provide an alternative workplace used for irregular, intermittent periods. Finally, a telework arrangement can be continuous but relatively short-term or it can be a long-term arrangement.[16] Although it would appear to be inconsistent with the purpose of the statute's call for facilitating 'teleworking to the maximum extent possible', at least one federal agency limits work-at-home and satellite office arrangements to no more than three days a week.[17]

A 2004 survey of federal agencies that employed about 1.7 million workers (about 65 per cent of all federal executive branch employees[18]) reported that 140,694 employees (a little over 8 per cent) teleworked.[19]

C. STATE GOVERNMENT SECTOR

Information respecting the employment practices of state and local governments is less complete. In 1990, California adopted what appears to be the first state law encouraging telecommuting by state government employees.[20] Its most recent report estimates that over 7,000 of those employed by the state of California participate in this program. In addition, over six local governments in California have similar programs.[21]

Since 1993, decrees issued by a succession of Governors of Arizona have encouraged teleworking arrangements for that state's public employees.[22] It

---

15. See, for example, Department of Defence, *Telework Guide* § 2.2.1, available at <www.telework. gov/policies/dodguide.asp#overtime> (accessed 20 December 2006).
16. General Services Administration, *OAD P 6010.4* ¶ 11(a)–(c), available at <www.telework.gov/ policies/gsapolic.asp> (accessed 20 December 2006).
17. Department of Housing and Urban Development, *Telework Guidelines* § 2.1.3, available at <www.hud.gov/offices/adm/jobs/telework/telwork4.cfm> (accessed 20 December 2006). This foot dragging in carrying out the telework statute is not exceptional. Despite the requirement of the federal law, as of 2005 about 15 per cent of federal agencies had not yet adopted a telework policy and close to 60 per cent neither provided employees with telework equipment nor shared in the costs of such equipment. Office of Personnel Management, *Report on the Status of Telework* (2005), p. 3.
18. In 2004, total civilian employment in the executive branch was about 2.6 million. Office of Personnel Management, *Employment and Trends* (November 2004), Table 1 – Federal Civilian Personnel Summary. Together with civilian employment in the judicial and legislative branches, total federal sector employment in November 2004 was over 2.7 million. Div. of Current Employ. Stat., Off. of Employ. and Unempl. Stat., Bureau of Labor Statistics, 'Comparison of All Employees, Seasonally Adjusted'.
19. Office of Personnel Management, *Report on the Status of Telework* (2005), p. 2.
20. California Government Code §§ 14200–14203.
21. California Dept. of Personnel Administration, 'The State of California Telework – Telecommuting Program 1983–21st Century' pp. 7, 12–13.
22. Ariz. Exec. Order 2003-11.

estimates that 3,442 employees, or more than 16 per cent of the state government's workforce employed in its most populous county, engage in telework, with the result that they annually drive 3.2 million fewer miles, generate 86,133 fewer pounds of air pollution, and endure 106,336 fewer hours of stressful automobile commuting time. It is asserted that this produces significant employee and employer fuel and vehicle maintenance cost savings, increases productivity, boosts employee morale and job satisfaction, and reduces employee turnover with resulting reduced recruitment and training expenditures.[23]

In 2003, the Governor of Georgia issued an Executive Order establishing a program to encourage telework for its state employees.[24] In Montana, a 1999 directive from the Director of the state's Department of Administration encouraged telework. That agency's most recent report estimates that close to four per cent of its workers now telecommute.[25] Statutes encouraging state agencies to allow telework have been adopted, as well, in Connecticut,[26] Florida,[27] North Carolina,[28] and Oregon.[29]

D. Private Sector

Some government programmes are designed to encourage telework in the private sector. For example, the US Department of Labour's Office of Disability Employment Policy gives financial grants to assist in the development of telecommuting programs that will help disabled workers obtain or maintain employment. In an effort to reduce transportation congestion and related problems, the Connecticut Department of Transportation established an agency called Connecticut Telecommute CT! This agency helps, without charge, Connecticut-based employers to design, develop, and implement programs for employee telecommuting.[30]

In addition, several private organizations in the US are dedicated to encouraging and facilitating the expansion of telework.[31]

---

23. See Arizona Department of Administration, 'Partnering to Make a Difference', available at <www.teleworkarizona.com/telefiles/program.htm> (accessed 20 December 2006).
24. Information is available from workaway@gms.state.ga.us.
25. Montana Audit Report 03-P01.
26. Conn. Gen. Stat. § 5-248i.
27. Fla. Stat. § 110.171.
28. N.C. Gen. Stat. § 143-215.107C.
29. Oregon Revised Statutes § 240.855.
30. <www.telecommutect.com> (accessed 20 December 2006).
31. For example, National Telecommuting Institute, Inc. is an educational and job-matching organization that encourages the development of telework jobs for Americans with disabilities.

III. LEGAL RULES AFFECTING TELEWORK

A. JURISDICTION[32] WITH AUTHORITY TO REGULATE OR DECIDE

Because the US is a federal system, state law often has a substantial effect on the employment relationship. This poses legal complications when telecommuting results in work being performed in one or more states other than that of the location of the office or headquarters to which a worker reports. There are two aspects to this problem: determining whether a particular jurisdiction has authority to regulate the employment issue and determining which jurisdiction's law should be followed in resolving a claim.

Under US law, the authority of administrative agencies and courts can be exercised only if there is jurisdiction over the parties involved in a conflict or over the subject matter at issue. Thus, if a person or business entity is physically present in a state or federal enclave or had significant contacts with that locality with respect to the basis for the claim, that person or entity is subject to the adjudicative authority of its courts and administrative agencies. Alternatively, courts and administrative agencies can exercise adjudicative authority over competing claims if the subject matter of the dispute, for example property, is located in that jurisdiction.[33] Federal administrative agencies and courts have authority to adjudicate a dispute if the Constitution gives Congress regulatory authority over the subject matter and Congress has adopted laws exercising that authority. Federal courts additionally can hear cases based on the identity of the parties, including cases in which the disputants are residents of different states.[34] This can result in more than one jurisdiction having competence to resolve a claim. For example, most states will process a claim for a work-related injury or illness if the causal event occurred in that jurisdiction, or if the parties entered into the employment agreement there, or if the work principally was performed there.[35] These alternative grounds for processing a claim, therefore, can result in multiple jurisdictions receiving the claim.[36] However, to avoid the problem of multiple recoveries, courts generally hold that the award granted by one jurisdiction is an offset against the recovery that is available when the same claim is presented in another jurisdiction.[37]

---

32. In the US, the term 'jurisdiction' is a broad concept that refers to the geographic area within which political and judicial authority may be exercised by co-ordinate governmental bodies; their power to regulate activities, persons and entities; their authority to make decisions respecting particular activities, persons or entities; and their authority to enforce regulations or decisions respecting particular activities, persons or entities. *Black's Law Dictionary* (7th ed., 1999), p. 855.
33. *Insurance Corporation of Ireland, Ltd. v. Compagnie Des Bauxites De Guinee* (1982) 456 US 694, 703–04; D. Tyler, 'Personal Jurisdiction via E-Mail: Has Personal Jurisdiction Changed in the Wake of *Compuserve, Inc. v. Patterson?*' (1998) 51 *Ark. L. Rev.* 429.
34. J. Nowak & R. Rotunda, *Constitutional Law* (2nd ed., 2004), § 2.1.
35. A. Larson, *Workers' Compensation Law*, §§ 142.03, 143.01, 143.02.
36. *Ibid.*, § 142.01.
37. *Sun Ship Inc. v. Pennsylvania* (1980) 447 US 715. State workers' compensation statutes often bar a claim if there has already been recovery under another jurisdiction's workers' compensation laws.

On the other hand, because states do not follow a uniform set of guidelines respecting the sufficiency of contacts that will justify processing a claim, where an employment relationship straddles more than one jurisdiction there is the potential that a claim will be rejected by each of them. To avoid the resulting injustice in one such situation, an authoritative source argues that when dealing with workers' compensation claims, the employee's contacts with the place of injury should always be treated as sufficient to require that jurisdiction to accept and process the claim.[38]

An additional important principle respecting potential jurisdictional overlap is that if when it created an employment standard or benefit the legislature assigned to an administrative tribunal the initial responsibility of interpreting and applying the standard or benefit, then, as a general rule, only the assigned administrative agency and the courts of that jurisdiction are legally competent to adjudicate questions concerning the interpretation of that legislation.[39]

Unemployment insurance claims filed by employees who work in one or more jurisdictions separate from the place from which their work is directed can pose a similar problem respecting which jurisdiction should accept and process the claim. For example, in one case a New York resident was hired by a financial information service provider to work in its New York office but later arranged with her employer to relocate to Florida and perform her work there by means of telecommuting from her Florida residence. Her work hours were set by the New York office which also controlled when she could take vacation and illness leave, and she maintained daily electronic contact with and submitted weekly reports to her New York based supervisor. On one occasion, at the employer's direction, she travelled to New York and worked there for two weeks. This arrangement continued for over 20 months at which time the employer elected to end the arrangement and offered her a job in New York which she declined. The employer then terminated her employment but when she filed in Florida for unemployment insurance benefits, the claim was administratively denied on the ground that she had voluntarily quit her job without good cause. She did not appeal that decision but instead filed a claim in New York. Her New York claim was administratively rejected on the ground that she was not employed there. This time she appealed the administrative determination to the state court. The New York court did not reach the question of whether she had just cause to decline a job that would require her to move back to that state. (Under the approach taken by all states, if she had just cause to decline that invitation, she would not have lost her entitlement to unemployment insurance benefits.) Instead, it agreed with the administrative agency that her claim was

---

38. A. Larson, n. 35 above, § 143.02[6].
39. See, for example, J. Hood, B. Hardy & H. Lewis, *Workers' Compensation and Employee Protection Laws*, (1990), p. 122. Other courts are constitutionally required to give full faith and credit to those decisions. However, federal courts can entertain collateral attacks on the constitutionality of an agency's authority over a claim or respecting the fairness or constitutional validity of the adjudicatory process. J. Hood *et al.* at pp. 124–25.

properly dismissed on the ground that the New York statute provides unemployment insurance benefits only if the employment is 'localized' in that state. The court explained that the central purpose of unemployment insurance is to reduce the economic impact on the community and that when work is performed in more than one state, that goal is best achieved by requiring that the claim be made in the locality where the unemployed worker was physically present when the job was lost.[40] The New York court did not discuss the more practical question of whether the New York employer paid or should have paid New York or Florida payroll taxes, including unemployment insurance premiums – a consideration that arguably should be of paramount importance in deciding whether a state should accept an unemployment insurance claim.

Another area in which jurisdictional authority is important respecting the employment relationship concerns the authority to regulate or tax the resulting remuneration. When a worker performs work tasks in one or more states other than that of the location of the office to which a worker reports, more than one jurisdiction may be able to claim authority to regulate or tax that part of the activity with which it has significant contacts.[41] For example, in one case a law professor who taught in New York three days a week, but for his own convenience and with his employer's consent worked from home the other two days, was denied the right to file a New York non-resident state income tax return that would have apportioned his income for state income tax purposes. The New York court held that all of the taxpayer's work income should be counted as New York work income because he was not obligated to work at home.[42] The court did not discuss whether it will treat work at home as a matter of the employee's own convenience if telework is medically necessary. The decision potentially exposes a worker's full income to taxation by both the tax payer's state of residence and the employer's state of residence. Unless Congress intervenes to remove the possibility of multiple

---

40. In *Re Allen* (NY 2003) 794 N.E.2d 18. The New York court's decision is criticized in D. Gregory, '19th Century Local Unemployment Compensation Insurance Law in the 21st Century Global Economy' (2004) 44 *Santa Clara L. Rev.* 1113; Note, 'Telecommuters and Their Virtual Existence in the Unemployment World' (2004) 33 *Hofstra L. Rev.* 785. As indicated in the above text at the end of this paragraph, the author thinks the commentator's criticism is misplaced if the employer had only been paying Florida payroll taxes, including Florida unemployment insurance taxes, on the wages paid to this employee.

41. J. Gabel & N. Mansfield, 'The Information Revolution and Its Impact on the Employment Relationship: An Analysis of the Cyberspace Workplace' (2003) 40 *Amer. Bus. L.J.* 305, 307; J. Nowak & R. Rotunda, *Constitutional Law* (2nd ed., § 8.6-7, 8.11, 2004).

42. *Zelinsky v. Tax Appeals Tribunal of the State of New York* (2003) 801 N.E.2d 840 (NY), *cert.* denied (2004) 541 US 1009. Accord, *Huckaby v. New York*, 829 N.E.2d 276 (NY), *cert.* denied (2005) 126 S. Ct. 546 (Tennessee resident who for his own convenience worked in that state for a New York employer and had to pay New York income tax on his full salary even though he worked in New York only about 25 per cent of the time). The New York court has been persuasively criticized for the inconsistency between its approach to teleworker unemployment insurance claims and teleworker income tax liability. Note, 'Telecommuters and Their Virtual Existence in the Unemployment World' (2004) 33 *Hofstra L. Rev.* 785, 803.

state tax levies on the same income,[43] eventually the US Supreme Court will have to determine whether this possibility of multiple state income taxation is an impermissible burden on constitutionally protected freedom to commute from state to state or on the constitutional privilege of selecting to live and work in different jurisdictions.[44]

B.   JURISDICTION[45] WHOSE LAW CONTROLS THE DECISION

Even if a jurisdiction has sufficient contacts with the parties or with the subject matter to justify its adjudication of the resulting dispute, a court will not necessarily apply its own law in resolving that dispute. Sometimes, under conflict of laws rules, a court will decide that the dispute being heard should be resolved in accordance with the law of another jurisdiction.

Generally, the law of the 'place of employment' controls a conflict arising out of an employment contract. As a result, if an employer operating in one state has a worker who performs work in a different state, a question can arise as to which state is that employee's place of employment – the place where the work is done or the place from which the work is directed? Complicating this issue is the principle that contracting parties generally are permitted jointly to select which state's substantive law will control the interpretation of their contract. This is known as a 'choice-of-law' provision. For example, in one case, a company headquartered in the state of Georgia which had 19 employees who performed their work in that state, hired a vice president of finance and business development who lived in Texas and did most of his work in Texas by means of telecommuting through mail, facsimile transmissions, electronic mail, telephone, and a networked computer. Less than a year after he was hired, he was dismissed on the ground that his performance was inadequate. When the dismissal was challenged, the employer contended that the vice president's employment was 'at-will'. Under that principle, a worker can quit or be dismissed at any time without the need to prove justification for the action.

---

43. In May 2005, a bill entitled 'Telecommuter Tax Fairness Act of 2005' was introduced in both the House of Representatives and the Senate. H.R. 2558, S. 1097. The bill, designed to nullify the New York court's decision, was referred to a subcommittee in both houses but, as of a year later, no further action had been taken by either subcommittee. The bill provides that income of a non-resident may be taxed by a state only for periods when the earner is physically working in the state and that 'no State may deem a non-resident individual to be present in or working in such State on the grounds that such non-resident individual is present at or working at home for the non-resident individual's convenience'.
44. A body of complex decisions holds both that federal jurisdiction over interstate commerce prohibits states from unduly burdening such commerce without federal consent and that the constitutional requirement that states grant non residents the privileges and immunities afforded to residents prohibits discriminatory commercial burdens, including tax burdens, on non residents. For example, *Complete Auto Transit v. Brady* (1977) 430 US 274; *Camp Newfound/ Owatonna, Inc. v. Town of Harrison* (1997) 520 US 564; J. Swain, 'State Income Tax Jurisdiction: A Jurisprudential and Policy Perspective' (2003) 45 Wm and Mary L. Rev. 319.
45. See n. 32 above.

The vice president, on the other hand, contended that he had a one-year employment contract. Under generally accepted principles in the US, if an employment contract is for a specific duration, the party terminating the relationship prior to the end of that duration must justify its action.[46]

The employer sought from a federal court located in Georgia a declaration of law that the employment relationship was 'at-will'. This raised two questions. First, whether the vice president could be sued in Georgia rather than in Texas; second, whether Georgia or Texas law should control the question concerning the 'at-will' or non 'at-will' nature of this particular employment relationship. Because judicial decisions vary from state to state respecting such matters as whether an employment contract for a specific term must be evidenced by a signed writing,[47] the court's selection of which state's law governed the relationship could determine the outcome, since an agreement had not been signed even though, prior to the start of work, the parties had exchanged proposed provisions for a written contract.

The federal court ruled that because the vice president made frequent trips to the company's Georgia headquarters and had responsibilities that affected the operations there, it was appropriate to allow the suit to be brought in the federal court located in that state. More importantly, the federal court also explained that because the parties had discussed including in a written contract a choice-of-law provision which selected Georgia law, and because a significant portion of the work was done in that state and affected business operations in that state, it was appropriate to let Georgia law control the result.[48]

Care must be taken to recognize the potential limits of the above federal court's holding inasmuch as the court's analysis implied that had the vice president not made frequent trips to Georgia, the court may have ruled that Texas law was controlling. Additionally, since there was no written contract, the fact that a choice-of-law proposal[49] had been made which would have selected Georgia law was ambiguous in its implications inasmuch as we must ponder whether the failure to adopt such a written provision indicated that it was not of material concern to either side.

When the legal issues at stake concern a tort, property or other category of dispute, the rules for determining which jurisdiction's law should control the case are not necessarily the same as those used for selecting the law to control contract disputes. For example, the general rule is that tort rights and liabilities are

---

46. A. Goldman & R. White, 'United States' in *International Encyclopaedia for Labour Law*, R. Blanpain (ed.) at ¶ 148–50.
47. See n. 46 above at ¶¶ 143–45.
48. *Carekeeper Software Development Co., Inc. v. Silver* (N.D. GA 1999) 46 F. Supp. 2d 1366, affirmed without opinion 264 F.3d 1146 (11th Cir. 2001).
49. Contractual choice-of-law provisions are enforced by US courts if the parties could have resolved the underlying dispute by means of a specific provision in their contract. In other situations the choice-of-law selection will be honoured only if the state whose law the parties selected has a substantial relationship to the parties or the transaction and there is no jurisdiction both with a materially greater interest in the transaction and the law chosen is not contrary to a fundamental policy of the latter state. See American Law Institute, *Restatement of Conflict of Laws* (2nd ed.), § 187.

determined by the law of the state which has the most significant relationship to the occurrence and the parties and that, presumptively, the law of the state in which the injury was suffered should control.[50] Accordingly, had the vice president in the above referenced case been injured when driving in Texas as a passenger in a vehicle driven recklessly by the visiting corporate president, it is unlikely that Georgia law would control a resulting personal injury suit brought by the vice president. In contrast, if the vice president filed a claim for workers' compensation benefits, case law indicates that recovery would be available and decided under the law of the state whose statute was invoked, whether Georgia, Texas, or both.[51]

For the above reasons, when telework involves multiple jurisdictions, some potential conflicts can be avoided if the parties include in the employment agreement an explicit choice-of-law provision. However, as observed, if it is to be honored by adjudicative bodies, that choice should be supported by the actual substantial contacts of the parties with the selected jurisdiction.

C.   Choice of Whether to Work at Home

Normally, deciding where work will be done is a prerogative of management unless the parties have specified the workplace or places in an employment contract or collective agreement. Although, as discussed below, general statutes that confine management's authority respecting the work situs have not been adopted in the US, management's determination of where work will be performed must be free from discrimination based on legally prohibited considerations. In addition, if the employer is a governmental entity, arguably the government employees cannot be required to work at home unless they voluntarily agree to that arrangement, because such compulsion would infringe on constitutional protection against government intrusions on the privacy of the home and might also constitute a taking of property without just compensation.[52] This protection is implicitly acknowledged in some federal agency regulations which emphasize that work-at-home arrangements must be voluntary.[53] However, publications of the General Services Administration (GSA) and the Department of Agriculture suggest that in emergency situations a federal employee may be required to work

---

50. American Law Institute, *Restatement of Conflict of Laws* (2nd ed.), § 145–46.
51. *Indus. Comm. of Wisconsin v. McCartin* (1947) 330 US 622; American Law Institute, *Restatement of Conflict of Laws* (2nd ed.), §§ 181–82. See, also, *Passantino v. Johnson & Johnson Consumer Prods.* (3d Cir. 2000) 212 F.3d 493, 505–06 (equal employment opportunity law of state where teleworker performed his duties was applicable even though the contested decision had been made in another state where his supervisors were located and from which his work was directed).
52. These protections are found in Amendments III, IV and V to the Constitution of the United States of America.
53. For example, Department of Housing and Urban Development, *Telework Policy*, § 1.2.4; General Services Administration, *Telework Policy*, Appendix A (sample telework contract); Department of Defense, *Telework Policy*, § D (d).

at home,[54] but no statutory or other authority is cited by either agency in support of that contention, and the doubtful constitutionality of such a requirement has not been tested in the courts. At least one state's law, perhaps reflecting recognition of the constitutional restraints on government intrusions upon household privacy, encourages telework for its employees but explicitly makes participation voluntary.[55]

An employer's pronouncement that telework is available to employees and its adoption of policies encouraging such arrangements are not the only factors that influence whether employees will elect to engage in that type of work activity. Studies show that the choice is affected by the attitude of individual supervisors toward such arrangements and the workforce's perceptions respecting management's willingness to assess teleworkers using the same standards applied when evaluating the work of those who do their jobs under direct supervisory oversight.[56]

An additional consideration that may affect the extent to which employers and workers can resort to the work-at-home telework format is the presence of zoning laws, home owners' association rules, or restrictive leasehold or deed covenants that potentially bar, limit or otherwise regulate work-at-home arrangements. In the US the purposes of such restrictions include preventing the noise and congestion of large numbers of people and vehicles that are deemed incompatible with a tranquil domestic setting, insulating living areas from unhealthy or dangerous emissions from commercial processes, reducing the number of strangers who might pose threats to personal security, and avoiding structural modifications and promotional activities that might affront aesthetic sensibilities. However, the details of such property use restrictions or prohibitions are widely varied.[57] They also are widely ignored.[58] In large measure they are ignored because too often they are written in broad, overly inclusive terms. Although enforcement efforts are unlikely to be initiated if no one is inconvenienced by a particular work-at-home activity that violates a zoning or covenant restriction, the existence of the restriction invites unequal enforcement for vindictive or corrupt purposes. Accordingly, in recognition of the growth in work-at-home activities, it has been urged that such restrictions should be amended to more specifically target only the underlying legitimate communal concerns.[59]

---

54. GSA, 'Telework – Frequently Asked Questions' and Department of Agriculture, Depart. Reg. 4080-811-002 at § 7(a) (5).
55. Fla. Stat. § 110.171(3)(c).
56. P. Berg, E. Applebaum, T. Bailey & A. Kallberg, 'Contesting Time: International Comparisons of Employee Control of Working Time' (2004) 57 *Ind. & Lab. Rel. Rev.* 331, 342.
57. N. Garnett, 'On Castles and Commerce: Zoning Law and the Home-Business Dilemma' (2001) 42 *Wm. and Mary L. Rev.* 1191, 1206–10, 1230–35.
58. N. Garnett, n. 57 above, 1198, 1228.
59. N. Garnett, n. 57 above, 1237–44.

D. TELEWORKER'S STATUS AS AN EMPLOYEE

Employers sometimes attempt to evade employee protective statutes by asserting that the telecommuter's enhanced independence transforms the relationship from employment to independent contractor, a relationship with fewer statutory protections. The earliest cases drawing a line between employees and independent contractors were largely actions respecting alleged liability of the employer (principal) for the employee's (agent's) tort. Those cases concluded that if the principal retains to a substantial degree the right to control the agent's work conduct, the principal is an employer and, in that capacity, has *respondeat superior* liability for the agent's errors.

Many courts have substituted an 'economic realities' approach when dealing with the question of whether a principal must provide statutorily based employment protections and benefits for a person who performs work that serves the principal's business interests.[60] American courts, however, do not fully agree on the factors to be weighed in testing the economic realities of whether there is an employment relationship. Some courts look to whether the alleged employer has the power to hire and fire the employees, supervises and controls employee work schedules or conditions of employment, unilaterally determines the rate and method of payment, and maintains employment records.[61] Other courts weigh additional factors, including whether the alleged employee has the opportunity for profit or loss and has a significant investment in the purported independent business, whether the working relationship with the principal is expected to be completed in a relatively short time or is intermittent as contrasted with being expected to be of long-term duration, what degree of skill is required to perform the work, and the extent to which the work is an integral part of the alleged employer's business.[62] These factors, which focus on the agent's dependency upon the principal to provide work, expand the notion of who is protected as an employee and are a more accurate reflection of the typical lofty platitudes pronounced by politicians when they introduce and adopt employee protective legislation.[63] Clearly, teleworkers are more likely to be treated as employees when their relationship is subjected to an economic reality test than if assessed under the right of control test.

If a teleworker is found to be an employee, the legal consequences go beyond issues of the protections owed to the worker. The employer may additionally have vicarious liability for injuries to business visitors who are at the employee's home,

---

60. *Armbruster v. Quinn* (6th Cir. 1983) 711 F.2d 1332, 1341–42.
61. *Watson v. Graves* (5th Cir. 1990) 909 F.2d 1549; *Carter v. Dutchess Community College* (2d Cir. 1984) 735 F.2d 8, 9; *Bonnette v. California Health and Welfare Agency* (9 Cir. 1983) 704 F.2d 1465, 1470.
62. *Henderson v. Inter-Chem Coal Co., Inc.* (10th Cir. 1994) 41 F.3d 567, 570. See, also, *Nat'l Resort Mart, Inc. v. Hitchcock* (Mo. Ct. App. 2002) 88 S.W.3d 459 (used 20 criteria set forth in a federal Internal Revenue Service ruling to decide whether claimants have employee status under the state's unemployment insurance law).
63. J. Hood, B. Hardy & H. Lewis, *Workers' Compensation and Employee Protection Laws* (1990), pp. 51–52.

to all visitors in the employee's at-home work area (including family members), and for injuries caused by the telecommuter's negligence at other locations.[64] On the other hand, there is no firm reason why courts could not continue to apply the traditional right of control test when addressing vicarious liability issues while using an economic reality test respecting responsibilities for employment standards and benefits.

E.   WAGE PAYMENT LAWS

Telework presents some legal issues that arise out of minimum wage and overtime pay legislation.

The Fair Labor Standards Act (FLSA) establishes federal minimum wage and overtime payment standards. Much of its impact is dependent on regulations adopted by the Secretary of Labor or by the Wage–Hour Administrator who is responsible for administrative enforcement of the Act. Although section 11(d) of Title 29 US Code authorizes the Wage–Hour Administrator to restrict, prohibit, and regulate 'industrial homework . . . to prevent the circumvention or evasion of and to safeguard the minimum wage rate', telework is rarely industrial in nature. Hence, generally, its availability is not subject to the administrative restrictions or regulations established under that statutory section.

On the other hand, regulations adopted under the FLSA specify that the Act applies whether work is performed in a factory, at home, or elsewhere.[65] Thus, the record keeping and wage calculation regulations adopted under that law must be satisfied by a telework arrangement.

A more difficult question is whether the Fair Labor Standards Act requires an employer to absorb the costs of establishing and equipping a home office or other remote office used for work. Regulations adopted under the FLSA allow an employer to make pay deductions for the reasonable cost of tools and equipment used in work so long as the net pay is at or above the federal minimum.[66] Thus, under federal law an employer is permitted to make pay deductions for the fair rental value of a computer, the cost of CD disks used by the employee, and the like, so long as the net weekly pay after those deductions still equals or exceeds the federal minimum wage. State wage payment laws often impose further limits on what can be deducted from pay by excluding all deductions except those specifically allowed. Typically, the above listed examples of deductions would not be allowed under such state laws.[67]

Although the federal minimum wage does not expressly prohibit an employer from conditioning the opportunity to engage in telework upon the employee

---

64. J. Mills, C. Wong-Ellison, W. Werner & J. Clay, 'Employer Liability for Telecommuting Employees' [August 2001] *Cornell Hotel and Restaurant Admin. Q.*, 48, 56.
65. 29 Code Fed. Reg. § 776.6.
66. 29 Code Fed. Reg. § 531.36(b).
67. For example, Cal. Lab. Code § 224; Ky. Rev. Stat. §§ 337.060-.070; Mass. Gen. Laws Ch. 149, §§ 150A, 152A, 178B.

purchasing the specially needed equipment or supplies, a Department of Labor regulation provides:

> [I]f it is a requirement of the employer that the employee must provide tools of the trade which will be used in or are specifically required for the performance of the employer's particular work, there would be a violation of the Act in any workweek when the cost of such tools purchased by the employee cuts into the minimum or overtime wages required to be paid him under the Act.[68]

It should be noted that under this Department of Labor regulation, because the reimbursement must only be sufficient to bring the worker's wages up to the hourly minimum, if the worker normally makes more than the minimum, the employer can require the employee to absorb the expenditure to the extent of the difference between the worker's normal wage for a week and the week's wages based on the hourly minimum.[69] The regulation does not address the more complex question of how to calculate the value of the required equipment if the employee has owned it for an extended period or uses it as well for personal benefit.

Courts give considerable deference to Department of Labor regulations but are not bound by them, and there is some basis for arguing that if Congress intended to impose a reimbursement requirement on employers for employee supplied equipment it would have specified it in explicit language.[70] On the other hand, one federal appellate court has given its approval to the interpretation adopted by the Labor Department in the above quoted regulation.[71]

Consistent with the concept of the employer's responsibility to fund the costs of productive activities, the federal agency with primary responsibility for promoting government employee telework takes the position that equipment, equipment maintenance, telephone lines and service, and the like, should be provided by the

---

68. 29 Code Fed. Reg. § 531.35.
69. The above cited regulation requires that reimbursement for the difference between the minimum wage and the amount expended by the employee be calculated for the week in which the expense was incurred. One court decision ruled that when hiring is conditioned upon the employee incurring such expenditure, the employer must reimburse the employee for that difference in the first pay week. *Arriaga v. Fla. Pac. Farms L.L.C.* (11th Cir. 2002), 305 F.3d 1228, 1237.
70. Temporary agricultural work visas are available under certain conditions when farmers cannot find US residents to perform needed work. One of the conditions is that the prospective employer agrees to pay the temporary worker at least the specially prescribed minimum wage and employs the worker for a stated duration. In such situations, if the worker completes 50 per cent of the contract work period, the farmer must reimburse the worker for the costs of travelling to the US for the job and subsistence costs incurred during the period of travel. The farmer is additionally required to reimburse the worker for the same costs incurred for the return trip to the worker's home country if the worker remains for the full contract period. 8 US Code § 1188(c) (3) (B) (i); 20 Code Fed. Reg. 655.102(b) (5) (i)–(ii). Because Congress has made this a specific compensation requirement for temporary foreign agricultural workers, arguably, by implication, similar payments are not required of employers respecting more general types of employment, since Congress has not adopted similar specific language regarding reimbursement for costs they incur to obtain their jobs.
71. *Arriaga v. Fla. Pac. Farms* (11th Cir. 2002) *L.L.C.*, 305 F.3d 1228, 1236–37.

employing government agency if these items are required for such work.[72] Nevertheless, the agency contends that incidental costs of at-home equipment operation (heating, electricity, water, and space usage) must be borne by the government employee. It justifies this position on the ground that these employee costs are more than offset by the savings which work-at-home employees gain from reduced commuting, parking, meals and clothing expenses.[73] However, no such mitigation of an employer's obligations is recognized by Department of Labor regulations, adopted for enforcement of the FLSA, which require that when determining whether wages satisfy the statutory minimum, expenditure made primarily for the employer's benefit must not be deducted from employee pay.[74] Thus, if challenged in court, federal agencies ultimately may be required to reimburse their teleworkers for those utility and rental expenses that are attributable to their telework activities.

Despite the minimum wage and overtime laws, workers are often paid less than is minimally required. It was estimated that in May 2004, over 10,189,000 American employees worked at home an average of 6.8 hours a week without receiving extra pay.[75] In many instances this was legal because the federal minimum wage and overtime laws exempt from overtime pay salaried employees who qualify as executive, administrative or professional employees. The FLSA has a variety of other exemptions, including higher paid computer software analysts. Nevertheless, some of the reported work performed at home was likely done by those who do not qualify for these exemptions and, therefore, was in violation of federal minimum wage and overtime pay requirements.

F.   EQUAL EMPLOYMENT OPPORTUNITY LAWS

Telecommuting can affect or be affected by equal employment opportunity laws in two ways. First, such laws may prohibit an employer from refusing to allow telework if the decision is unlawfully motivated. Secondly, under some circumstances, laws that require reasonable accommodation of employees who are in protected classes may entitle the protected employees to engage in telework. ('Protected classes' refers to those groups of workers who are often victimized by discrimination and, therefore, are afforded statutory protections from such discrimination. Federal laws prohibit discrimination based on race, gender, religion, national identity, disability, age 40 and above, union activity, and participation in reporting or

---

72. S.1348 of Title 31 of the US Code, with just a couple of narrow exceptions, prohibits federal funds from being spent to install or maintain telephones in private residences. However, Title VI § 620 of Public Law 104-52, adopted November 19 1995, permits federal funds to be used for such purposes if an employee is duly authorized to work at home in accordance with policies established by the Office of Personnel Management.
73. General Services Administration, OAD P 6010.4 (15) (i–l).
74. 29 Code Fed. Reg. 531.32(c).
75. BLS, *Work at Home – 2004* (US Department of Labor Document 05-1768, September 22 2005), Tables 4 and 6.

assisting in the enforcement of various worker protective laws. The duty to provide reasonable accommodation, however, is limited to disabled employees and those whose religious practices restrict certain work activities or work environments.[76])

For example, female workers who telework to facilitate being able to care for their children are entitled to equal treatment with male employees who telework for other reasons. However, an employer is not required to permit telework merely because that arrangement removes some of the complications of an employee's childcare responsibilities. Thus, in one case a court ruled that it was not evidence of sex discrimination when an employee, who worked from home two days a week where she cared for her two young children, was asked whether she could do a higher paid job for which she was being interviewed if it had to be performed entirely on the employer's premises and, therefore, would require her to place her children in day care during work hours. The court explained that the question was not illogical or unnecessary because it concerned potential time conflicts and was not based on the stereotyped assumption that a female has primary responsibility to provide care for children.[77]

Similarly, in a case in which a pregnant manager asserted that she could satisfactorily perform her job from home, a trial court concluded: '[A]s a matter of law an employer may mandate that those in leadership positions come to the office to do their job. On its face that is an entirely reasonable requirement and one dictated by principles of sound management'.[78] In contrast, refusal to permit an employee to telework is evidence of discrimination if the privilege is granted to similarly situated employees who are not in a protected classification.[79] Accordingly, in the previously quoted case, the court added: 'Of course, if an employer has permitted a manager in a nonprotected class to work from home but has denied that opportunity to a manager in a protected class, it must demonstrate that there is a legitimate, non-pretextual basis for its discrimination'.[80]

It has been argued that because women generally have far more family care responsibilities than men, they are in greater need to avail themselves of work-at-home options. Therefore, in theory, a gender discrimination claim can be made if offered work-at-home arrangements entail reduced earning or promotion opportunities that cannot be functionally justified. In that situation the arrangement has a disparate impact on female workers and, therefore, should support a discrimination claim seeking equalization of the opportunities for earning or promotion.[81]

Laws protecting employees from disability discrimination pose an additional complication with respect to telework since such laws impose on the employer a duty to make reasonable efforts to accommodate the disabled worker's special

---

76. A. Goldman & R. White, 'United States' in *International Encyclopaedia for Labour Law*, R. Blanpain (ed.) at ¶¶ 347, 356; R. White, *Employment Law and Employment Discrimination* (1998).
77. *Stahl v. St. Anthony Med. Ctr.* (7th Cir. 2004) 2004 App. LEXIS 12890.
78. *Rafeh v. University Research Co. L.L.C.* (D. MD. 2000) 114 F. Supp. 2d 396, 399.
79. *Bassett v. Minneapolis* (8th Cir. 2000) 211 F.3d 1097, 1109.
80. *Rafeh v. University Research Co. L.L.C.*, n. 78 above at 399.
81. M. Travis, 'Equality in the Virtual Workplace' (2003) 24 *Berkeley J. Empl. & Lab. L.* 283, 346–54.

needs. An often cited appellate court decision, issued in 1995, stated: '*general-ly*...an employer is not required to accommodate a disability by allowing the disabled worker to work, by himself, without supervision, at home'.[82] However, care must be taken to not read more into that statement than was intended by the court. First, the court qualified its statement by noting that this proposition was *generally* applicable; it did not present the statement as an absolute rule. Secondly, the court's conclusion was based on its observation that:

> Most jobs in organizations public or private involve team work under supervision rather than solitary unsupervised work, and team work under supervision *generally* cannot be performed at home without a substantial reduction in the quality of the employee's performance. *This will no doubt change as communications technology advances, but is the situation today.*[83]

Thus, with the improvement of real time methods of group communications among those in remote locations, and increased experience with the success and efficiency of telecommuting, it may no longer be appropriate to presume that reasonable accommodation of disabilities does not include work-at-home arrangements. Accordingly, the question of the reasonableness of acceding to a disabled employee's work-at-home request should be approached as an issue of fact to be decided case by case, an approach taken by at least some courts.[84] Nevertheless, with frequency, work-at-home requests by disabled workers have been rejected by the judiciary for reasons such as too many of the worker's core responsibilities required physical presence at the employer's facility, excessive expense would have been entailed in operating under that arrangement, the worker had shown that he or she could not be relied upon to perform diligently without direct supervision, and the like.[85]

---

82. *Vande Zande v. Wisconsin* (7th Cir. 1995) 44 F.3d 538, 544 (emphasis supplied).
83. *Ibid.* (emphasis supplied).
84. For example, *Mason v. Avaya Communications, Inc.* (10th Cir. 2004) 357 F.3d 1114, 1124; *Humphrey v. Memorial Hosps. Ass'n* (9th Cir. 2001) 239 F.3d 1128; *Howard v. Gutierrez* (2005) US Dist. LEXIS 38672 (D. DC 2005); *Hernandez v. City of Hartford* (D. CN 1997) 959 F. Supp. 125.
85. For example, *Mason v. Avaya Communications, Inc.* (10th Cir. 2004) 357 F.3d 1114, 1121 (supervisors could not adequately monitor productivity of work performed at home and at-home worker would not be available to assist or cover for others who were faced with a work overload); *Morrissey v. General Mills, Inc.* (8th Cir. 2002) 37 Fed. Appx. 842 (per curiam) (cost of accommodation excessive where several times a day a courier would have to bring documents to the disabled worker's home); *Kvorjak v. Maine* (1st Cir. 2001) 259 F.3d 48 (job required physical presence with other employees at centre because an essential responsibility involved on-the-spot collaborative efforts, including guiding less experienced workers in doing data research); *Heaser v. The Toro Co.* (8th Cir. 2001) 247 F.3d 826 (accepted employer's summary assertion that using memos generated at home by computer instead of using chemically treated copy paper to which the claimant was allergic was operationally unsatisfactory even though there was no complaint of unsatisfactory performance during the worker's three months of at-home performance); *Black v. Wayne Ctr.* (6th Cir. 2000) 2000 US App. LEXIS 17567; *Phillips v. Farmers Insurance Exchange* (2006) US Dist. LEXIS 5130 (N.D. TX. 2006) (unreasonable to

Occasionally, it is the employer who wants to accommodate a disabled worker's needs through a work-at-home arrangement to which the employee objects. For example, in one case a worker who suffered severe allergic reactions to airborne environmental irritants requested the employer to provide her with a smoke-free work environment. The employer offered to reduce some of her exposure to irritants by assigning her to do significant portions of her work by telecommuting. The employee objected on the ground that such an arrangement would isolate her socially and deprive her of access to amenities provided for employees at the work site. The court ruled that the Americans with Disabilities Act requires only a reasonable accommodation, not the accommodation preferred by the employee and, therefore, since the offered telecommuting arrangement eliminated exposure to the irritants, it satisfied the employer's obligation.[86]

Although federal legislation also prohibits age discrimination against most workers who are age 40 or older, there have been few reported telework related claims pertaining to such discrimination. Nevertheless, in one case a federal government employee alleged that in retaliation for filing age and other discrimination claims against the agency, he had been subjected to a hostile work environment that included denying him permission to telecommute, and that this and other harassment forced him to retire. Accordingly, he sued to set aside his signed agreement stating he was retiring voluntarily in exchange for receiving a $25,000 retirement incentive payment. The case report does not indicate any justification offered for the telework request other than the claimant's desire to spend more time at the beach. The court summarily agreed with an administrative decision that the claimant's retirement was uncoerced. It apparently considered the lack of legal merit for the work-at-the-beach request to be self-explanatory and, hence, the employer's rejection of the request could not be treated as discriminatory.[87]

G. FAMILY AND MEDICAL LEAVE ACT

The Federal Family and Medical Leave Act (FMLA) entitles workers who have at least a year of longevity on the job to take, during a twelve-month period, up to twelve weeks of unpaid leave for their own or an immediate family member's medical care when there is a serious health problem, or for care of a newborn, or to receive adoption of a child or placement of a foster child. The Act applies only if

---

require work at home as an accommodation where the disabled employee repeatedly failed to perform job duties satisfactorily when she worked at home); *Becerra v. EarthLink, Inc.* (2006) US Dist. LEXIS 2383 (D. KS 2006) (deficiencies in disabled worker's communication ability and initiative plus adverse impact on morale of other workers justified employer's rejection of work-at-home request); *Nanette v. Snow* (D.MD. 2004) 343 F. Supp. 2d 465, affirmed 2005 US App. LEXIS 20320 (4th Cir. 2005) (job could not be fully performed from home because the essential responsibilities required office meetings, personal interaction with customers, and travel).

86. *Chan v. Sprint Corp.* (D. KS 2005) 351 F. Supp. 2d 1197.
87. *Boyd v. Department of Transportation* (Fed. Cir. 2001) 21 Fed. Appx. 906.

the employer employs at least 50 workers within a 75 mile area. The Department of Labor has adopted a regulation stating that for the purpose of determining whether an employee is covered by the Act, a telecommuter's worksite is the office to which the worker reports and from which assignments are made.[88]

A potential issue under the FMLA, one the courts apparently have not yet decided, is whether an employer can require an employee to telework in lieu of taking FMLA leave if the telework arrangement will not interfere with receiving or giving the needed medical care.

H.   WORKER ADJUSTMENT AND RETRAINING NOTIFICATION ACT

The Worker Adjustment and Retraining Notification Act (WARN) requires employers to give advance notice of an impending mass layoff at a 'single site of employment' if the employer has at least 100 workers. A Department of Labor regulation designates that those 'who are outstationed' are treated as working at the site 'to which they are assigned as their home base, from which their work is assigned, or to which they report'.[89] 'Outstationed' employees include those who telecommute.[90] Hence, teleworkers are to be counted as employed at the site from which their work is assigned, both to determine whether the impending layoff meets the statutory criteria of a mass layoff[91] and whether they are entitled to the statutory advance notice of such a layoff.

I.   OCCUPATIONAL SAFETY AND HEALTH REGULATIONS

The federal Occupational Safety and Health Act (OSHA) requires employers to furnish employees with employment and a place of employment free from recognized hazards likely to cause serious injury. It also gives the Department of Labor authority to adopt specific safety and health standards. Enforcement is through an administrative process which includes on-site inspections. Resulting citations require employers to correct violations and can result in fines and even imprisonment.[92]

On its face, the Act is applicable to virtual workplaces, including at-home work sites. Because the US Constitution generally requires a court issued warrant in order for a home to be searched lawfully, the Department of Labour has issued an ambiguous directive respecting home work site inspections by its enforcement personnel. On the one hand, the directive states that the agency will not take formal action to inspect a home office work site even upon the specific request of an employee. (The directive does not explain how the privacy concern justifies

---

88. 29 Code of Fed. Reg. 825.111(a) (2).
89. 20 Code of Fed. Reg. § 639.3(i) (6).
90. *Kephart v. Data Systems Intl., Inc.* (D. KS 2003) 243 F. Supp. 2d 1205.
91. 29 US Code § 2102.
92. 29 US Code §§ 654, 662, 666.

refusing to inspect when an employee-home owner has made the request.) On the other hand, the directive states: 'Employers are responsible in home worksites for hazards caused by materials, equipment, or work processes which the employer provides or requires to be used in an employee's home'.[93] The directive also requires employers to include home work site related incidents in maintaining required records respecting work-related illnesses and injuries.[94] Generally, this directive nullifies the Act's protection of teleworkers because the Act's protections can only be enforced by the Department of Labor. Since telework equipment can pose serious safety hazards such as exposed electrical wiring, overloaded power circuits, unstable platforms, and cables placed without protection against tripping, the directive reduces the safety and health protections of those who work at home. However, it is theoretically possible for an endangered employee to obtain a federal court order granting temporary relief and requiring the Department of Labor to proceed with enforcement if the court is persuaded that the employee is faced with imminent danger of serious physical harm.[95] Nevertheless, the prospect of a telework employee undertaking and succeeding with such a suit is remote.

The Occupational Safety and Health Act provides for the criminal prosecution of an employer if an employee dies as a result of the employer's willful violation of the requirement that it provide a place of work free from recognized hazards that may cause serious injury or illness.[96] However, because proof of such wilfulness is difficult to establish if the hazard was not previously cited to the employer and the covered incidents are rare, especially in a home setting, the Department of Labor's directive against at-home inspections largely eliminates the encouragement which that provision was intended to give employers to try to correct reported hazards of the most serious kind. Thus, federal law, as enforced, gives teleworkers less safety and health protection than is provided to those who work at a non-residential site.[97]

When, with the employer's knowledge, work is performed at a worker's home, related injuries or illness are generally treated as covered by workers' compensation benefits. Accordingly, injuries connected to at-home telework are covered.[98] Because premiums for such insurance are based in part on the employer's claims experience, the desire to keep claims to a minimum provides some incentive for employers to reduce work-related safety and health hazards. Accordingly, even if federal OSHA enforcement policies do not aggressively protect at-home teleworkers, employers have some financial incentive to not neglect their safety and health

---

93. Dept. of Lab. Dir. CPL 2-0.125(X), eff. February 25 2000.
94. Dept. of Lab. Dir., n. 93 above, at (XI).
95. 29 US Code § 662.
96. 29 US Code § 666(e).
97. States can enforce their own occupational safety and health codes if those codes are certified as being at least as protective of employees as is the federal code; that is, they can give workers greater protection than is given by the federal program. About half of the states have such certified codes. An effort was not made to determine, on a state-by-state basis, whether any of these codes or announced enforcement policies provide such greater protection for teleworkers. However, the general treatises covering that area of law do not call attention to any state safety and health legislation particularly directed at telecommuters, an indication that none has yet been adopted.
98. Larson, *Workers' Compensation Law*, § 16.10.

needs. However, that incentive is limited since the insurance premiums often spread risk costs among broad groups of employers. Thus, diligent employers often pay part of the costs attributable to indifferent employers. In addition, the least scrupulous employers can reduce their premiums by coercing workers to not file claims.[99]

J.   EMPLOYEE SOCIAL INSURANCE BENEFITS

Telework complicates unemployment insurance law, not only with respect to the previously discussed issue of determining which jurisdiction or jurisdictions should entertain the claim, but also with respect to the substantive issue of whether the employee is disqualified from receiving benefits because he or she voluntarily quit or declined a reasonable job opportunity that required discarding or accepting a telework arrangement.[100]

Qualification for unemployment insurance benefits starts with the proposition that the benefit applicant must be ready, able and willing to work. Unwillingness to work can be established by showing that a worker was dismissed from the most recent employment for work connected misconduct. It can also be established by showing that the worker's attendance at the most recent job was inadequate.[101] In addition, a worker can be deemed unwilling to work, and therefore disqualified from unemployment insurance benefits, if the worker voluntarily left the most recent job, or after being dismissed did not seek or refused to accept available employment. However, under a federally imposed standard, disqualification cannot be based on refusing work if 'the wages, hours, or other conditions of the work offered are substantially less favourable to the individual than those prevailing for similar work in the locality'.[102]

Although federal law imposes various other restrictions on a state unemployment insurance system's rules for disqualifying claimants, it permits states to be more lenient in making benefits available.[103] Accordingly, many state courts have ruled that an unemployment insurance claimant cannot be disqualified for declining work that is clearly unsuitable to the employee's circumstances. Suitable work has been held to mean work that the employee customarily performs or is reasonably fit to perform to best utilize earning capacity gained by past experience, talents or training. Nevertheless, this is a fact specific finding and may be influenced by considerations such as the relative availability of employment that fully utilizes the worker's ability, and by the sympathy or lack of

---

99. M. Finkin, C. Summers, A. Goldman & K. Dau-Schmidt, *Legal Protection for the Individual Employee* (3rd edition, 2002), pp. 680–81, 720–21.

100. R. Covington & K. Decker, *Employment Law* (2nd ed., 2002), p. 384.

101. R. Covington & K. Decker, n. 100 above, pp. 384–89.

102. 26 US Code § 3304(a) (5) (B). Congress imposes on most employers a significant payroll tax, but most of that tax is excused if the state's unemployment insurance system satisfies a number of federally imposed criteria such as those found in s.3304.

103. 26 US Code § 3304(a).

sympathy of the state court judges toward those who are unemployed.[104] In the context of telecommuting, therefore, whether an unemployment insurance benefit claim will be granted may turn on such considerations as whether the most recent job was lost for failure to adjust to the new virtual workplace arrangement, or whether a worker has the capacity to learn how to use the new technology, or whether a worker had adequate justification to decline available telework.

With some frequency, workers become unemployed because family responsibilities either require them to be at home or close to home to provide child or health care, or because a spouse must relocate to obtain employment or remain employed. When workers leave jobs or reject offered jobs because of the incompatibility of the work site with the worker's perceived family responsibilities, American courts have been divided as to whether the worker's decision should be treated as voluntary and, therefore, a basis for disqualification from claiming unemployment insurance benefits.[105] An example is provided by the previously discussed case in which the financial information service provider in New York was initially allowed to continue her work by telecommuting from Florida. It will be recalled that Florida's denial of her application for unemployment insurance benefits was based on the contention that she was unqualified because she refused her employer's offer to return to an assignment at the New York work site.[106] Although the court stated that the employee's original request to telework was based on the fact that her spouse was located in Florida,[107] the case report does not tell us whether she had newly married a Florida resident, or whether her spouse had recently relocated to Florida and, if so, whether he had moved there despite an option of remaining in the New York area. Nor does the New York court's decision describe the personal circumstances respecting the choice of residence of the claimant and her spouse when, after 20 months, her employer directed her to cease telecommuting and resume work at the New York work site. If the decision to remain in Florida was necessitated by the husband's employment there, the claimant was ill advised to take her claim to New York and abandoned the Florida claim in as much as the latter's courts have been somewhat more sympathetic than the New York courts in finding that family responsibilities compelled the unemployment insurance claimant to leave the prior job and, therefore, did not disqualify the claim.[108]

---

104. See, for example, *Murphy v. Employment Security Department* (WA 1987) 734 P.2d 924; *Uvello v. Director of Division of Employment Security* (MA 1986) 489 N.E.2d 1999; *Wojcik v. Div. of Employment Security* (NJ 1971) 277 A.2d 529; *Swanson v. Minneapolis-Honeywell Regulator Co.* (MN 1953) 61 N.W.2d 526, 531; *Pacific Mills v. Director of Division of Employment Security* (MA 1948) 77 N.E.2d 413.
105. Case decisions are collected and described in G. Blum, 'Unemployment Compensation: Eligibility as Affected by Claimant's Refusal to Work at Particular Times or on Particular Shifts for Domestic or Family Reasons' (2004) 2 *A.L.R.5th*, 475.
106. In *Re Allen* (NY 2003) 794 N.E.2d 18.
107. In *Re Allen* (NY App. Div. 2002) 741 NYS2d 342.
108. Compare *Barclay v. Quail Ridge Property Owners Association* (FL Ct. App. 4th Dist. 2004) 867 So. 2d 508, with *In re Claim of Epps* (NY App. Div. 3d Dept. 2000) 715 N.Y.S.2d 89.

15. United States of America

Income benefits provided by employer funded private disability and life insurance are typically only available to the extent that the claimant is wholly incapacitated from earning a livelihood and became incapacitated or died while engaged in employment. A number of US case decisions have examined the impact of telework on such claims. For example, one case involved a work arrangement under which, for a week at a time, technical support staff were assigned to be on call after they left the employer's premises and, if paged on the employer provided pager, were required to promptly solve the employer's operational computer problem using either the employer's laptop computer which they carried with them or their own at-home computer in which the employer's software had been installed. When an on-call member of the technical support staff was killed while going to her home after leaving work, her estate claimed benefits under an employer provided insurance policy that covered its employees while travelling on business and in the course of business. Reinstating the estate's suit to collect the insurance, an appellate court held that a reasonable fact finder could easily conclude that at the time of her accident, the technical support employee's return to her home constituted travelling to the place where she and her employer expected her to continue her day's work for the employer.[109]

Similarly, in another case, a state court held that under its workers' compensation law, benefits were available to a work-at-home employee who was injured while returning home to work after making his weekly visit to the employer's office.[110]

Although there is no legal barrier to providing disability or life insurance benefits to teleworkers, in some cases benefits have been denied because the specific language of the insurance agreement is more narrowly structured. For example, in one case benefits were denied for an executive who continued to perform his duties while hospitalized. The court dismissed a suit to recover on the insurance contract because the insurance policy specifically stated that it covered an employee 'only when performing the duties of his occupation at his Participating Employer's business establishment or other location to which his Participating Employer's business requires him to travel'.[111]

Case decisions have denied long-term disability benefits based on the claimant's ability to telework. In one case, for example, income benefits under a long-term disability insurance policy were held to have been properly terminated where a laboratory research scientist's post-trauma history demonstrated her ability to do scientific editing work at home and continued insurance benefits were conditioned on her being unable to perform the material duties of any occupation for which she

---

109. *Lifson v. INA Life Ins. Co.* (2d Cir. 2003) 333 F.3d 349.
110. *Bentz v. Liberty Northwest* (MT 2002) 57 P.3d 832. Workers' compensation benefits are generally not available for injuries suffered while commuting to or from an employee's principal work site, an analogous situation weighed by the court. However, workers' compensation does cover travel from one work site to another during the course of a work day. R. Covington & K. Decker, *Employment Law* (2nd ed., 2002), pp. 78–79.
111. *Burnham v. Guardian Life Ins. Co. of America* (1st Cir. 1989) 873 F.2d 486, 487.

was qualified based on her education, training, or experience.[112] On the other hand, it has been held that where the intrusion of a home office would unduly encumber his living arrangement, a workers' compensation claimant was not disqualified from receiving benefits merely because he had rejected a work-at-home opportunity that he could perform despite his disability.[113]

K. ORGANIZING AND REPRESENTING WORKERS

The National Labor Relations Act (NLRA) protects the right of employees to organize for the purposes of achieving collective representation. That right is protected regardless of whether the employees work for the same employer. However, case decisions allow employers to prohibit organizing activities if they are conducted by employees or directed at employees while they are engaged in work. In addition, case decisions permit employers to exclude non employees from using their property for union organizing unless there are no other means of accessing the workers.[114]

Efforts to organize employees who telecommute are complicated by the lack of, or reduced opportunities for, face-to-face contact at or near the employment establishment. In one case in which employees telecommuted, the National Labour Relations Board (which enforces the NLRA) ruled that the employer violated the Act when a supervisor implicitly warned a telecommuter to not use his employer provided communications terminal to urge others to support a labour organization. However, the Board emphasized that the employer allowed workers to use the terminals for non-business purposes and indicated that because the union supporters had means of contacting the other workers by telephone and had opportunities to meet with their counterparts at various work-related meetings, it would have been permissible for the employer to ban union organizing use of the communications terminals if it enforced a business-use only rule respecting such terminals.[115] On the other hand, the Board has held that unless it can prove a compelling business justification, an employer violates the Act if in response to learning of a

---

112. *LaMarco v. CIGNA Corp.* (2000) US Dist. LEXIS 14341 (ND CA 2000), affirmed 33 Fed. Appx. 301 (9th Cir. 2002).
113. *Bussa v. Workers' Comp. Appeal Bd.* (PA Comm. Ct. 2001) 777 A.2d 126, 130 ('given that the computer is located in the bedroom, Claimant would not be able to perform his job if his wife would happen to be sick or bedridden again, as she had been several months previously'). Also, compare *Allegheny Power v. Workers' Comp. App. Bd.* (Pa. Comm. Ct. 2004) 841 A.2d 614 (mobile home in which the claimant lived with his wife and child could not accommodate a home office without disrupting their family life) with *Medved v. Workers' Comp. App. Bd.* (Pa. Comm. Ct. 2001) 788 A.2d 447, *cert.* denied 538 US 908 (2003) (benefits denied to a registered nurse who suffered a severe back injury and refused to accept a job requiring her to solicit information and charitable donations from a telephone the employer would install in her home).
114. A. Goldman & R. White, 'United States' in *International Encyclopaedia for Labour Law*, R. Blanpain (ed.) at ¶ 444.
115. *Technology Serv. Solutions* (2000) 332 NLRB 1096, 1101. See, also, *Media General Operations*, Inc. (2005) 346 NLRB No. 11.

union organizing effort it institutes a rule prohibiting non-business access to the internet.[116]

It has been argued that the National Labor Relations Board should not allow any employer interference with employee use of the employer's internet for union organizing during non work time. This contention is based on the proposition that email has become an integral forum for workplace communication in the same way as locker rooms and rest areas. Thus, it is argued that because the latter have long been recognized as locations where employees have a statutory right to engage in organizing activity during non work time, unless the employer can show compelling operational needs to bar such use, employee access to the employer's electronic network for union organizing during non work time should be wholly free from employer restraints.[117]

IV. CONCLUSION

Telework is making its mark on American labour and employment law just as it is making its mark on the American workplace. Although there has been little US legislation directed at customizing employment standards and benefits law to the unique characteristics of telework, courts and administrative agencies, faced with specific issues, have resolved many of the inevitable questions. However, as is typical in American law, the answers have not been consistent. Since the heads of administrative bodies in the US, including their highest level adjudicative panels, are generally appointed by elective officials for a limited term of office, their choices tend to reflect the appointing authorities' political preferences for increased or decreased employee protection. Similar propensities, though often a bit more tempered, are found in the decisions of judges whether popularly elected or politically appointed – even when they have lifetime tenure. Hence, because legislation has not been tailored to the special circumstances of telecommuting, the need for interpretation offers decisional leeway that results in divergent choices reflecting the decision-makers' perception of economic and social dynamics. Accordingly, as we have seen, although many decisions provide reasonable accommodations between the new work setting and the worker protective goals of underlying legislative or juridical principles, some decisions reflect indifference toward the worker's plight.

---

116. *Gallup, Inc.* 334 NLRB 366 (2001).
117. N. King, 'Labor Law for Managers of Non-Union Employees in Traditional and Cyber Workplaces' (2003) 40 *Amer. Bus. L.J.,* 827, 869–72.

Chapter 16

IBM's on Demand Workplace Strategy in a Nutshell

Christian Dirkx

I. INTRODUCTION

IBM (*International Business Machines*) was founded about a hundred years ago, and maintained its place as a business spearhead ever since, thanks to its power of innovation. For instance, IBM has been filing the highest number of patents in the U.S. for the thirteenth year in a row, and it counts amongst its staff five Nobel Prize Winners! IBM has a workforce of 355.000 highly skilled people and revenue over 2006 was $91.4 billion. IBM activities focus on services ($48 billion of revenue), hardware, software and financing. Its research and development budget exceeds 5 billion dollars.

In Belgium and the Grand Duchy of Luxemburg (*www.ibm.com/be*) IBM employs 2434 employees, mainly in consulting and services activities; a quarter works in sales, distribution and support activities. In 2006 IBM Belgium/ Luxembourg hired 300 people.

IBM's most important innovation is the *IBMer*. Our Company is a values-based business driven by values-based leadership: dedication to every customer, innovation that matters, for our company and for the world, and trust, and personal responsibility, in everything we do. IBM's policy is to make sure that every employee can decide where, when and how to work. 95% of all IBMers in Belgium

Blanpain et al., European Framework, Agreements and Telework, pp. 273–284.
©2007, Kluwer Law International BV, The Netherlands.

and Luxembourg can, with the approval of their manager, work on any other place than their traditional office. This implies that nominative, individualized office space has disappeared: on average, one desk is foreseen for 1.35 employees. The collaborators can use all available means and tools including mobile communication tools and a well designed set of process and reporting tools enabling them to perform their work remotely.

IBMers take more time for flexible working.[1]

II. ON DEMAND WORKPLACE

On Demand Workplace is a totally different way of working. With its On Demand Workplace strategy, IBM aims at enabling its collaborators to work any time, any place of his or her choosing, in function of the professional objectives and the results to be attained. This is made possible thanks to an advanced set of internal tools and processes which allow work to be organized towards the end user (process management) in such a way that people don't have to 'go to the office', but (so to speak) work 'comes to them' via mobile technology.

Thanks to this advanced process technology, they can work where, at that moment, their presence is required, which most of the time is closest to their customers or to the team they are working with.

It means that a majority of the employees still work regularly at an IBM office. On average, one or two work days per week are spent outside the traditional office (this is an average, so the time spent in teleworking can vary between 0 and 90 per cent depending on the function): either at a customer site, or in IBM premises in Belgium or abroad (including satellite offices called 'proximity centres'), or occasionally at home. This implies that people performance is evaluated based upon result rather than upon presence at the office.

Mobility is at the core of this strategy: not only spatial mobility (optimizing travel and minimizing traffic jams), but also temporal mobility (dynamic management of working time, enabling a better balance between work and private life), and functional mobility (managing skills and career development).

In this respect, On Demand Workplace is a key driver of IBM's Human Resources (HR) strategy: mobility enables better *employability*. The 'deal'[2] between IBM and its collaborator implies a commitment on behalf of the employee to optimize his/her skills and experience, hence 'market value'. IBM commits to provide all tools, means, support and coaching to reach this objective, in order for the company to attract, retain and motivate the best talent in the industry. On Demand Workplace plays an essential role in this strategy.

---

1. Usually, the term 'telework' is used to designate any form of work which takes place outside the traditional office space. IBM's On Demand Workplace strategy enables teleworking in this definition.
2. Also called 'psychological contract'.

III. OBJECTIVES AND DESCRIPTION OF ON DEMAND WORKPLACE

A. NEEDS

- The employees of IBM Belgium/Luxembourg want a healthier balance between work and private life. They also look for ways to become more efficient, for instance, by avoiding time in traffic jams or in superfluous meetings.
- Customers request IBM talent to be available as long and as close to their business as possible, and to respond more quickly to their needs.
- Service and administrative costs need to be reduced, necessitating drastic savings in occupancy costs.

B. MISSION

The set up of On Demand Workplace has the following core characteristics:

- Enabling the IBM Belgium/Luxembourg employee to work where and when needed and increase productivity.
- Revising office infrastructure.
- Providing any facilities and tools available at a traditional office.
- Implementing change management programmes to coach the managers and collaborators in the transition towards On Demand Workplace.

C. THE PROJECT

On Demand Workplace was implemented almost completely using IBM internal competencies and skills and with a high degree of team work between people from various competency horizons, such as:

- IBM Strategy and Change consultants;
- HR consultants IBM Global Services;

- IBM RESO (Real Estate and Site Operations);
- IBM Integrated Technology Services.

The following steps were implemented to realize On Demand Workplace:

1. Employee Survey and Communication of the Concept

Flexible work means a big deal of change for each employee. Therefore, IBM put communication and education of its workforce at the centre of the project from day one. After a first employee survey, an On Demand Workplace Board was created, involving the general manager, the HR manager and the communications manager, but also leaders of the major business units, and of course the real estate, security and IT leaders. Three groups were created: one with the mission of making the specifications of the project (called the Architects), a second with the mission to build the infrastructure based upon these specifications (the Builders), and a third group focusing exclusively on communication and change management.

Throughout the whole project, the employees were coached via specific change management sub-projects. A manager training enabled to educate managers in understanding their new role as coach of mobile and more autonomic employees. Resistance against change needed to be addressed, and new ways of thinking and organizing processes and management styles needed to be learned.

Via the IBM intranet, a portal was created and consistent communication was held permanently. Information sessions were held, and channels were created to field questions and answers permanently.

2. Building and Office Infrastructure

All IBM office premises were completely revised and rebuilt (including a brand new building to house IBM's Belgian head office) to make sure every IBM employee could work in every location. Office premises were conceived the same everywhere so that the employee could log on and use the IT and building infrastructure transparently. Logical units like toilets, shared office tools and coffee spaces were created uniformly.

3. Proximity Areas

In every IBM location (Antwerp, Brussels, Ghent, Liège, Charleroi, etc.) specific proximity zones have been created. Apart from the office spaces reserved for specific departments of the company, these spaces offer the possibility for any employee to work in another location. The Proximity Centre in Rotselaar, near Leuven, goes a step further. This office has no secretarial or other support, but offers a possibility to avoid traffic jams.

4. Technological Changes

The importance of having the right technology at your disposal to work remotely cannot be underestimated, albeit that it is only a means to serve a purpose: to work differently. As an IT company, IBM is, of course, well positioned to offer the best of its products and services to its employees in an efficient and cost effective way.

More than 95 per cent of our workforce has a laptop computer; and broadband communication facilities from home are offered, as well as wireless and mobile (GPRS) communication. Most of the employees use their GSM phone and get their expenses reimbursed. Various tools are implemented, such as electronic conversation and meeting tools, VOIP (Voice Over IP) telephony, and teamware, and other advanced functions are at their disposal to communicate anywhere, anytime in the most efficient way.

Education modules have been developed by the On Demand Workplace community.

IV. LEGAL ASPECTS

The labour contract remains unchanged: the employee commits to work at one of IBM's office buildings in Belgium or the Grand Duchy. The work regulations remain unchanged as well, offering fixed or flexible working schedules. Home is not a workplace. Meetings at home are not allowed. Home is not equipped, except with ADSL, and the work accident insurance coverage has been extended to home (extra premium was paid).

The conditions to be eligible for teleworking are:

- There needs to be an agreement between manager and reportee. Teleworking is on a voluntary basis.
- The job must allow for mobile working.
- There is no 'statute', no acquired rights.

Structural home working is not part of policy.

V.   RESULTS OF THE PROJECT

Here's how the employees evaluate the project:
   The On Demand Workplace concept is well accepted and implemented:

1.   80 per cent of the workforce confirm it offers good flexibility to decide where, when and how to work.
2.   66 per cent consider on demand workplace an important benefit.
3.   60 per cent want more mobility.
4.   58 per cent believe on demand workplace can improve their work/life balance.
5.   50 per cent use proximity centres.

Furthermore, 50 per cent of employees have experienced improvement in productivity.[3]

> I can take the children to school, return home, work through my e-mails, then leave for a customer – go to the office after the rush hour, and even end my day at the location closest to home. Definitely one of the reasons I want to work for IBM!

A.   CONCLUSION: A 'WIN-WIN-WIN'

IBM's On Demand Workplace strategy definitely benefits its customers and employees, but also IBM's own income and expenses statement.
   Company benefits:

- Attracts and retains skilled people.
- Less absenteeism.
- Employees spend more time with customers.
- Enhances profitability thanks to substantial real estate savings. (IBM Belgium saved EUR 8 million with more rational use of space; this amount was partially reinvested in better communication and printing infrastructure.)

Employee benefits:

- Employee satisfaction improved.
- More 'face time' with internal or external clients.
- Better balance of personal/family life.
- More productivity (estimated at 5 to 15 per cent improvement).

Customer benefits:

- Increased customer satisfaction.
- Better accessibility to IBM teams.
- More 'face time' with IBM.

---

3. 'E-place' survey, November 2002: 1100 respondents.

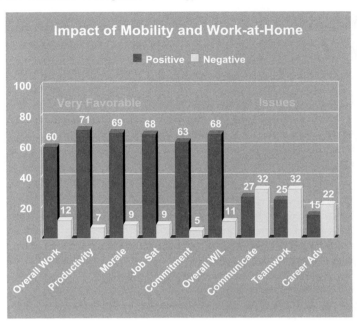

Figure 1: Impact of mobility and work-at-home

- Faster response to enquiries.
- Improved reaction time and delivery of critical information.

B.   BUT NOT WITHOUT PITFALLS

The benefits of mobile working (field, home or client based) are well documented. New levels of flexibility, work/life balance, proximity to customers, and increased responsiveness and productivity – not to mention the reduced need for commuting and travel – have all been cited as advantages of this new way of working.

However, a survey from IBM's Institute of Business Value (IBV) and the Economist Intelligence Unit (EIU) revealed that these benefits have to be balanced against a number of pitfalls that threaten to undo some of these gains. If these issues are not addressed, the survey indicates that remote employees can end up feeling mistrusted by colleagues, alienated and under appreciated.

The primary objective of this research was to better understand the perspectives and experiences of employees who are mobile workers.

Study objectives:

- Understand the key issues and challenges facing mobile workers;
- Provide guidance to organizations as to where and how they should focus their time, attention and resources as they look to improve the productivity and work experience of mobile workers.

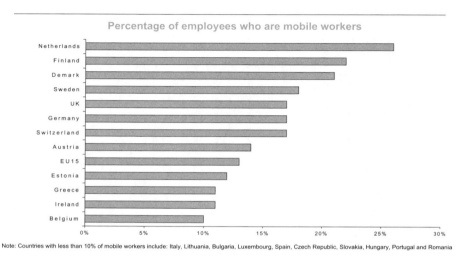

Figure 2: Percentage of employees who are mobile workers

Study methodology:

- 351 mobile workers surveyed by the EIU;
    - ○ represent 29 countries across Europe;
    - ○ various industries, job functions and organizational sizes;
- Interviews with academics and practitioners who have been involved in mobile working programmes.

The study demonstrated that mobile workers are beginning to represent a significant percentage of the European workforce:

Further, there is significant interest among many European employees to work remotely in some fashion.

Here are the key findings from this study:

- First, mobile workers are beginning to represent a significant percentage of the European workforce.
- There has been a rise in the number of individuals who have recently begun working in a mobile environment.
- Mobile workers face significant difficulties in communicating and collaborating with colleagues.

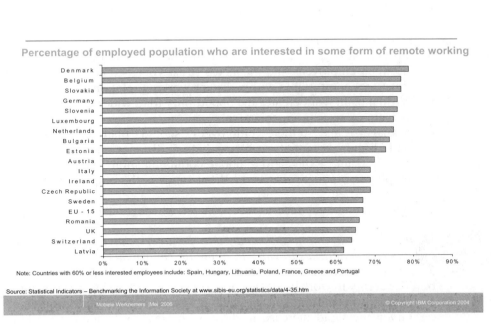

Figure 3: Percentage of employed population who are interested in some form of remote working

- Mobile workers believe they are in danger of becoming disconnected from the informal networks (feeling out of touch).
- Mobile workers feel there is a perceived need to remain accessible to colleagues (feeling of losing corporate visibility/credibility)
- Separating work and home life is one important area where mobile workers express difficulty.
- For many employees, the technological infrastructure in many organizations does not adequately serve the needs of mobile employees.

Source: *IBM Institute for Business Value in Cooperation with the Economist Intelligence Unit*, May 2005.

From the above, the following recommendations to the challenges that companies face with the mobile workforce have been derived:

1. *Improve the reliability and functionality of remote working technology.*
   a. Use technologies that allow mobile employees to more easily collaborate (higher bandwidth tools, web-based electronic meetings, instant messaging, and video conferencing).
   b. Technology facilitates virtual team work between workers around the globe.

    c.   Effective use of technology requires additional employee training – employees must know how to operate the technologies.

    d.   Technology must be reliable and readily available in order to be effective.

2. *Provide visible corporate and managerial support for mobile working.*

    a.   Provide strong company support for mobile working to instil trust between employees and managers (trust your people). The manager must feel comfortable with a distant working relationship.

    b.   Virtual team work creates the opportunity for a wider network of partnerships across an organization.

    c.   Managers and remote employees should plan communication and discuss potential problems before distance managing begins. Set the same expectations about communication (which days will employee report to manager? What times is the employee available by phone? etc.).

    d.   Always maintain face-to-face contact whenever there is an opportunity.

3. *Make sure that employees (and their managers) have the appropriate skills and capabilities to work in a mobile environment.*

    a.   Train employees and their managers to work in a mobile environment.

    b.   The ability to work independently, organize work tasks and collaborate in a virtual environment are seen as key skills for mobile workers.

    c.   Given the rapid increase in those who are new to mobile working, companies need to find ways to reduce the learning curve associated with effectively collaborating using virtual technologies.

4. *Develop an outcome-based performance management system that levels the playing field between remote and office-based workers.*

    a.   Establish a performance-based culture, assessing employees on their results, not on the number of hours spent in the office.

    b.   Develop results-oriented objectives/explicit requirements for work deliverables.

    c.   Have clearer measurements in place/well define performance standards.

    d.   Have frequent monitoring and feedback.

In order to address the pitfalls, IBM Management has taken several initiatives to encourage meetings between people, apart from the classical business meeting. For instance, IBM invites all of its people on a regular basis to meet for a 'happy hour' drink; IBM office buildings are open plan, with coffee corners for informal contact; IBM Management has organized informal employee get-togethers to discuss the practicalities of teleworking and listen to testimonials; in order to address 'office etiquette', several campaigns have been launched in the past few years to control the 'e-mail monster', to clear the paper 'invasion' (Blue Jeans Days), to encourage office etiquette and for team building (Code of Conduct).

VI. CONCLUSION – REVISITED?

Teleworking has been a success so far at IBM Belgium, but the biggest pitfall would be to look at it as a purpose in itself. It is not. It is not more or less than another way of working. It is not a solution to all problems either. It sometimes makes life easier, but creates other complexities – not the least in terms of management of infrastructure (be it office space, parking, catering or IT). It cannot be abstracted from the culture and strategy of the entity which wants to implement it. Communication and leadership are two essential ingredients for its sustainable success.

At IBM, On Demand Workplace was used as a vector for change in company strategy and culture. As such it proved to be very powerful. It also proved to be a success in terms of customer coverage, employee satisfaction and company benefits. We definitely want to maintain that Win-Win-Win.